Korean Society

Citizens' groups and social movements have been crucial in transforming South Korea from a military authoritarian regime to one of the most dynamic democracies in Asia. Taking the innovative theme of 'civil society' – voluntary organizations outside the role of the state which have participated in the process of political and social democratization – the essays collected here examine Korea as one of the most dramatic cases in the world of ordinary citizens participating in the transformation of politics.

Topics include:

- comparisons of Korean democratization with the experiences of post-authoritarian regimes elsewhere in the world;
- the legacy of Korea's Confucian past for contemporary politics and society;
- close examinations of various civil society movements, including the labor movement, the student movement, the women's movement and religious organization;
- the possibilities for political change and the emergence of civil society in North Korea.

Including both new and revised material, this second edition remains conceptually innovative, topical and fully up to date, providing an interdisciplinary study that will be an invaluable resource for students of contemporary Korea, Asian politics and society.

Charles K. Armstrong is Associate Professor of History and Director of the Center for Korean Research at Columbia University, New York.

Asia's Transformations
Edited by Mark Selden
Binghamton and Cornell Universities, USA

The books in this series explore the political, social, economic and cultural consequences of Asia's transformations in the twentieth and twenty-first centuries. The series emphasizes the tumultuous interplay of local, national, regional and global forces as Asia bids to become the hub of the world economy. While focusing on the contemporary, it also looks back to analyse the antecedents of Asia's contested rise. This series comprises several strands:

Asia's Transformations aims to address the needs of students and teachers, and the titles will be published in hardback and paperback. Titles include:

Confronting the Bush Doctrine
Critical views from the Asia–Pacific
Edited by Mel Gurtov and
Peter Van Ness

China in War and Revolution,
1895–1949
Peter Zarrow

The Future of US–Korean Relations
The imbalance of power
Edited by John Feffer

Working in China
Ethnographies of labor and workplace
transformation
Edited by Ching Kwan Lee

Asia's Great Cities. Each volume aims to capture the heartbeat of the contemporary city from multiple perspectives emblematic of the authors' own deep familiarity with the distinctive faces of the city, its history, society, culture, politics and economics, and its evolving position in national, regional and global frameworks. While most volumes emphasize urban developments since the Second World War, some pay close attention to the legacy of the *longue durée* in shaping the contemporary. Thematic and comparative volumes address such themes as urbanization, economic and financial linkages, architecture and space, wealth and power, gendered relationships, planning and anarchy, and ethnographies in national and regional perspective. Titles include:

Bangkok
Place, practice and representation
Marc Askew

Beijing in the Modern World
David Strand and Madeline Yue Dong

Shanghai
Global city
Jeff Wasserstrom

Hong Kong
Global city
Stephen Chiu and Tai-Lok Lui

Representing Calcutta
Modernity, nationalism and the
colonial uncanny
Swati Chattopadhyay

Singapore
Wealth, power and the culture of
control
Carl A. Trocki

Asia.com is a series which focuses on the ways in which new information and communication technologies are influencing politics, society and culture in Asia. Titles include:

Japanese Cybercultures
Edited by Mark McLelland and
Nanette Gottlieb

Asia.com
Asia encounters the Internet
Edited by K. C. Ho, Randolph Kluver
and Kenneth C. C. Yang

The Internet in Indonesia's New
Democracy
David T. Hill and Krishna Sen

Chinese Cyberspaces
Technological changes and political
effects
Edited by Jens Damm and
Simona Thomas

14 **Popular Culture, Globalization and Japan**
Edited by Matthew Allen and Rumi Sakamoto

15 **medi@sia**
Global media/tion in and out of context
Edited by Todd Joseph Miles Holden and Timothy J. Scrase

* Now available in paperback

Critical Asian Scholarship is a series intended to showcase the most important individual contributions to scholarship in Asian Studies. Each of the volumes presents a leading Asian scholar addressing themes that are central to his or her most significant and lasting contribution to Asian studies. The series is committed to the rich variety of research and writing on Asia, and is not restricted to any particular discipline, theoretical approach or geographical expertise.

Southeast Asia
A testament
George McT. Kahin

China's Past, China's Future
Energy, food, environment
Vaclav Smil

Women and the Family in Chinese History
Patricia Buckley Ebrey

The Chinese State in Ming Society
Timothy Brook

China Unbound
Evolving perspectives on the Chinese past
Paul A. Cohen

Korean Society

Civil society, democracy and the state

Second Edition

Edited by Charles K. Armstrong

Routledge
Taylor & Francis Group

LONDON AND NEW YORK

First published 2002 by Routledge

This second edition first published 2007
by Routledge
2 Park Square, Milton Park, Abingdon, Oxon OX14 4RN

Simultaneously published in the USA and Canada
by Routledge
270 Madison Ave, New York, NY 10016

Routledge is an imprint of the Taylor & Francis Group, an informa business

Typeset in Times by
HWA Text and Data Management, Tunbridge Wells

British Library Cataloguing in Publication Data
A catalogue record for this book is available from the British Library

Library of Congress Cataloging-in-Publication Data
Korean society : civil society, democracy and the state / edited by
    Charles K. Armstrong. – 2nd ed.
        p. cm. – (Asia's transformations)
    Includes bibliographical references and index.
    1. Civil society – Korea (South)   2. Democracy – Korea (South)
    3. Democratization – Korea (South)   4. Korea (South) – Politics and
    government – 1988–   I. Armstrong, Charles K.   II. Series.
JQ1729.A15K68 2006
300.95195–dc22   2006014584

ISBN10: 0–415–77057–2 (hbk)
ISBN10: 0–415–77058–0 (pbk)
ISBN10: 0–203–96664–3 (ebk)

ISBN13: 978–0–415–77057–6 (hbk)
ISBN13: 978–0–415–77058–3 (pbk)
ISBN13: 978–0–203–96664–8 (ebk)

Contents

x *Contents*

Contributors

Charles K. Armstrong is Associate Professor of History at Columbia University, where he specializes in modern Korean, East Asian and international history. His recent books include *The North Korean Revolution, 1945–1950* (2003), *The Koreas* (2006), and, as co-editor, *Korea at the Center: dynamics of regionalism in northeast Asia* (2006). He is currently completing a book on the history of North Korean foreign relations.

Donald N. Clark is Professor of History and Director of International Programs at Trinity University in San Antonio, Texas. He is the author or editor of various articles and books including *Christianity in Modern Korea* (1986), *The Kwangju Uprising: shadows over the regime in South Korea* (1988), and *Culture and Customs of Korea* (2000). His latest books are entitled *Living Dangerously in Korea, 1900–1950* (2003) and *Modern East Asia*, co-authored with Conrad Shirokauer. He has also published a chapter on Sino-Korean tributary relations in the *Cambridge History of China*.

Bruce Cumings is Norman and Edna Freehling Professor of History and East Asian Political Economy at the University of Chicago. He is the author of *The Origins of the Korean War* (1981, 1990), *War and Television* (1992), *Korea's Place in the Sun: a modern history* (1997), *Parallax Visions: making sense of American–East Asian relations* (1999), and *North Korea: another country* (2003) and is the editor of the modern volume of the *Cambridge History of Korea* (forthcoming).

John Duncan is a Professor and Chair of the Department of Asian Languages and Cultures, Professor of History, and Director of the Center for Korean Studies at the University of California – Los Angeles. He is the author of *The Origins of the Chosŏn Dynasty* (2000) and co-editor of *The Journal of Korean Studies*.

Sunhyuk Kim is an Associate Professor in the Department of Public Administration at Korea University. He has previously taught at the University of Southern California, Claremont-McKenna College, and the State University of New York-Buffalo, and has been a research fellow at the Center for International Security and Arms Control at Stanford University and the Asiatic Research Center at Korea University. He is the author of *The Politics of Democratization* *in Korea: the role of civil society* (2000) and *Economic Crisis and Dual Transition in Korea: a case study in comparative perspective* (2004).

Hagen Koo is Professor of Sociology at the University of Hawaii. He is the author of the award-winning book, *Korean Workers: the culture and politics of class formation* (2001). Currently, he is working on a book project on globalization and the middle classes in South Korea.

Namhee Lee is an Assistant Professor of Modern Korean History at the University of California – Los Angeles. Her previous publications include "Representing the Worker: worker–intellectual alliance of the 1980s in South Korea," in *The Journal of Asian Studies* (November, 2005) and "Between Indeterminacy and Radical Critique: Madang-guk, ritual, and protest," in *Positions: East Asia cultures critique* (Winter, 2003). She has recently completed a book manuscript entitled "The Making of Minjung: the South Korean Democratization Movement".

Linda S. Lewis is an Associate Professor of Anthropology and Director of the East Asian Studies Program at Wittenberg University (Ohio). A cultural anthropologist specializing in contemporary Korean society, she holds a PhD from Columbia University. Her publications have dealt with mediation and the Korean courts, and women in elite occupations. Her most recent book is *Laying Claim to the Memory of May: a look back at the 1980 Kwangju Uprising* (2002).

Seungsook Moon is Associate Professor of Sociology and Director of the Asian Studies Program at Vassar College. She has published widely on the issues of nationalism, militarism, democratization, and women's movements, and is the author of *Militarized Modernity and Gendered Citizenship in South Korea* (2005), and a co-editor of *Gender, Race, and Sexuality in the Global U.S. Military Empire* (Duke University Press, forthcoming).

cratic politics and civil society activism remain both vibrant and contested within South Korea today, 20 years after the "democratic breakthrough."

The political scientist Larry Diamond defined civil society as "the realm of organized social life that is voluntary, self-generating, (largely) self-supporting, autonomous from the state, and bound by a legal order or set of rules." [8] Whether or not we choose to use the term "civil society" in the classic Western sense, it is certainly the case that various kinds of voluntary associations fitting Diamond's definition have existed in South Korea since liberation from Japanese colonial rule in 1945, if not before.[9] For much of the post-liberation period, however, civil society under successive authoritarian regimes in South Korea has had to struggle to maintain its autonomy from the state, and has often been in direct conflict with the state. But by the 1990s this state/society conflict model no longer fit the circumstances of the ROK, and the older conceptual frameworks for understanding Korean politics needed to be revised. The opposition between "state" and "society", in which the latter was often conceptualized in the 1970s and 1980s as the *minjung* or "popular masses," is no longer a useful framework for understanding Korea today.[10] Throughout the 1990s, South Korea witnessed the growth of intermediate, voluntary associations which influence the political process but are not of it: citizens' groups, environmental movements, religious organizations, new kinds of student, worker, and farmer organizations, the movement for local political autonomy – in short, there has been a general emergence of new and diverse forms of association (i.e., civil society) in a revitalized "public sphere".[11] Issues of political change are no longer focused primarily on changing the nature of the state, which is widely perceived to have passed through the stage of democratic transition into the stage of democratic consolidation, but on specific policies and their implementation – although democracy in South Korea, as elsewhere, remains far from perfect.

The concept of civil society is clearly Western, and more specifically Western European, in its origins and early development; one of the key questions, therefore, is how well this term and the tradition of political thought with which it is associated can be applied to contemporary non-Western societies. Not long ago, the social stability and successful capitalist development in the absence of democratic politics in several East Asian countries were seen by some as evidence of a social consensus, derived from deep-seated cultural norms often associated with "Confucian" historical legacies, that mitigated against Western liberal democracy and favored authoritarian governments.[12] The debate on so-called "Asian values", carried on by scholars and politicians on both sides of the Pacific since the 1980s, has centered on the question of cultural values that supported collectivity, consensus, harmony, and strong government against Western liberal notions of individualism, conflict, and openness.[13] Opponents of "Confucian Authoritarianism," including then-opposition leader and later South Korean President Kim Dae Jung, argued on the contrary that Asian cultural heritages, and Confucianism in particular, supported democracy and the freedom of the individual.[14] The rise of democracy in South Korea and Taiwan has contributed to a re-examination of Confucian culture as the possible well-spring of an indigenous tradition of democracy, civility, and human rights.[15] Historically, East Asian societies, it is argued, also had a "public sphere" that, if not precisely analogous to that of early modern and modern Europe, could nevertheless serve as a basis for democracy in contemporary East Asia.[16] Confucianism, long seen both by Western observers and by East Asians themselves as a hindrance to civil society in East Asia, may in fact be a boon.[17]

During the Chosŏn dynasty (1392–1910), Korea was the most thoroughly "Confucianized" state in Asia, surpassing Japan, Vietnam, and perhaps even China itself in its adherence to Confucian institutions, rituals, and values. Thus, the relationship between Confucian values and civil society is perhaps best explored in Korea, which has the strongest Confucian heritage and has experienced the most dramatic process of recent democratization among the East Asian countries. Against this background, the current volume seeks to contribute to the comparative study of civil society in (East) Asian democratization.[18] A more regionally-based comparative approach, rather than the bilateral comparisons with "the West" that underlie most studies of individual East Asian countries, might reveal considerable commonalities and interconnections – especially among the East Asian democracies of South Korea, Japan, and Taiwan – that distinguish this region from the types of civil societies that have developed in Europe and America.

Democratic transformations: from workers to netizens

The South Korean democracy movement of the 1980s, culminating in the extraordinary events of June 1987 that brought hundreds of thousands of South Koreans into the streets to protest against the Chun Doo Hwan regime, involved a broad coalition of social groups, professions, and classes. Students, intellectuals, and religious leaders played a prominent role, as they had in earlier anti-authoritarian protests. Middle-class, white-collar professionals joined as well, with their own demands for political and economic rights, particularly unionization.[19] And constituting a critical new element in the democratic movement were the blue-collar workers, a more visible, vibrant, and militant labor force than South Korea had ever seen before, a direct product of the country's rapid industrialization since the 1960s.[20]

Bowing to this popular pressure, as well as to American warnings that the U.S. would not support a violent crackdown on the protestors, General Chun announced that he would step down and hold elections before the 1988 Seoul Olympics, not after as he had previously declared.[21] Chun's announcement was followed by a Presidential election in which the two major opposition figures, Kim Young Sam and Kim Dae Jung, both ran, splitting the opposition vote and handing the election to Chun's chosen successor, former General Roh Tae-woo, who won the presidency with less than 37 percent of the vote. Despite its limitations, however, the 1987 elections represented a milestone in South Korea's transition to democracy, and President Roh would play an important role in laying the groundwork for future democratization. In 1992, Kim Young Sam was elected as the first civilian president in 30 years, as the candidate of the Democratic Liberal Party (DLP), which combined Kim's former opposition party with Roh's ruling Democratic Justice Party. In 1997, Kim Dae Jung became the first president elected from the opposing party in the history of the Republic.

The changes of political leadership in South Korea in the late 1980s and 1990s were accompanied and promoted by new forms of civil associations and non-governmental organizations (NGOs). Collectively, these organizations constituted an emerging civil society, engaged with and yet apart from the political system. Few countries in the world surpassed South Korea in the number, extent, and involvement of civil society groups, which often played key roles in advocating and enabling the political involvement of ordinary citizens.[22]

By the end of the 1990s there were literally thousands of NGOs operating in South Korea. Among their activities has been the monitoring of public officials, campaigning for judicial reform and economic justice, and "disqualification" of candidates deemed unfit to run for office. Grass-roots mobilization was made even more rapid and efficient in the early 2000s through the use of the Internet, as South Korea attained one of the world's highest per capita rates of broadband usage and the term "netizen" (for "Internet citizen") entered the discourse of Korean democratization.[23] "NGO" also became part of regular South Korean vocabulary; Kyung Hee University in Seoul, for example, established what may be the only Department of NGO Studies in the world.

In December 2002 Roh Moo-hyun, a self-taught human rights lawyer and protégé of Kim Dae Jung, won the Presidency over his conservative rival Lee Hoi-chang of the Grand National Party (GNP). Roh survived an impeachment challenge early in his presidency and established a new party, the Yŏllin Uri Dang ("Our Open Party") which won a majority in the 2004 National Assembly Elections. The Uri Party, as it was called, seemed to represent the left-of-center, young and "progressive" elements of South Korean society, with a regional base in the Southwestern provinces (although Roh himself, unlike Kim Dae Jung, is from the Southeast). Its rival, the GNP, had an older and more conservative constituency with a base in the Southeast. It remains to be seen whether these developments represent the coming of a more stable and ideologically-based two-party system, over the highly volatile, personalized and regionally divided politics that have driven South Korean political parties for most of the Republic's history.[24]

Democratic prospects and civil society

At the procedural level, democracy in South Korea seems firmly consolidated. Barring a catastrophic event such as war – not a possibility to be ruled out on the Korean peninsula – it seems highly unlikely that a military-led or other strongly authoritarian government will come to power in the foreseeable future. Still, there are those who are skeptical about the depth of South Korea's democratic transformation. Among the most frequently cited limitations to South Korea's democracy are the persistence of individualized party politics, centered on a leader rather than a platform, and strong regional sentiments that impede truly national and issue-oriented parties from consolidating. Another limitation is the National Security Law, which bars any speech or action that supports North Korea or shows it in a positive light, a law that not only curtails freedom of speech but is also highly problematic in a time of growing North–South contacts. But there are also more fundamental criticisms of South Korean democracy. Choi Jang-jip, one of South Korea's leading political scientists, argues that South Korean democracy remains "minimalist" and conservative, not expressing the true range of political options and opinions among its citizens. Choi argues that, indeed, democracy is in danger of moving backward – not to authoritarianism, but to a political system characterized by a largely apathetic electorate dominated by a small number of conservative elites and special interests. Rapidly declining voter turnout, among other evidence, supports Choi's thesis.[25]

It may be precisely because of the conservative nature of democratic transition to date that civil society and social movement organization remain active and visible in South Korea. Rather than fade away as one might expect in a mature democracy, activism has persisted well into the post-authoritarian period. Social movements have become institutionalized – part of the fixed landscape of South Korean society – but not politically incorporated, despite the closeness of some social movement groups to the Roh Moo-hyun administration. Thus, politics writ large in South Korea, including both formal political parties and civil society groups, continues to be contentious, dynamic, and at times explosive.[26]

Civil society has therefore not disappeared with South Korea's democratization. The two co-exist and contend, each influencing the other. The authors in this volume view the relationship among civil society, democracy, and the state in contemporary South Korea from a variety of perspectives. In Chapter 1, Bruce Cumings takes a broadly comparative view, observing South Korea's experience of democratization through the lens of civil society theory as developed in the West, arguing that the former has much to contribute to the latter. In Chapter 2, John Duncan explores the historical roots of Korean civil society in the Chosŏn period (1392–1910). In Chapter 3, Sunhyuk Kim looks closely at South Korea's democratic breakthrough and the role of civil society in establishing and consolidating democracy. The following five chapters analyze different civil society actors: Hagen Koo writes on South Korean workers, Namhee Lee on students, Seungsook Moon (in a chapter new to this volume) on gender and civil society, Linda S. Lewis on the memory of the 1980 Kwangju massacre, and Donald N. Clark on the Protestant church. My own chapter, also a new addition, moves beyond South Korea to explore the possibility of civil society within North Korea, given the recent economic and social changes in the Democratic People's Republic of Korea (DPRK).

Both North and South Korea emerged out of Japanese colonialism in the late 1940s determined to construct a strong state as an answer to foreign domination, military weakness and economic "backwardness."[27] But the South Korean state, based in theory on a democratic political model toward which its critics could try to make it accountable, was unable either to absorb or to permanently suppress civil society, despite decades of attempting to subordinate civil society to the state's goals, especially the goal of economic growth. The limits of the authoritarian state in South Korea allowed for a space, however constrained at first, for civil society to develop in opposition to the state, a course which eventually led to the authoritarian state's demise.[28] As of yet, no such opposition has emerged in the North, with its very different kind of state, one that absorbed rather than merely repressed the nascent civil society of the late1940s. By effectively organizing and drawing support from large segments of the peasantry, working class, students and other social elements that later developed into an active civil society in the South, the North Korean regime co-opted a potentially critical civil society and created an extremely powerful and penetrative state.[29] To this day, there is no sign of overt, organized opposition in North Korea. In the case of South Korea, an active civil society and a strong state have been at odds for much of the Republic's history. But the state–society relationship in South Korea is hardly a zero-sum game. For civil society to flourish, a state that guarantees legal rights, democratic freedoms, and the satisfaction of basic social needs is indispensable.[30] Effective democracy, in short, requires both a viable state and a vibrant civil society. If the former was overdeveloped in South Korea in the past, the latter has come into its own in the last 20 years, which is a hopeful sign for the future of Korean democracy.

Notes

1 Samuel P. Huntington, *The Third Wave: Democratization in the Late Twentieth Century* (Norman: University of Oklahoma Press, 1991); Larry Diamond *et al.* eds. *Consolidating the Third Wave Democracies: Themes and Perspectives* (Baltimore: Johns Hopkins University Press, 1997).

2 Although some theorists would trace the origins of civil society theory in the West as far back as Aristotle, it is in the Enlightenment and post-Enlightenment work of Locke, Kant, and especially Hegel that the notion of "civil society" (for Hegel, *bürgerliche Gesselschaft*, or "bourgeois society") receives full analytical attention. In the twentieth century, although the Italian Marxist Antonio Gramsci discusses civil society in the 1920s, it is only in the 1960s that Jürgen Habermas brings civil society once again to the center of theoretical inquiry. See especially Habermas, *The Structural Transformation of the Public Sphere: An Inquiry into a Category of Bourgeois Society*, trans. Thomas Burger (Cambridge: MIT Press, 1989 [1962]).

3 See especially John A. Hall, ed. *Civil Society: Theory, History, Comparison* (Cambridge, UK: Polity Press, 1995), and numerous works by John Keane, including *Democracy and Civil Society* (London: Verso, 1988); *Civil Society and the State: New European Perspectives* (London: Verso, 1988); and *Civil Society: Old Images, New Visions* (Stanford: Stanford University Press, 1998).

4 Most (in)famously by Frances Fukuyuma in his article of that name, later expanded into the book *The End of History and the Last Man* (New York: The Free Press, 1992).

5 This disillusionment with civil society has occurred even in the parts of Europe where the democratic breakthrough has been an unambiguous success. See Clive Tempest, "Myths from Eastern Europe and the Legend of the West," *Democratization* vol. 4, no. 1 (Spring 1997), special issue on "Civil Society: Democratic Perspectives"; Bill Lomax, "The Strange Death of 'Civil Society' in Post-Communist Hungary," *The Journal of Communist Studies and Transition Politics* vol. 13, no. 1 (March 1997).

6 David L. Blaney and Mustapha Kamal Pasha, "Civil Society and Democracy in the Third World: Ambiguous and Historical Possibilities," *Studies in Comparative International Development* vol. 28, no. 1 (Spring 1993).

7 Cohen and Arato, for example, call for an attempt "to thematize a program that seeks to represent the values and interest of social autonomy in face of *both* the modern state and the capitalist economy" in Jean L. Cohen and Andrew Arato, *Civil Society and Political Theory* (Cambridge: MIT Press, 1992), p. 30.

8 Larry Diamond, "Rethinking Civil Society: Toward Democratic Consolidation," *Journal of Democracy* vol. 5, no. 3 (July 1994), p. 5.

9 Andrew Weller, an anthropologist specializing in Taiwan, pointedly rejects the term "civil society" for the type of civil associations he finds in Taiwan, preferring to see these associations in their own terms rather than measuring them against a putative Western ideal. See Weller, *Alternate Civilities: Democracy and Culture in China and Taiwan* (Boulder, CO: Westview Press, 1999), p. 16. Both in Taiwan and South Korea, civil associations have local roots and distinctive forms that are often quite different from such associations in the West. Nevertheless, Korean civic leaders and intellectuals *themselves* have come to use the term "civil society" (*simin sahoe*) to refer to their groups and activities, whatever the provenance of the term or appropriateness of the concept.

10 *Minjung* was a widely used term for the non-elite and increasingly politicized elements of South Korean society in the 1970s and 1980s. See Namhee Lee in this volume, and Kenneth Wells, ed. *South Korea's* Minjung *Movement: The Culture and Politics of Dissidence* (Honolulu: University of Hawaii Press, 1995). The contributors to Hagen Koo, ed. *State and Society in Contemporary Korea* (Ithaca: Cornell University Press, 1993), explore "the complex, dynamic, and dialectical relationships between the state and society" in post-1945 Korea (p. 8), a relationship that was often, if not usually, one of conflict.

11 Im and Yang, *Han'guk ŭi simin sahoe.*

12 The proponents of Asian market authoritarianism tended to neglect the fact that, before the take-off of East Asian capitalist economies in the latter part of the twentieth century, the general consensus of Western observers was that Confucianism was an *impediment* to the development of capitalism. The most famous argument for Confucianism *contra* capitalism is of course in the work of Max Weber, especially *The Religion of China: Confucianism and Taoism*, ed. and trans. Hans H. Gerth (New York: Free Press, 1951), but many others, including Karl Marx, held a dim view of capitalism's potential in East Asia (other than Japan) that influenced Western thinking on the subject well into the twentieth century.

13 See especially the interview with Lee Kwan Yew, then prime minister of Singapore, in *Foreign Affairs* (March/April 1994) on the subject of "Asian Values."

14 Kim Dae Jung, "Is Culture Destiny? The Myth of Asia's Anti-Democratic Values," *Foreign Affairs* (November/December 1994), rebutting Lee Kwan Yew.

15 See, among others, Thomas B. Gold, "Civil Society in Taiwan: The Confucian Dimension," in Tu Wei-ming, ed. *Confucian Traditions in East Asian Modernity* (Cambridge: Harvard University Press, 1996); Wm. Theodore De Bary and Tu Weiming, eds. *Confucianism and Human Rights* (New York: Columbia University Press, 1998); and Daniel E. Bell, *East Meets West: Human Rights and Democracy in East Asia* (Princeton: Princeton University Press, 2000).

16 Philip C.C. Huang, " 'Public Sphere'/ 'Civil Society' in China? The Third Realm between State and Society," *Modern China* vol. 19, no. 2 (April 1993).

17 It is arguable that, in fact, the places in East Asia where democracy is most readily observable, such as Japan, Hong Kong, and Taiwan, are precisely where Confucian traditions are ambiguous, weak, or marginal. The same cannot be said of Korea, however.

18 For perspectives on the (still largely nascent) civil society in China, see Timothy Brook and B. Michael Frolic, eds. *Civil Society in China* (Armonk, NY: M.E. Sharpe, 1997). For Asia as a whole, including East, Southeast, and South Asia, see Muthiah Alagappa, ed. *Civil Society in Asia: Expanding and Contracting Democratic Space* (Stanford: Stanford University Press, 2004).

19 Doowon Suh, "From Individual Welfare to Social Change: The Expanding Goals of Korean White-Collar Labor Unions, 1987–1995," PhD Dissertation, University of Chicago, 1998.

20 Hagen Koo, *Korean Workers: The Culture and Politics of Class Formation* (Ithaca: Cornell University Press, 2002).

21 Don Oberdorfer, *The Two Koreas: A Contemporary History* (Reading, MA: Basic Books, 1997), p. 166.

22 Sunhyuk Kim, *The Politics of Democratization in Korea: The Role of Civil Society* (Pittsburgh: University of Pittsburgh Press, 2000).

23 The term "netizen" was apparently coined in the U.S. in the late 1990s, but became more widely used in East Asia, especially Japan and South Korea. See Michael Hauben and Ronda Hauben, *Netizens: On the History and Impact of Usenet and the Internet* (Los Alamitos, CA: IEEE Computer Society Press, 1997). In 2002, the South Korean weekly *Sisa Journal* named the netizen as "Person of the Year."

24 David Scofield, "The Dawning of Pluralism in South Korea," *Asia Times*, March 30, 2004. http://www.atimes.com.

25 Choi Jang-Jip, *Democracy after Democratization: The Korean Experience* trans. Lee Kyung-hee (Seoul: Humanitas, 2005).

26 This is the thesis of Sun-Chul Kim's PhD research in the department of sociology at Columbia. Kim examines what he calls "defiant institutionalization" of social movements in post-authoritarian South Korea.

27 For Chosŏn Korea as a relatively weak state, see James Palais, *Politics and Policy in Traditional Korea* (Cambridge: Harvard University Press, 1975).

28 The role of the United States in the process of South Korea's democratization has been ambiguous. On the one hand, the U.S. provided the most important model of democratic political institutions for the Republic of Korea from the latter's founding in 1948, and the idea of democracy on the American model was often the inspiration for anti-authoritarian protests in South Korea. On the other hand, the actual behavior of U.S. military and government representatives within South Korea, from the 1945–48 military occupation until the 1990s, was often in support of repressive political leaders in the name of security and the defense against communism. After the May 1980 massacre of civilian demonstrators in Kwangju, for which many Koreans held the U.S. partly accountable, anti-government protests in Korea took a distinctly anti-American tone for the first time. See Gi-Wook Shin, "Marxism, Anti-Americanism, and Democracy in South Korea: An Examination of Nationalist Intellectual Discourse," *Positions: East Asia Cultures Critique* vol. 3, no. 2 (Spring 1995), and Linda Lewis in this volume.

29 Charles K. Armstrong, *The North Korean Revolution, 1945–1950* (Ithaca: Cornell University Press, 2003).

30 Keane, *Civil Society: Old Images, New Visions*, p. 9.

1 Civil society in West and East

Bruce Cumings

Thinking about the differences between Korea and the United States is an inevitable career by product for Americans who study Korea or Koreans who study America, because they are, or they become, people who have a foot in both cultures. Such scholars also change, and they become people with both feet planted firmly in neither culture, that is, feet planted nowhere, or in an indefinable space existing between the two countries. But what is always so striking to such a person is the contrast between his or her daily life, where thoughts and images of Korea and America mingle profusely, and the stark contrast exemplified by the two peoples: Americans and Koreans were joined together as allies and friends since 1945, but they rarely think about each other (although this generalization is more true of the American people, who know little about Korea), and even more rarely do they actively compare each other on the same plane. In a recent book I tried to understand the complexity of perception that results from these juxtapositions, using metaphors of vision: clear, blurred, and double vision, and also the complex vantage point afforded to a person who is poised between two cultures, reflecting critically on both of them.[1]

Since the collapse of the Berlin Wall and the fall of Western communism, a ubiquitous trope has emerged in American scholarship on the meaning of these critical events: *civil society*, as in the title of this book. This term, which was central to an older political sociology but had fallen into disuse, reappeared in two contexts: (1) what the former communist countries needed most was what the communists had respected least, namely civil society; and (2) what Americans needed was to repair and restore their own civil society. Meanwhile, in the Republic of Korea a strong civil society emerged for the first time in the 1980s and 1990s, as a product and also a gift of the extraordinary turmoil of Korea's modern history. And few if any Americans noticed. It is this theme that I wish to dwell on, primarily from an abstract or theoretical perspective.[2]

For much of the past decade the American political spectrum from right to left was suffused with an assortment of concerns about American civil society. Most commentators pointed to the same symptoms: the pathologies and dangers of cities and (remarkably) the suburbs where the majority of Americans now lived, but where astonishing and unprecedented events occurred (like the killings at Columbine High School); high rates of crime amid a more general breakdown of morality, with arguments on both the right and left about what caused this presumed moral breakdown; the disintegration of nuclear families, amid increasing divorce rates, growing numbers of Americans choosing to remain unmarried, and the rise of gay rights movements; citizen apathy and lack of interest in politics, symbolized by less than half the people voting in national elections; the decline of the "group life" that Alexis de Tocqueville and others had thought so characteristic of American democracy, and the like.

A symbol of this kind of thinking was Robert Putnam's famous article (and subsequent book), called "Bowling Alone." A Harvard political scientist, Putnam gained national renown for his argument that Americans had become a nation of alienated individuals, lacking in public spirit and a willingness to join civic groups; they even went bowling by themselves, instead of joining the bowling teams that were a staple of American life in the 1950s, when Putnam grew up. If this discourse waned somewhat during the years of economic boom in the late 1990s, the fractured outcome of the 2000 presidential election brought it back. Indeed, President George W. Bush and his advisors fret about the problems of American civil society almost as much as their predecessors did, in the Clinton administration. As one article on this presidential commonality put it,

> It has been difficult to pin an ideological tail on the nascent Bush White House. One day the president is called a staunch conservative … and the next he's labeled a bleeding heart for helping prisoners' children and promoting literacy programs. The problem, some Bush advisers and friends say, is that conventional political definitions do not adequately explain what the president is trying to do. His actions have less to do with the left vs. right, they say, than with his embrace of many of the ideas contained in the movement known as "communitarianism," which places the importance of society ahead of the unfettered rights of the individual.
>
> "This is the ultimate Third Way," said Don Eberly, an adviser in the Bush White House, using a favorite phrase of President Bill Clinton, who also sought, largely unsuccessfully, to redefine the debate with an alternative to the liberal-conservative conflict.

The writer went on to link communitarianism, to "'civil society' thinking," which he said is a term with many interpretations:

> but at its center is a notion that years of celebrating individual freedom have weakened the bonds of community and that the rights of the individual must be balanced against the interests of society as a whole. Inherent in the philosophy is a return to values and morality, which, the school of thought believes, can best be fostered by community organizations. "We need to connect with one another. We've got to move a little more in the direction of community in the balance between community and the individual," said Robert D. Putnam of Harvard University, a leading communitarian thinker.

Bush's inaugural address "was a communitarian text," according to his advisors, using key words like "civility," "responsibility," and "community"– and that was "no accident," because Bush's advisors consulted Putnam about the speech. Another advisor said that Bush wanted to move Republicans away from the libertarian idea that individuals are "lone atoms" apart from their community: the President, he said, "is a civil society guy ."[3]

This wave of concern about American civil society coincided with a quite different idea, namely, that civil society is inherently a Western concept, and that it is absent in the remaining communist countries, that it is the thing most in need of creation in post-communist countries, and the thing mostly absent in East Asia – whether in authoritarian Singapore, democratic Japan, or rapidly democratizing South Korea and Taiwan. Samuel Huntington, also a political scientist at Harvard, made this view notorious in his essay (and subsequent book), *The Clash of Civilizations*, which sought to fashion a new paradigm for post-Cold War global politics. His assumption was that several distinct bodies of inherited ideas and practices existed in our world, and that they either already had or soon would constitute themselves in opposition to each other; as they did so, the new axis of global politics would spring forth.[4] On closer reading, one finds in this account a nostalgic reprise of 1950s modernization theory and a disillusioned lament on the passing of the Eastern establishment and its Anglo-Saxon counterparts in Europe, thus yielding a plea for a renewed Atlanticism. For Huntington there is but one great civilization, the West's, and a host of competing civilizations that are, or may become, threats to Western civilization.

Francis Fukuyama had a similar perspective in his influential book, *The End of History*.[5] Fukuyama sprinkles criticisms of American liberalism through his text, especially the American inability to come to agreement on moral issues, the failures of American leaders (if mostly those from the Democratic Party), and the perils of community in a time of atomized individualism. But like Huntington he privileges the West, and the United States: "a contemporary liberal democracy like the United States permits considerable scope for those who desire to be recognized as greater than others." He ended the book with his hope that "the idea of a universal and directional history leading up to liberal democracy may become more plausible to people"; human history will come to seem like "a long wagon train" that finally reaches the end of its journey, which is, for him, free-market liberalism. Like other celebrants of liberalism and "the West," Fukuyama substitutes for actually existing liberalism an ideal version, drawn from the fine words and high-minded phrases of iconic figures like John Locke, John Stuart Mill, and Alexis de Tocqueville.

In Karl van Wolferen's *Enigma of Japanese Power*[6] this comparison between the West and all-the-rest is explicitly related to the failings of East Asian politics. Essentially his argument is that East Asia modernized without civil society and without an Enlightenment. For van Wolferen "the West" connotes a site of "independent, universal truths or immutable religious beliefs, transcending the worldly reality of social dictates and the decrees of power-holders"; Japan, however, is a place where people adjust their beliefs to situations, in "a political culture that does not recognize the possibility of transcendental truths." As in nineteenth century accounts of "the Orient," for van Wolferen Japan is an enigma, opaque, led by a mysterious "System," and "single-mindedly pursuing some obscure aim of its own." The System "systematically suppresses individualism," he writes, and the Japanese do not accept Western logic or metaphysics, going all the way back to "the Greeks." The "crucial factor" that proves these generalizations is "the near absence [in Japan] of any idea that there can be truths, rules, principles or morals that always apply, no matter what the circumstances."[7] Koreans might think the same thing of Japan, but van Wolferen does not like any of the East Asian political systems: "The Japanese, Korean and Taiwanese experiences show that a third category of political economy can exist, beside the Western and communist types." These states represent "a largely uncharted economic and social-political category."[8]

In this discourse, which is quite common in the U.S., the ills and pathologies of American civil society curiously disappear, to be replaced surreptitiously by an idealized construction drawn from Locke and Tocqueville. Of course no one can claim that East Asian countries have the social pathology obvious on almost any street in any American city, and recent elections in Korea and Taiwan had rates of voter turnout and exuberant participation far above those of American elections. But all that is forgotten in the conjuring of a Western civil society where well-informed citizens debate the important questions of politics and the good life without fear or favor, in contrast to the limited democracies, authoritarian systems and general illiberalism of East Asia, with the People's Republics in China and North Korea taking the cake as the worst-case outcomes of the pathologies of Asian politics.

In an earlier work called *Making Democracy Work*, Robert Putnam began this study of civil society in general and Italian civil society in particular with a discussion of the widespread despair in the U.S. about public institutions and democratic possibilities, then went on to analyze the exemplary civic virtue of northern Italy and the lack of it in the south, and ended on a note suggesting that non-Western societies shared many of the pathologies of southern Italy:

> Where norms and networks of civic engagement are lacking, the outlook for collective action appears bleak. The fate of the Mezzogiorno is an object lesson for the third World today and the former Communist lands of Eurasia tomorrow, moving uncertainly toward self-government.[9]

In this book Putnam also rehabilitated Almond and Verba's 1963 book, *The Civic Culture*, calling it "a modern classic" in the vein of Tocqueville's *Democracy in America*.[10] Indeed Putnam's own theory draws heavily on the Weberian/ Parsonian pattern variables that Almond and Verba used forty years ago, renaming them as "norms of civic engagement," "social structures of cooperation," and the like. Good civil societies depend on civic engagement, political equality, the attenuation of individual striving in the interests of community, "solidarity, trust, and tolerance," and a network of civic or secondary associations: indeed, a key indicator of "civic sociability" is the "vibrancy of associational life."

Jürgen Habermas is the world's pre-eminent theorist of the public sphere (*Öffentlichkeit*), and in his work the concerns of scholars like Huntington and Putnam reach their highest, most sophisticated level. Habermas is the opposite of a romantic reactionary or a skeptical post-modernist: his thought is thoroughly shaped by belief in the Enlightenment project, the uses of human reason, the validity and abundant yield of progress, and the (still unrealized) utopian potential of the modern – however much it may be difficult to believe in that potential in today's world. His life work has combined a deep knowledge of the continental tradition and its heights (especially for him in the work of Kant, Hegel, Marx, Nietzsche and Weber), with an unusual interest in positivist and systematic Anglo-Saxon social science. From the latter he draws upon precisely the Parsonian concern with norms, roles, and systems that influenced Almond, Verba, and Putnam.[11]

Habermas's primary concern is civil society – or what he calls the public sphere, "the definitive institution of democracy," according to an American theorist:

> A public sphere is an arena in which individuals participate in discussions about matters of common concern, in an atmosphere free of coercion or dependencies (inequalities). … Habermas' institutional concerns center on empowering voice, and on disenabling other means of collective judgment within democratic arenas – coercion, markets, and tradition.[12]

But for Habermas the public sphere consists not merely of the commonly designated sites of political discussion, like parliament or the newspapers; it is a vast (and theoretically universal) communications network that nonetheless bases itself in procedural democracy – especially in guarantees of basic human rights and political freedoms – and in a pluralism of groups. Autonomous public spheres are formed through the self-organization of a myriad of social groups, entering into a moral and political relationship with each other through communicative networks, yielding an egalitarian, open, and uncoerced debate. All who participate must be equal, each to the other; the sphere must be completely open, with no barriers to entry; the resultant debate is ipso facto both political and *moral*, since Habermas recognizes no separation of fact and value, or politics and morality (at least in the sphere of debate and decision). But it is also a *rational* sphere, where facts and values can be known: Habermas distinguishes between "'three domains of reality:' outer nature, inner nature, and society, to which correspond the objective, the subjective, and the intersubjective dimensions of rationality."[13] For Habermas democracy is an intersubjective communicative process featuring dialogue, debate, and even conflict, and this is the only medium allowing us to know rationally the uses and ends of civil society. Habermas's ideal-typical public sphere thus has much in common with the economists' marketplace, where all enter equally to truck and barter according to self-interest and supply and demand, free of coercion or regulation. His insistence on the pathologies of violence in politics, however, is most reminiscent of the Quaker pacifist tradition in America, where all problems must – by definition – be debated and talked through, no matter how long it takes, until that point where consensus is achieved:

> Habermas announced that a rational basis for collective life would be achieved only when social relations were organized "according to the principle that the validity of every norm of political consequence be made dependent on a consensus arrived at in communication free from domination."[14]

Any intervention by violence, or by the organs of power, necessarily short-circuits the deliberative process necessary to a democratic public sphere.

Only in "the West"?

The most disturbing aspect of this literature is the cavalier identification of civil society and communitarian democracy with the West: these things originated in Western Europe, migrated to North America and the British Commonwealth, and hardly anywhere else. Non-Western societies are simply not suitable settings for civil society and republican democracy, Putnam suggests. *The Civic Culture* reported these Western conceits straightforwardly in 1963, a time of higher American self-confidence and less self-awareness; it was only in the U.S. and England that the authors found "a pattern of political attitudes and an underlying set of social attitudes that is supportive of a stable democratic process." In the other nations they studied (West Germany, Italy, and Mexico), "these patterns are less evident."[15]

Habermas, a person who certainly ought to know better, also privileges the West as the site of the origin of his "public sphere" and its contemporary problematic, as well as its ultimate redemption. He concluded one of his books on "modernity" with this statement:

> Who else but Europe could draw from its own traditions the insight, the energy, the courage of vision – everything that would be necessary to strip from the … premises of a blind compulsion to system maintenance and system expansion their power to shape our mentality.[16]

This is by no means an unusual emphasis for Habermas, even if it is unusually blunt; his whole work is imbued with "the claim that the modern West – for all its problems – best embodies" the values of rationality and democracy,[17] with a now-evident, now-hidden discourse about modern German history (which I think pushes him toward the privileging of norms of political interaction that are evident in postwar West Germany, but nowhere else in German history – and for that reason may be temporary or precarious in their staying power), and an apparent lack of concern for the non-Western experience, except as a species of occasional counter-hegemonic practice in the "Third World." Thus he shares the same prejudices as his cherished predecessor Max Weber (Habermas is most of all a Weberian), but not Weber's passionate and intelligent comparativist project

– and in a time when Weber would certainly recognize his own provincialism, were he still talking about "only in the West ...." But perhaps we had better sample the original Weber, what he said then, since we don't know what he would say now:

> Only the occident knows the state in the modern sense, with a professional administration, specialized officialdom, and law based on the concept of citizenship. ... Only the occident knows rational law .... Furthermore, only the occident possesses science. ... Finally, Western civilization is further distinguished from every other by the presence of men with a rational ethic for the conduct of life.

Habermas is much more aware than Huntington and Putnam of critical alternatives to his work, however, which is not to say they make a big impact on him. Nancy Love is right to point out that the public sphere of Habermas's construction "asks us to be Gods," to enter the public space free of property, inequality, recourse to force, or even to anger; thus is born an arena of "ideal speech," recognizing "no sides"– no classes, genders, or races to be transcended.[18] In that respect, Habermas's public sphere is no different than the ideality of liberalism. Still, that is an easy criticism, and Habermas is right that in public debate, we do not want the shadow of our class, race, or gender to overwhelm the message we wish to impart. Nor is Habermas's Western essentialism something that distinguishes him from any number of Western theorists. We should try harder to develop an effective critique of Habermas in his own terms.

We have been examining an Anglo-Saxon discourse about civil society, even if the German Habermas agrees with it; now let us examine the continental European discourse of the mid-nineteenth century. If we return to original European debates about state and civil society, in Hegel's work and Marx's critique of it, we see that the first modern representative state also just happened to be found in the hegemonic power of the nineteenth century, England. Its primary industrial rival, Germany, could only produce some unavailing, pale reflection of the liberal state, according to Marx. So, in reality, it produced a strong state that was the flip side of a weak civil society – a "fused state." But at the level of theory Germany could work an elegant and sublime substitution for Anglo-Saxon dominance: namely, Hegel – who towered over any English thinker in his time.

For Hegel, modern society establishes the distinction between public and private, and because individuals are atomized by the market (as Marx says of Hegel's theory), the state itself must provide a new form of unity – in Hegel, an abstracted unity that substitutes for a lost organic community. Whereas John Locke presents the state (or "civil government") as the separated "impartial judge" of private conflicts, for Hegel this separation of state and civil society was a contradiction of his deepest understanding of human society,[19] and so he hypothesized a state that will restore the lost wholeness for which he yearned, yielding a fusion of what we call state and society.

Hegel seeks to overcome the division between state and civil society also through representative government, whereby delegates are chosen and entrusted to "superintend the state's interests" in civil society. Marx points out that this hardly solves the problem of the state's alienation from civil society: it is the civil service in the form of administration, or judiciary, or police, that in turn represent the state in civil society, and often with *force majeure*. Hegel thinks he gets around this objection by arguing that the civil servant is not loyal to the monarch but instead a neutral figure, chosen on the basis of his specialized knowledge; if every citizen has the opportunity to join "the class of civil servants," and there are specified procedures for deciding who joins (civil service examinations), then we need not worry about the arbitrary exercise of state power.[20] Guarantees against arbitrary power are lodged in the official himself – in, for example, the civil servant's "dispassionate, upright and polite demeanor." The reader will note that Hegel's reasoning is quite compatible with contemporary doctrine.

Hegel introduces a confusion, however, by saying that not just anybody ought to be a bureaucrat. Where do we find such people? Generally speaking, Hegel says, in the middle class – the "pillar" of the state. Likewise, the bureaucrats are part of the definition of what it means to be middle class. Marx then intrudes Hegel's idea that the state should also develop the middle class, or "grow it," to use a Clintonesque term, if it is weak. And with that Hegel's argument reveals its circularity and its bourgeois presuppositions, a dog biting its own tail: a government of the middle class, by the middle class – and for the middle class?

Marx took Hegel (and not Locke) to be the exemplary theorist of the representative state, and instantly took his measure: however dazzling he was, Hegel merely recapitulated Germany's position *vis-à-vis* the advanced economies:

> The German *status quo* is the *undisguised consummation of the ancien régime and the ancien régime* is the *hidden defect of the modern state*. The struggle against the German political present is the struggle against the past of modern nations ... the present German regime ... [is] an anachronism, a flagrant contradiction of universally accepted axioms. ...
>
> In Germany, therefore, we are about to begin at the point where France and England are about to conclude. ... This is a good example of the *German* form of modern problems, an example of how our history, like some raw recruit, has up to now been restricted to repeating hackneyed routines that belong to the past of other nations.

As for Hegel, he supplied the ideality for which there was no reality:

> We Germans have lived our future history in thought, in *philosophy*. We are the *philosophical* contemporaries of the present without being its *historical* contemporaries. ... What for advanced nations is a *practical quarrel with modern political conditions is for Germany, where such conditions do not yet exist, a critical quarrel with their reflection in philosophy.*

I have purposely left out Marx's most important statement, which has a prescience founded in genius and requires no emphasis: in England and France "it is a question of the solution; here [in Germany] it is only a question of the collision."[21] Why a collision? Because a middle class brought into being in hothouse conditions could never establish its hegemony short of a bloody reckoning with its reactionary enemies, like the Prussian Junkers, classes forged in the long run of "real" history. Germany thus combined the "civilized defects" of the modern world with the "barbaric defects" of the old regime. How can such a country, in one great leap, overcome "not only its own limitations but those also of the modern nations"?[22]

History's answer was that it could not, and those who enjoy pointing out the progressive teleology in Marx's thought need also to reckon with Germany's trajectory (Bismarck-to World War I-to Weimar-to Hitler-to catastrophe and then and only then to liberalism) and the diabolical unfolding of barbarism within "civility," foregrounded by Marx in 1844.

Antonio Gramsci, writing in the twentieth century, extended the conception of civil society by arguing that it was not just the sphere of debate, disputation and politics (that is, the sphere primarily of the intellectuals), but a vast space existing between the ruling groups who inhabit the state, and the normal or commonsensical routines of everyday life in the society. It is in this space that state and society come together, with the outcome indeterminate: it might be an organic unity of one and all, or a sharp cleavage of every man for himself, held together by the forces of order. For civil society to have legitimacy, or even to function at all effectively, the goals of the dominant groups must be translated into the quotidian reality of each person, so that civil and political behavior becomes habitual and no longer a matter of conscious reflection.

Gramsci's well-known definition of hegemony emerged from this logic: that civil society is organic which teaches its master ideas through the metaphors of mother's milk or the air we breathe – it is no longer ideology, but ethos (ether, the-air-we-breathe). Absent such hegemonic mediation, and the state must exist over and above civil society as a coercive form of domination. State and civil society, therefore, coexist in a curious zero-sum fashion: the less the civil society functions as it ought to, the more the state must grow in power to remedy this defect. The intellectuals are the primary carriers of a self-conscious civil society and therefore populated the salons of eighteenth-century France as the modern conception of civil society developed, but modern society can only be whole when the intellectuals abandon their protected sphere (resting implicitly on state guarantees of basic freedoms, which often do not exist for other people) and constitute themselves as organic with the people. This is for him the only acceptable "fused state."[23]

From Marx we learned that civil society is a construct of the early industrializers, and the abortively fused state the product of late industrialization, a political entity seeking to make up for lost time, to substitute for a lost historical evolution. Gramsci understood this historical substitution of the state for the unevolved civil society, but argued that modern society can only become whole when civil society is no longer the vested interest of the intelligentsia, but the common property of all. Clearly American theorists of civil society, as well as Habermas, have much to learn from this critique on the left.

A critique of the Anglo-Saxon discourse on civil society from the right, or the Catholic tradition, can be found in Alasdair MacIntyre's influential book, *After Virtue*, and in Roberto Unger's *Knowledge and Politics*. MacIntyre begins his account with the incapacity of Americans to decide questions of morality in the public sphere. Of moral and political debate there is plenty, but the debates are never resolved: they are interminable, because we have "no rational way of securing moral agreement."[24] The debate over abortion, for example, "the right to life" versus "the right to choose," is but one of many such irresolvable issues. MacIntyre and Unger trace the origin of this problem to Anglo-Saxon positivism and its separation of fact and value, of objective knowledge and normative preference. Where Habermas establishes a distinction between instrumental and intersubjective relations in civil society (usually identified as the technocratic rationality of a bureaucracy as contrasted to the I–thou relations of a true political community), MacIntyre says that the separation of fact from value leaves us with nothing but instrumental relationships in American civil society. You have your moral or political preference and I have mine, but in choosing between values, reason is silent: therefore we must agree to disagree, and fashion a procedural politics that is unconcerned with substantive ends. Such a politics will then mediate conflicting moral/political positions.

MacIntyre contrasts this procedural regime, which is only concerned with "man as he happens to be," with the Aristotelian notion of "man as he could be if he realized his essential nature": "To say what someone ought to do is at one and the same time to say what course of action will … lead toward a man's true end and to say what the law … enjoins."[25] Politics, for MacIntyre, is that sphere where human beings realize their true or essential nature. The question must be, "what sort of person am I to become?" Liberals wish to avoid this question, because reason must be silent before questions of what constitutes the good for human beings; instead, the liberal asks "what rules ought we to follow," what procedures will enable us to reach a rough form of justice between conflicting claims of right. But this does not avoid the question of what sort of people we are: every day we answer that question in our practice, through the lives that we lead. Ineluctably, therefore, MacIntyre argues that the presupposition of any civil society must be "the exercise of the virtues and the achievement of the good."[26]

Through this contrast between the liberal and the Aristotelian position, MacIntyre and Unger arrive at a devastating conclusion about the possibilities of civil society in America: we cannot form an intersubjective political community (Habermas's ideal), because not only do we not know what its purpose would be, but we have already agreed not to raise this question. As Unger puts the point,

> The political doctrine of liberalism does not acknowledge communal values. To recognize their existence, it would be necessary to begin with a vision of

the basic circumstances of social life that took groups rather than individuals as the intelligible and primary units of social life.[27]

Or as MacIntyre argues, "a modern liberal political society can appear only as a collection of citizens of nowhere who have banded together for their common protection."[28]

MacIntyre goes on to argue that the civic community is not one defined by a single, reigning conception of virtue: if people sincerely assert their conceptions of the substantive ends of human community in their daily practice, there will inevitably be conflict. Instead of submerging that conflict as an insoluble normative problem, or expecting it somehow to dissolve in the consensus of the ideal public sphere, it is "through conflict and sometimes only through conflict" that we will learn "what our ends and purposes are."[29] But however a community chooses to reach moral or substantive ends, it must do so or risk becoming a mere collection of anomalous individuals:

> In any society where government does not express or represent the moral community of the citizens, but is instead a set of institutional arrangements for imposing a bureaucratized unity on a society which lacks genuine moral consensus, the nature of political obligation becomes systematically unclear.[30]

From this insight we can understand the increasing tendency of Americans to assume that they have no obligations, from the simplest one of voting to the more important task of shaping a political community that is also a moral bond between people.

From the Catholic Right we have learned that liberalism cannot create the civil society that it privileges as its birthright, because of the inherent presuppositions of liberalism itself. MacIntyre and Unger agree that civic community must be a value over and above the individual and his liberty, but argue that such a community cannot exist without an agreement on its substantive end – which must be to fashion human beings who realize the community's conception of the good. What about Habermas?

It turns out that a person we can call "the early Habermas" had already figured all this out. His 1961 book, *The Structural Transformation of the Public Sphere*, is a *tour de force* analysis of how the liberal (or bourgeois) public sphere, a limited but vital civil society in the eighteenth century, turned into a bureaucratized, alienated public space still marching under the banner of the French *philosophes'* ideals of civic virtue.[31] Here we find Habermas saying essentially what Gramsci did, that civil society exists *between* the state and the mass of the people; as it developed in the eighteenth century it bid fair to be the ideal political space that liberals have always claimed it should be, with the spread of newspapers, journals, salons, and coffee houses. But by the late nineteenth century it had become what it is today, a space for competition between plural interests who "negotiate and compromise among themselves and with government officials, while excluding the public from their proceedings."[32] The bourgeois public sphere is thus limited to a particular epoch, and is not synonymous with the historical development of civil society itself.

Habermas rather agrees with Marx that Hegel "took the teeth out of the idea of the public sphere in civil society"; Marx's blistering critique "demolished all fictions to which the idea of the public sphere" appealed, a sphere which "contradicted its own principles of universal accessibility."[33] Whether it was German "late" development or the arrival of masses of laborers in England's cities, "the bourgeois self-interpretation of the public sphere abandoned the form of a philosophy of history in favor of a common sense meliorism":

> the critique of the idea of the bourgeois public sphere as an ideology was so obviously correct that under the altered social preconditions of "public opinion" around the middle of the [nineteenth] century, when economic liberalism was just reaching its peak, its social-philosophical representatives were forced almost to deny the principle of the public sphere of civil society even as they celebrated it.[34]

There is a bourgeois public sphere, in other words, but also a "*plebeian* public sphere" that represents the entrance of the masses onto the political stage – as with Robespierre and his followers.[35] Habermas thought the Chartist movement was the specific cause of this change, i.e., the moment when organized labor first burst upon the industrial scene.

The denial and evasion that followed is best evidenced in John Stuart Mill's reaction to the "pressure of the street" in the form of laborers, women, and (American) blacks pushing for the voting franchise. He was, by all means, in favor "of all movements rebelling against the aristocracy of money, gender and color"; they should all have the franchise. But the arrival of this new, flooded public sphere of loud and divided opinion also struck Mill as a new kind of "coercive force" violating the open, non-violent nature that should characterize the public space, and so he began deploring "the yoke of public opinion" and the compulsion to conformity that the new majority threatened. Or as Tocqueville put the point (in full if unacknowledged agreement with Mill),

> In democracies public opinion is a strange power. ... It uses no persuasion to forward its beliefs, but by some mighty pressure of the mind of all upon the intelligence of each it imposes its ideas ...

Now Mill called neither for participation without-fear-or-favor nor for critique of the powers-that-be by the tribunes of the people, but for tolerance – mostly of the now-slim stratum of intellectuals, i.e., the elect of the liberal public sphere. Meanwhile Tocqueville came to understand the genius of the American founding fathers in dividing the political public sphere, through checks and balances and the voluntary associations that mediate between leaders and led.[36]

There is a direct line from this surreptitious denial and evasion, this historically-shaped "yes" and "no" to the massed laborers and the non-elect by Mill and Tocqueville, through Bentley, Dahl, Almond and Verba, and Putnam, down to Huntington's exasperated attack on "the democratic distemper" of the 1970s. Habermas summarizes his account of the decomposition of the liberal public sphere as follows:

> Marx shared the perspective of the propertyless and uneducated masses who ... would employ the platform of the public sphere, institutionalized in the constitutional state, not to destroy it but to make it into what, according to liberal pretense, it had always claimed to be. In reality, however, the occupation of the public sphere by the unpropertied masses led to an interlocking of state and society which removed from the public sphere its former basis without supplying a new one.[37]

Is this a better explanation of the democratic malaise that Putnam and other analysts point to, or not? In my view Habermas delivered in 1961 an unanswerable critique of actually-existing liberalism.[38]

Democracy and its discontents in East Asia and Korea

The East Asian state–society configuration that van Wolferen and others find so wanting from a Western standpoint today, bears close comparison to a particular Western experience, if not *the* Western experience – namely continental European development – and therefore is by no means *sui generis*. As we saw, Marx and Hegel could hardly have been more explicit about Germany's predicament: for Marx, it was that Germany "did not pass through the intermediate stages of political emancipation at the same time as modern nations";[39] for Hegel, the optimist of course, it was the task of the state to overcome Germany's debilities:

> It is a prime concern of the state that a middle class should be developed, but this can be done only if the state is an organic unity ... i.e., it can be done only by giving authority to spheres of particular interests, which are relatively independent, and by appointing an *army of officials* whose personal arbitrariness is broken against such authorized bodies.[40]

This is a theory of "late" state formation, and of "late" democratization; Marx places the German domestic configuration in the time and space of the world system and declares the task hopeless, whereas Hegel conjures it in the thin air of an ideal type, and then foists the problem off on the bureaucrats. What is the problem? To create the middle class that is the presumed basis of democracy.[41]

In German "state science" (*Staatswissenschaft*) the conception of the *fused state* was thus born, in the aftermath of the French Revolution, as a point of definitional anxiety and political reality. It is then a short step to observe the disorders of that same revolution, to relate them to novel ideas about "popular will," and to conclude, well, who needs that? To put the point baldly, of what value is civil society in a race for industrialization? The Germans invented the fused state not to solve the problems of liberty, equality, and fraternity at the dawn of the industrial epoch, but to solve the mid-nineteenth century problems of the second industrial revolution and, more importantly, to catch up with England. A fused state is one that both subsumes civil society, and tries to build it up – but not if these efforts get in the way of industrialization.

Here, in short, is a political theory of late development that put off to a distant future the magnificent obsession of the Anglo-Saxon early industrializers with questions of popular will, democratic representation, public vs. private, or state vs. civil society. It is also a theory that explains much about East Asia's democratic trajectory: Japan, a democracy after 1945 but only after the cataclysm of war and occupation; South Korea, a democracy in 1993 but only after the cataclysm of revolution, war, division, and decades of military dictatorship (1961–1987) and sharp political struggle; Taiwan, a democracy in 1996 but only after revolution, war, national division, and forty years of martial law (1947–1987).

Viewed from the complacent standpoint of the 1990s, one analyst after another celebrated South Korea and Taiwan as victories for democracy, coming (predictably) toward the end of a process of "modernization," in which a middle class emerged triumphant. So do we have the "fused state," or emergent democracy and civil society? The answer is this: we had the fused state in South Korea and Taiwan, and now we have a limited form of procedural democracy – just like Japan and Germany. But the path to this end was hardly smooth; instead it was filled with decades of torment and turmoil, *Sturm und Drang*, and then-and-only-then, democracy.

The struggle for Korean civil society and democracy was precisely situated in MacIntyre's "site of conflict." Democratic struggles began in Korea on the day that Japan surrendered in August 1945, and have continued down to the present.[42] The popular forces of the late 1940s wanted both democracy and social justice, that is, a cleansing revolution that would wipe away the influences of Japanese imperialism. They got a cleansing in North Korea but no democracy, little if any cleansing in South Korea and little if any democracy, and after a massively destructive civil war, a thoroughly divided and disjointed nation.

Within the constricted politics of the Rhee regime (1948–1960), where any sign of a leftist orientation meant a jail term if not death (the inconsequential progressive Cho Pong-am was executed in 1958, one of the better-known of many similar examples), a space for the intelligentsia cracked open enough such that students, faculty, and intellectuals could be the vanguard for an overthrow of the First Republic, albeit when Syngman Rhee was on his last legs and the U.S. wanted him out. The tepid opposition organized the Second Republic through a weak cabinet system of government, where for a year (April 1960–May 1961) civil society on the liberal model mushroomed rapidly. At this time South Korea had more college students per capita than England, more newspaper readers per capita than almost any country in the world, and a concentration of administrative, commercial, industrial, and educational energies in one great capital city – much

like Paris.[43] A very lively salon society animated the capital, publishers brought
out thorough rewritings of modern Korean history, and students began to imagine
themselves the vanguard of unification with the North.

General Park Chung Hee was the Korean agent of the Hegelian conception
of the fused state, shutting down civil society with his *coup d'état* in 1961 and
the three-year emergency junta that followed, and deploying the state as the
initiator, guide, and financier of a classic type of "late" industrialization. Strong
American pressure from the Kennedy administration forced Park to drop his
plans for instant heavy industrialization and to don mufti and run for election
(in 1963), yielding "export-led development" and the contentious public sphere
that I first encountered in 1967. The Nixon administration enlarged the sphere
of Korean autonomy through the Guam doctrine and Nixon's neo-mercantilist
"New Economic Policy" of August 1971, enabling Park to shut down civil society
completely in 1971–1972 with barely a murmur from Washington.[44]

To make a long and bloody story very short, we can say that Park misjudged
the hidden strengths and growing maturity of the public sphere, which was
overdeveloped in relation to the economy but still underdeveloped compared
to the ubiquitous agencies of the expanding Yusin state: a vast administrative
bureaucracy, huge, distended armed forces, extensive national police, a ubiquitous
Central Intelligence Agency with operatives at every conceivable site of potential
resistance, and thorough ideological blanketing of every alternative idea in the
name of forced-pace industrialization. If you want to visit Korea in the early
1970s, you can go to China today and see all the same things.

Park's fused state thus set up an unending crisis of civil society that culminated
in the disorders of Masan and Pusan in August and September 1979, leading to
Park's assassination by his own intelligence chief in October, which led to the
"*coup*-like event" mounted by Chun Doo Hwan and Roh Tae Woo in December
1979, and the denouement at Kwangju in May 1980. The period 1980–1987 will
appear in history as a classic Brumairean event,[45] with the luckless "nephew"
(Chun) acting on behalf of the dispatched "uncle" (Park), using the jail and
the gnout all the way, but compounding into farce the tragedy of Park Chung
Hee (who truly was Korea's industrial sovereign, if not its Napoleon). The real
tragedy, of course, had taken place at Kwangju, where an aroused, self-organized,
and intersubjective citizenry (i.e., not a bunch of rioters and miscreants) sought
desperately to save itself from the new martial law regime that Chun had just
announced, only to be slaughtered (a minimum of 600 killed, maximum of 2,000
– like Tiananmen in 1989).

Chun Doo Hwan had himself designated President shortly after Kwangju. In
the next year he purged or proscribed the political activities of 800 politicians,
8,000 officials in government and business, and threw some 37,000 journalists,
students, teachers, labor organizers, and civil servants into "Purification Camps"
in remote mountain areas where they underwent a harsh "re-education"; some 200
labor leaders were among them. The "Act for the Protection of Society" authorized
preventive detention for seven to ten years, yet more than 6,000 people were
also given "additional terms" under this Act in 1980–1986. The National Security

Law defined as "anti-state" (and therefore treasonable) any association or group "organized for the purpose of assuming a title of the government or disturbing the state," and any group that "operates along with the line of the communists," or praises North Korea; the leader of such an organization could be punished by death or life in prison.

Amid this squalid history, it would be difficult to overestimate the lack of concern for democracy and human rights in Korea evinced by one American president after another. Kwangju occurred on President Jimmy Carter's watch, who prided himself on his "human rights" policy; his main response was to send an aircraft carrier task force to Korean waters as a warning to North Korea, and (within a week of the rebellion) to send the U.S. Ex-Im Bank chairman to Seoul to assure the junta of American economic support, including a $600 million loan that Carter had just approved. Carter told the *New York Times* that "the Koreans are not ready for democracy ... according to their own judgment." Meanwhile for decades a chorus of praise met every new gain in South Korea's GNP. Multitudes of American economists, business pundits, and political scientists thought it their solemn duty to extol Korean capitalism to the heights – not once but a thousand times. "Miracle" became the trope on everyone's lips, with "dynamic" not far behind. In September 1977 *Fortune* magazine had this to say about business in Korea:

> What positively delights American business men in Korea is the Confucian work ethic. ... Work, as Koreans see it, is not a hardship. It is a heaven-sent opportunity to help family and nation. The fact that filial piety extends to the boss–worker relationship comes as a further surprise to Americans accustomed to labor wrangling at home.[46]

Civil society began to waken again with the February 1985 National Assembly elections, and by spring 1987 an aroused, self-organized, and intersubjective citizenry took over the streets of the major cities, with late-coming but substantial middle-class participation, thus forcing Chun from office in June. A few months later the always-tepid opposition again split, allowing the emergence of an interim regime under the other, somewhat shrewder "nephew" (Roh Tae Woo), a regime that first accommodated and then sought to suppress a newly energized civil society now including the liberated and very strong forces of labor (more strikes and labor actions occurred in 1987–1988 than at any point in Korean history, or most national histories).

In 1990 this regime sought to fashion the Japanese solution to democratic pressures, a "Democratic Liberal Party" (reversing the characters of Japan's Liberal Democratic Party) that would encompass the moderate opposition in the form of Kim Young Sam and his Pusan-based political machine, bringing them under the tent of the southeastern Taegu-Kyŏngsang elites (or "T-K Group") that had dominated the ROK (Republic of Korea) since 1961, thus to form a single-party democracy that would rule for the ages – or at least for the next generation. A host of analysts (not the least being the U.S. Embassy in Seoul) came forward to laud this "pact" between softliners and hardliners among the elite, which seemed to mimic the democratic transitions of the 1980s in Latin America.[47]

This was the Schumpeterian solution to the problems of an enlivened and growing civil society. About mass democracy, the Austrian aristocrat Schumpeter never cared much; he was a classic elitist. He valued a democratic system that provided a circulation of elites through periodic elections, enough funds mediated by the banks or the state to keep business growing, enough cash from big business to keep the politicians happy, an occasional circus by the politicians to keep the people entertained, and little more than that. The Liberal Democratic Party (LDP) followed this model closely in the period 1955–2001, perhaps too closely given its temporary loss of power in the summer of 1993; the Democratic Liberal Party (DLP) was the same (although no one quite imagined that it would provide such a circus!). Soon the DLP was gone, replaced by factions representing the T-K Group, and Kim Young Sam's Pusan-based group.

The DLP solution could not last, because unlike Japan's system it excluded labor (still today no political party has roots in Korea's massive working class, and until 1998 labor unions were prevented by law from involving themselves in politics), it failed to reckon with unresolved crises in postwar Korean history (especially Kwangju), and merely masked over sharp splits within the political elite – above all, the continuing exclusion of representation for the southwestern Chŏlla people in the politics of Seoul, but also the continuing repression of anything smacking of a serious left (through the National Security Law), and the restiveness of the *chaebŏl* (conglomerate) groups under continuing strong state regulation.

In 1995 a series of dramatic events and actions unfolded, with consequences no doubt unforeseen at the time, but having the result of an audacious assault on the military dictators who ruled Korea from 1961 onward and their legacies, a reckoning that goes beyond anything in the global transition from authoritarianism that the world has witnessed in the past two decades. It goes beyond the Latin American cases, where (often at the urging of American political scientists) the new regimes decided to let bygones be bygones and let the military go back to the barracks; it goes beyond Romania, where a rough summary justice dispatched dictator Ceausescu but let his system remain; and it went beyond East Germany, where Honecker was overthrown and expelled but where West Germany merely absorbed the old East German system, rather than achieving a consensual merger between two rather different civil societies.

Most commentary focused on the actions of President Kim Young Sam in cashiering the generals, with his backers arguing that he was a sincere reformer all along who now wanted to right the wrongs of modern South Korean history, and his detractors saying he allowed the prosecution of Chun and Roh on charges of bribery because that would help him overcome the influence of the Taegu-Kyŏngsang group within the ruling party, and then was forced in November 1995 to allow both of them to be indicted for the December 1979 coup and the suppression of the Kwangju citizenry because the "slush fund" scandal was lapping too close to his own door. More important, in my view, has been the emergence of a new generation of prosecutors, formed by the struggles of civil society as they got educated and came of age, and who now ingeniously use "the rule of law" to go after their dictatorial antagonists. What conclusions can we draw from this?

First, no "LDP" solution could work for the reasons given above, and thus we are back to political parties grouped around prominent leaders (namely the "three Kims" who dominated Korean politics in the 1990s), based in regional political machines and patron–client ties as always in postwar Korean history; second, with the continuing suppression of the non-violent left under the National Security Law, the ROK still falls short of either the Japanese or the American models of democracy and civil society; third, the falling out among the ruling groups and the trials of Chun and Roh, as well as the full glare of publicity on the slush fund scandals, bathing the state and the *chaebŏl* groups in a highly critical light, opened the way to another assertion of civil society and perhaps an authentic democracy that would finally give Korea the non-coercive, intersubjective public sphere it has long deserved, a politics that would go beyond the halting and temporary, jerry-built transitions to weak democracy in Latin America, the former Soviet Union and Eastern Europe, and the Philippines.

In December 1997 long-time dissident Kim Dae Jung was elected to a five-year term, amid a capitalist panic that no one – least of all the cheerleaders for the "Korean miracle"– had predicted. Since he suffered so much in the past from the security organs of the state, one would expect him finally to dismantle them. But he also had to revive the Korean economy while accommodating very strong labor unions. His solutions to these problems will determine the future of Korean democracy for a long time to come.

Kim Dae Jung embodied the courageous and resilient resistance to decades of dictatorship that marked Korea as much as its high-growth economy. Paradoxically, this maturing civil society was a key enabling mechanism for Washington and the IMF getting their way in Korea. Why? Because Kim's election brought to power people who have long criticized the state–bank–conglomerate nexus and who, like the president, were long its victims. The irony grows in that the global managers feared Kim's election (he might be a "populist") and Washington long backed the dictators who tormented him, with one U.S. ambassador after another refusing to meet Kim Dae Jung publicly, while bad-mouthing him in "off the record" conversations with reporters.

For the first time it appeared that a former dissident, a person of unquestioned democratic credentials with a base in the abused and underdeveloped southwest, might finally come to power. And so Washington and Wall Street insiders openly suggested that Kim was the wrong leader at the wrong time in the wrong place: a U.S. diplomat told a reporter:[48]

We could be in a position in which Kim Dae Jung takes office in the midst of a financial emergency that is going to require a lot of pain and downsizing of South Korean businesses. … Almost no one thinks he will command the authority to pull it off.

In fact no other conceivable political leader was better positioned than Kim truly to change the Korean system; indeed he had called for reforms analogous to those of the IMF throughout his long career.

Kim Dae Jung has never been a radical, and has not had a strong base in labor for two reasons: first, until 1998 it was illegal for labor to involve itself in politics; second, over the years Kim has been much more a champion of the southwestern region and of small and medium business than he has of labor (and, of course, supporting labor was a ticket to political oblivion in Korea's McCarthyite milieu). It is true that he is more sympathetic to labor demands than previous leaders, and labor clearly prefers him to the past run of dictators. But that isn't saying much, given the harsh anti-labor environment of the past fifty years.

Today Korea has two large unions, each claiming the membership of about half a million workers. The Korean Federation of Trade Unions (KFTU) was for decades the only legal union – because it was controlled by the state in the interests of owners, through what the late James West called "corporatism without labor" whereby the state, the conglomerates and the banks worked hand-in-glove, but labor was systematically excluded. From 1970 to 1987 the state also controlled the recognition of unions at foreign-invested companies, banning strikes and all unapproved union organizers – thus "to placate uneasy foreign investors."[49] The other large union is the Korean Confederation of Trade Unions (KCTU), which grew rapidly after 1987 but was illegal until early 1998. Both have about half a million members, but the KFTU was built upon an enterprise union base controlled from the top down, which allowed but one union per enterprise and thus dispersed horizontal solidarity across sectors. The Trade Union Act in force for decades barred intervention in the workplace by "third parties" (anyone who is not an employed worker or manager), and banned political activities by unions – making support of a specific political party illegal. All unions had to be approved by the Ministry of Labor.[50]

President Kim got labor's acquiescence to his reforms if not outright support with a master stroke in January 1998, one that made for far-reaching political changes: under his direction, for the first time in Korean history labor leaders met with leaders of business and government to work out fair and equitable policies to deal with the IMF crisis, a kind of "peak bargaining" arrangement that represents labor's biggest gain ever. After tough negotiations Kim got labor to agree to large layoffs (which ultimately quadrupled the pre-crisis unemployment rate, albeit from 2 to 8 percent, not a high rate by Western standards)[51] in return for the right to exist legally and to participate in politics and field candidates for elections. When labor leaders took this deal back to the rank and file it was soundly rejected, and many called for a general strike. The ROK has virtually no social security or unemployment compensation system; a puny unemployment law passed in 1995 allows 50 percent of wages for 30 to 210 days, depending on how long a worker has been employed – measures that are well below ILO (International Labor Organization) standards. But months of labor peace followed the January 1998 agreement, punctuated by sudden day-long shutdowns and sporadic actions

that continued as unemployment approached nearly 7 percent of the workforce by mid-summer 1998.

Other democratic reforms have proceeded rapidly under Kim Dae Jung. Kim Young Sam did nothing to change Korea's ubiquitous ANSP (Agency for National Security Planning), merely putting his own allies in control of it. This intelligence agency prosecuted hundreds of cases under the National Security Law in the mid-1990s, including labor organizer Pak Chŏng-yul, who was arrested in the middle of the night in November 1995 when ten men rushed into his home and dragged him off to an unheated cell, where for the next 22 days his tormenters beat him, poured cold water over him, and limited him to 30 minutes sleep a day, all to get him to confess to being a North Korean spy – which he wasn't. A government official told a reporter such measures were necessary because "We found the whole society had been influenced by North Korean ideology"; he estimated that upwards of 40,000 North Korean agents existed in the South.[52]

An investigation in early 1998 proved that the ANSP had run an operation just before the election to tar Kim Dae Jung as pro-communist, and incoming officials also unearthed for reporters the list of KCIA (Korean Central Intelligence Agency) agents who had kidnapped Kim in 1973. In February 1998 the *Sisa Journal* published for the first time the full administrative structure of the ANSP, showing that it had more than 70,000 employees (and any number of informal agents and spies), an annual budget of around 800 billion wŏn (about $1 billion), and almost no senior officials from the southwest (three from among the 70 highest-ranking officials, one among 35 section chiefs). It controlled eight academic institutes, including several that provide grants to foreign academics and that publish well-known English-language "scholarly" journals. Kim Young Sam's son, Kim Hyŏn-ch'ŏl, ran his own private group inside the ANSP and gave critical information to his father; many therefore blamed Kim's inattention to the developing Asian crisis on the arrest of his son in mid-1996 (for arranging huge preferential loans and massive bribery), thus depriving the President of reliable information. The new government cut the "domestic" arm of the ANSP by 50 percent, reduced the rest of the agency's staff by 10 percent, fired 24 top officials and many lesser people, and reoriented the agency away from domestic affairs, toward North Korea. A top official said the ANSP was to be "reborn to fit the era of international economic war"[53] (not a bad characterization of the contemporary world economy).

Today South Korea is a remarkable country where even white collar bank employees strap on identical headbands saying "Down with IMF trusteeship!" and march through the streets yelling slogans in unison. Students on the raucous campuses ten years ago, they are now united with blue collar workers in the KCTU. But because of labor's strength even in white collar ranks, foreign companies are reluctant to buy firms without rights to reduce employees. An anonymous senior official of a foreign brokerage firm remarked, "There's no point in taking over a [Korean] bank if you can't lay off anyone."[54]

We can conclude this brief consideration of recent Korean history with the observation that the contribution of protest to Korean democracy cannot be overstated; it is a classic case of "the civilizing force of a new vision of society … created in struggle."[55] A significant student movement emerged in Western Europe and the United States in the mid-1960s, and had a heyday of perhaps five years. Korean students were central activists in the politics of liberation in the late 1940s, in the overthrow of the Rhee regime and the politics of the Chang regime in 1960–1961, the repudiation of Korea–Japan normalization in 1965, and the resistance to the Park and Chun dictatorships in the period 1971–1988. Particularly in the 1980s, through the mediation of *minjung* ideology and praxis (a kind of liberation theory stimulated by the Latin American example), Korean students, workers, and young people brought into the public space uniquely original and autonomous configurations of political and social protest – ones that threatened many times to overturn the structure of American hegemony and military dictatorship. This was a classic example of Habermas's characterization of student protest in terms of a blurring of borderlines "between demonstration and civil disobedience, between discussion, festival, and expressive self-presentation."[56] Many students also adopted the Gramscian position, leaving the campuses to merge organically with the working class, often to find themselves jailed and tortured as "disguised workers," and always at the risk of their careers. Even if that part of the Korean public sphere is relatively quiescent now, it made an indelible contribution to Korean democracy in the past two decades.

Notes

1 Bruce Cumings, *Parallax Visions: Making Sense of American–East Asian Relations* (Duke University Press, 1999).
2 My first publication on this theme appeared in Seoul: "Pigyojŏk simin sahoe wa minjujuŭi" [Civil Society and Democracy: A Comparative Inquiry], *Ch'angjak kwa Pip'yŏng* [Creation and Criticism], (Seoul, May, 1996).
3 Dana Milbank, "A Marriage of Family and Policy," *Washington Post*, April 15, 2001, p. A1.
4 Samuel P. Huntington, *The Clash of Civilizations and the Remaking of World Order* (New York: Simon & Schuster, 1996).
5 Francis Fukuyama, *The End of History and the Last Man* (New York: Avon Books, 1992).
6 Karl van Wolferen, *The Enigma of Japanese Power: People and Politics in a Stateless Nation* (New York: Alfred A. Knopf, 1989).
7 Ibid., pp. 1–10, 23–24.
8 Ibid., pp. 5–8, 23–24.
9 Robert D. Putnam, *Making Democracy Work: Civic Traditions in Modern Italy* (New York: Princeton University Press, 1994), p. 183. In my reading no reviewer of this book pointed out that many or even most northern Italian cities have had communist mayors in the postwar period.
10 Putnam, *Making Democracy Work*, p. 11.
11 See, for example, his "Toward a Reconstruction of Historical Materialism," in Habermas, *Communication and the Evolution of Society*, trans. Thomas McCarthy (Boston: Beacon Press, 1984). Habermas is eminently more sophisticated about such matters than Almond and Verba or Putnam, however; for an interesting discussion of Habermas and Parsons, see Anthony Giddens, "Reason Without Revolution?

Habermas's Theorie des kommunikativen Handelns," in Richard J. Bernstein, ed., *Habermas and Modernity* (Cambridge: MIT Press, 1985), pp. 95–121.

12   Mark E. Warren, "The Self in Discursive Democracy," in Stephen K. White, ed., *The Cambridge Companion to Habermas* (New York: Cambridge University Press, 1995), p. 171.

13   Peter Dews, *Logics of Disintegration: Post-Structuralist Thought and the Claims of Critical Theory* (London: Verso, 1987), p. 103.

14   White, "Reason, Modernity and Democracy," in *Cambridge Companion to Habermas*, p. 6.

15   Gabriel Almond and Sidney Verba, *The Civic Culture: Political Attitudes and Democracy in Five Nations* (New York: Little, Brown and Company, 1963), p. x. *The Civic Culture* makes interesting reading forty years later. Seeking to quantify the Tocquevillean propensity of Americans to join voluntary associations, the authors found that 57 percent of Americans were joiners, compared to only 44 percent in West Germany. Union membership was at 14 percent in the American stratified sample of 970 respondents, and 15 percent among 955 West Germans. Today union membership in the U.S. is still at about 14 percent, whereas 40 percent of German workers are members of unions. No doubt a similar survey today would find that far more Germans are members of voluntary associations than are Americans. If, for Almond and Verba, "weak democracy" is characterized by "the passive citizen, the nonvoter, the poorly informed or apathetic" (*Civic Culture*, pp. 246–476, 338), the U.S. would certainly qualify today, according to many authors.

16   Habermas, *The Philosophical Discourse of Modernity*, trans. Frederick Lawrence (Cambridge, Mass.: MIT Press, 1987), p. 367.

17   White, "Reason, Modernity and Democracy," p. 9.

18   Nancy S. Love, "What's Left of Marx," in White, ed., *Cambridge Companion to Habermas*, pp. 58–61.

19   Lucio Colletti, "Introduction," in *Karl Marx: Early Writings*, trans. Rodney Livingstone and Gregor Benton (New York: Vintage Books, 1975), pp. 31–32.

20   Marx, *Critique of Hegel's Doctrine of the State*, in Colletti, pp. 111–112.

21   Marx, *Critique of Hegel's Philosophy of Right* (1844), in Colletti, pp. 247–249.

22   *Critique of Hegel's Philosophy of Right*, p. 252.

23   Antonio Gramsci, *The Prison Notebooks* (New York: Columbia University Press, 1992).

24   Alasdaire MacIntyre, *After Virtue: A Study in Moral Theory* (Notre Dame, Ind.: University of Notre Dame Press, 1984). For analogous points in Unger's work see *Knowledge and Politics* (New York: The Free Press, 1975), pp. 38–49. For Habermas's critique of *After Virtue* (which struck me as quite weak), see Dews, ed., *Autonomy and Solidarity*, p. 248.

25   MacIntyre, *After Virtue*, pp. 50–51.

26   Ibid, pp. 110–112, 149.

27   Unger, *Knowledge and Politics*, p. 76.

28   MacIntyre, *After Virtue*, p. 147.

29   Ibid., p. 153.

30   Ibid., p. 236.

31   Habermas, *Strukturwandel der Öffenlichkeit* (Hermann Luchterhand Verlag, 1961), trans. by Thomas Burger as *The Structural Transformation of the Public Sphere* (Cambridge, Mass.: MIT Press, 1989). This book was published around the same time as Almond and Verba's *Civic Culture* and represents a profound (if implicit) critique of their project. But it was not translated into English until 1989.

32   Thomas McCarthy, "Introduction," in *Structural Transformation*, p. xii.

33   Ibid., pp. 122–124.

34   Ibid., pp. 130–131.

35   Ibid., pp. xvii–xviii.

36 Ibid., pp. 133–136, quoting Tocqueville. And quoting Mill: he "turned against the idea of a public sphere," advocating instead that political questions be decided not by "an uninformed multitude," but only "by appeal to views, formed after due consideration, of a relatively small number of persons specially educated for this task" (p. 136). The Chartist newspaper was the first one with a mass edition of over 50,000 copies (p. 168).

37 Habermas, *Structural Transformation*, p. 177.

38 The early Habermas is also brilliant on suburbs (pp. 157–164), seeing in them a "refeudalization" according to the "technical requirements of traffic flow," and "the shrinking of the private sphere into the inner areas of a conjugal family largely relieved of function and weakened in authority." The resultant "travesty" turned the privacy of the eighteenth-century bourgeois sphere, whose only reference was the public, into a privacy for the sake of refuge from that same sphere (a privacy whose only referent is shelter from the madding crowd), with the raucous new public sphere violating the hallowed family space via a mass media that was part of the sphere of consumption, not the sphere of civility and political debate. Habermas was under the influence of the Frankfurt School at this time, of course, but his conclusion that "the world fashioned by the mass media is a public sphere in appearance only" (p. 170) perfectly anticipates the post-modernist argument that the mass media do not convey reality, but only a semblance of reality. It becomes in his words "the manipulated public sphere" (p. 217).

39 Marx, *Critique of Hegel's Philosophy of Right*, p. 252.

40 Hegel, quoted in Marx, *Critique of Hegel's Doctrine of the State*, in *Early Writings*, p. 116.

41 Scholars as diverse as Zygmunt Bauman and Immanuel Wallerstein have argued that Stalinist states took the German fused state project to its logical conclusion in their "late-late development," which was to strangle civil society altogether while building the sinews of industry and modern urban society (Wallerstein, *After Liberalism* [New York: The New Press, 1995], pp. 220–226). Meanwhile they created a middle class in spite of themselves, by virtue of bringing forth a new generation of young people in the 1980s – their children.

42 See Cumings, *Korea's Place in the Sun: A Modern History* (New York: W. W. Norton, 1997), chapters 4 and 7.

43 A good source on this period is Gregory Henderson, *Korea: The Politics of the Vortex* (Cambridge, Mass.: Harvard University Press, 1968). One would never understand Seoul at this time by examining aggregate or per capita economic figures, which placed South Korea around $100 per capita GNP. Middle-class families all had maids, and wealthy families employed phalanxes of maids, cooks, drivers, and handymen. Masses of the population were dirt poor, of course, but the society had a material wealth that could not be measured using the empirical methods of developmental economists.

44 The best source on this is Jung-en Woo, *Race to the Swift: State and Finance in Korean Industrialization* (New York: Columbia University Press, 1991).

45 Karl Marx, *The Eighteenth Brumaire of Louis Bonaparte* (New York: International Publishers, 1966).

46 George E. Ogle, *South Korea: Dissent within the Economic Miracle* (Atlantic Highlands, N.J.: Zed Books, 1990), p. 76.

47 The key texts in this literature are Guillermo O'Donnell, Phillipe C. Schmitter, and Laurence Whitehead, eds, *Transitions from Authoritarian Rule: Comparative Perspectives* (Washington: Johns Hopkins University Press, 1986); same authors, *Transitions from Authoritarian Rule: Latin America* (Washington: Johns Hopkins University Press, 1986); same authors, *Transitions from Authoritarian Rule: Tentative Conclusions About Uncertain Democracies* (Washington: Johns Hopkins University

Press, 1986). For my critique, which compared several Latin American cases with South Korea, see "The Abortive Abertura," *New Left Review* (spring 1989).

48   Quoted by David Sanger, *The New York Times*, November 20, 1997.

49   James M. West, "South Korea's Entry into the International Labor Organization: Perspectives on Corporatist Labor Law During a Late Industrial Revolution," *Stanford Journal of International Law* 3, 2 (1987), pp. 494–495.

50   KCTU, "Struggle for Labor Law Reforms Campaign News no. XXIV," February 28, 1997.

51   The rate increased dramatically from November through July 1998 to 6.5 percent, with nearly 1.5 million unemployed (according to many Korean newspaper accounts); as of early 2001 it was just over 7 percent.

52   Andrew Pollack, *New York Times*, Feb. 22, 1997.

53   *The Korea Herald*, March 19, 1998.

54   Namju Cho, *The New York Times*, Jan. 15, 1998.

55   Raymond Williams, *The Country and the City* (New York: Oxford University Press, 1975), p. 231.

56   Jürgen Habermas, *Autonomy and Solidarity: Interviews* (London: Verso, 1992), p. 234.

2 The problematic modernity of Confucianism

The question of "civil society" in Chosŏn dynasty Korea

John Duncan

Introduction

There has been an upsurge of interest in the past few decades in the relationship between Confucianism and modernity in East Asia. This began in the arguments about "Confucianism and capitalism" which have sought to overturn Max Weber's verdict on the incompatibility of Confucianism and capitalism and explain the exceptional economic success of the East Asian region in terms of certain "Confucian" values such as respect for authority and self-development through education. In the past few years this effort to understand the links between Confucianism and modernity has expanded to a much wider scope, as seen in the 1997 launching in South Korea of a new journal, *Chŏnt'ong kwa hyŏndae* (*Tradition and Modernity*), whose inaugural issue was devoted to the question of "Confucianism and Twenty-first Century Korea."[1]

One of the areas in to which this inquiry has now moved is politics. The attainment of somewhat more democratic regimes in such countries as Taiwan and South Korea has prompted a number of scholars to explore the possibility of what we might call "Confucian democracy," rejecting older notions about Oriental despotism and seeking antecedents of democracy in Confucian political thought and practice. With respect to Korea, the issue has been brought to the foreground by the recent debate in the pages of the *Korea Journal* between Cho Hein and David Steinberg.[2] It is my intention here to reconsider some of the arguments put forth by Cho, Steinberg, and some other scholars engaged in this debate in hopes of contributing to a more nuanced and historically specific understanding of the question of Confucianism and political modernity.

The plasticity of Confucianism

Before I turn to the examination of specific issues relating to the possibility of "Confucian democracy," I think it important to note that the debate on Confucianism and modernity in East Asia and in Korea is hardly new. It has been going for over a century, with protagonists from all across the political spectrum staking out a bewildering array of positions regarding Confucianism.

The rhetoric of anti-Confucianism

Historians often remark on the anti-Confucian rhetoric of the Westernizing reformers of late-nineteenth- and early-twentieth-century East Asia, be it Fukuzawa and the Bunmei kaika movement in Meiji Japan, the May 4th activists in early Republican China, or the Independence Club in Korea. What has received less attention in the case of Korea, however, is the way in which anti-Confucian polemics have been deployed by activists on all sides of the progressive versus conservative and nationalist versus collaborationist binaries that historians routinely use to talk about the political and intellectual history of late-nineteenth- and twentieth-century Korea.

The most famous and influential of the early anti-Confucianists in Korea was the scholar and revolutionary Shin Ch'aeho (1880–1936), who laid the blame for Korea's loss of independence squarely on Confucianism. Shin's anti-Confucianism is given its clearest expression in his 1925 article, "The Biggest Event in the Last 1,000 Years of Korean History," where he decried the slavishness and weakness of contemporary Korean society and culture and attributed it to the destruction of a vigorous indigenous culture by Sinophilic Confucianists following the victory of the renowned scholar and official Kim Pushik (1075–1151) over the nativist rebel monk Myoch'ŏng (?–1135) in the mid-twelfth century.[3] Shin, of course, was a staunch anti-imperialist whose 1936 death in a Japanese prison has made him a virtual icon of Korean nationalism. Furthermore, his turn toward radicalism in the 1920s and his call for a direct popular revolution has been a source of inspiration for the *minjung* nationalists of recent years.[4]

But anti-Confucian rhetoric can also be found among thinkers who collaborated with the Japanese. Yun Ch'iho (1864–1946), for one, was a man who had been an important member of the Independence Club in the 1890s before later becoming an active supporter of Japanese colonial rule. Yun, in an 1895 essay decrying the baneful effects of Confucianism on Korea, argued:

> With diffidence yet with conviction I dare say that it [Confucianism] has done very little, if anything, for Korea. What Korea may have been without Confucian teachings, nobody can tell. But what Korea is with them we too well know. Behold Korea, with her oppressed masses, her general poverty, her dirt and filth, her degraded women, her blighted families – behold all this and judge for yourselves what Confucianism has done for Korea.[5]

Another such example can be found in the novelist Yi Kwangsu (1892–?), perhaps the most notorious of all colonial collaborators. Yi incorporated a strong critique of traditional social values in his fiction, but perhaps his harshest attack on Confucianism came in his controversial 1922 treatise "On Remaking the Nation" (*Minjok kaejoron*) in which he decried certain "national traits," such as excessive formalism and neglect of commerce and industry, that were commonly attributed to Confucian teachings.[6]

Anti-Confucianism continued to be an important theme in post-1945 Korea, with scholars in both the progressive and the conservative camps staking out anti-Confucian positions. As Michael Robinson has shown, post-liberation intellectuals such as Hyŏn Sangyun, Yi Sangŭn, and others continued to blame Confucianism for the lack of economic development and the persistence of authoritarian politics in South Korea throughout the 1940s, 1950s, 1960s and beyond.[7] But during the same period, the man who was to become president-for-life, Park Chung Hee, also launched a harsh critique of the negative effects of Confucianism on Korean society shortly after coming to power in 1961. According to Park, Confucianism was to blame for a whole host of ills in Korea, including the lack of an independent and enterprising spirit, indolence, malicious selfishness, and undemocratic political practices, which latter item he characterized – undoubtedly with the intent of justifying his coup and discrediting his political opponents – as sectarian party strife.[8]

More recently, the *minjung* scholars who struggled in opposition to the Park and Chun regimes have also engaged in a negative critique of Confucianism, depicting the Confucian learning of the Chosŏn period as a tool by which the yangban ruling class rationalized its oppression of the commoners,[9] and generally regarding Confucianism as an obstacle to the realization of democracy and social justice.[10]

These examples show that throughout the late nineteenth and twentieth centuries Confucianism has been used as a polemical target by individuals with what appear to be mutually incompatible political agendas. In the colonial period, Shin Ch'aeho was seeking to debunk Confucianism in order to facilitate the rediscovery of an original native spirit that would allow Korea to resist imperialist aggression and strengthen itself without succumbing to Westernization while Yi Kwangsu and Yun Ch'iho were seeking to discredit Confucianism in order to pursue a Westernizing reconstruction of Korean society under Japanese tutelage. In the post-liberation period, liberals and progressives were lamenting the way in which Confucianism contributed to authoritarian or dictatorial politics while Park Chung Hee appears to have been attacking Confucianism not only to foster a more entrepreneurial spirit for capitalist economic development but also to discredit the democratic Chang Myŏn regime, which he overthrew.

The pro-Confucian arguments

What then of the pro-Confucianists? Here, too, the picture is quite complex. A number of scholars have remarked on the way the Japanese made selective use of Confucian social values to legitimize their rule and supported various Confucian institutions, as well as on the way in which many Korean elites, both unreconstructed rural Confucian literati and the new urban bourgeoisie, responded positively to those efforts.[11]

But there were also pro-Confucianists who were bitterly anti-Japanese. There were, of course, the Confucian literati who took to the field at the head of guerrilla forces (righteous armies) to fight against the Japanese during the late 1890s and the

1900s. But there were also intellectuals striving to find some sort of reconciliation between their Confucian heritage and the new learning of the West. One such man was Pak Ŭnshik (1859–1926), a nationalist propagandist who wrote such stirring patriotic works as *Han'guk t'ongsa* [The Painful History of Korea] and *Han'guk tongnip undong chi hyŏlsa* [The Bloody History of the Korean Independence Movement]. In 1909, Pak wrote his "Treatise on the Reform of Confucianism," in which he decried the stifling effects of *Ch'eng-Chu* Neo-Confucian metaphysical philosophizing and called for a revitalization of Confucianism through the Wang Yang-ming school whose stress on unity between intuitive knowledge and direct action made it better suited to cope with the rapid changes that were descending on Korea. Pak concluded his treatise by contending that this would lead to a time when "Confucianism will illuminate the entire world."[12]

Other scholars of the colonial period who sought to find relevance for modernity in Confucianism include Chŏng Inbo (1892–?) who, like Pak, criticized the sterile metaphysics of the *Ch'eng-Chu* school. Chŏng, however, argued that the alternative was to be found in the empirically oriented scholarship of eighteenth-century advocates of Practical Learning (*shirhak*) such as Yi Ik (1681–1763), whose great contribution, according to Chŏng, was that he "sought creativity based in facts."[13] Chŏng's argument was further developed by An Chaehong (1892–?), a journalist and political activist devoted to independence and social democracy who spent several years in colonial jails because of his anti-Japanese activities. An sought to find antecedents to Korean modernity by comparing the ideas of the well-known late Chosŏn reform Confucianist, Chŏng Yagyong (Chŏng Tasan, 1762–1836), with modern Western thought and concluded that Chŏng Yagyong's ideas were often parallel to the nationalism, egalitarianism, economic thought, and scientific learning of the early modern West.[14]

Despite the general anti-Confucian consensus among intellectuals in the late 1940s and 1950s noted by Michael Robinson, pro-Confucian attitudes persisted in South Korean society after liberation from Japanese rule in 1945. In the capital, Sŏnggyun'gwan University, located on the site of and taking its name from the old Royal Confucian Academy, established a college of Confucian studies, but it was in the towns and villages of rural Korea where Confucianism remained particularly strong. Men in the countryside continued to join Confucian associations and participate in Confucian rites while clinging to the factional alignments of their ancestors.

These Confucian factional identities became an issue in presidential politics in the 1960s, when Park Chung Hee praised Yi I (Yi Yulgok, 1536–1584) of the Westerner faction for his commitment to strengthening the country's defenses and criticized Kim Sŏngil (1538–1593) of the Easterner faction for failing to warn of the impending Japanese invasion in the early 1590s. This brought an outcry of protest from southeastern Korea, the historical stronghold of the Easterners, which in turn prompted Park to repair his relations with the southeast by praising Easterner achievements.[15] Whether it was due to this particular incident or to a realization of the utility of Confucian social ethics for his particular brand of authoritarian politics, by the 1970s Park Chung Hee made a rather spectacular

U-turn and began to promote Confucian social and political values, eventually making his daughter the head of his New Spirit (*saemaŭm*) movement and sending her around the country to address mass rallies on the importance of such cardinal Confucian virtues as loyalty and filial piety.

Another instance of conservative espousal of Confucian values came in the early 1990s, when concern over an outbreak of violent crime generated a debate on ways to create a healthier social order. Among the leaders of this debate was Hong Ilsik, then president of one of South Korea's most prestigious universities, who proposed to have all freshman students reside in dormitories where they would be taught traditional social values by faculty head-residents and to have them take a required general education course on the fourteenth-century Confucian morals handbook *Myŏngshim pogam* (in Chinese, *Ming xin bao jian*, "Valuable Mirror for Illuminating the Mind").[16]

On the other hand, however, there have also been Confucian-oriented intellectuals who have fought against South Korea's military dictators and have sought to find in Confucianism the basis for a more just and egalitarian society. One such thinker is Kim Ch'ungnyŏl, who argues that the authoritarian aspects of Confucianism developed from the time of the Former Han dynasty of China (206 BCE–8 CE) and calls for a return to early Confucianism (*wŏnshi yugyo*), which he believes prescribed a more equal and reciprocal social order, as a way to reconcile the East Asian cultural heritage with Western liberal democracy.[17] Another example of contemporary Confucian efforts to resist authoritarian politics is one thinker's gallant attempt to theorize a "*minjung* Confucianism," which critiques the authoritarian tendencies of official Confucianism and literati Confucianism before concluding with a prolonged discussion of *minjung* Confucianism and the goals of a *minjung* Confucian revolution: "the free and equal liberation of humans, the establishment of a democratic and republican independent state, and the construction of a world of peaceful coexistence."[18]

Thus we can see that just as anti-Confucianism has been used by a wide variety of people for what are often diametrically opposite purposes, so, too, has pro-Confucianism been used by different groups and individuals for mutually contradictory goals. In some cases, such as that of Park Chung Hee, this may mean nothing more than the cynical manipulation of Confucian values for crass political purposes. But in other instances, such as those of Pak Ŭnshik and Chŏng Inbo who criticized one strand of Confucian learning while upholding others, it hints at the richness of the Confucian tradition, which included many different schools and many competing ideas about how best to order society. In short, what we call Confucianism is complex, difficult to define, and subject to appropriation for a wide range of political and social purposes.

This means that we must be very careful when discussing the Confucian tradition and its relationship, positive or negative, to modernity. To give a rather simple example, it is quite commonplace to attribute the factional politics that arose in late imperial China and Chosŏn dynasty Korea to Confucianism. Eisenstadt, however, has shown that such factionalism was a common feature of historical bureaucratic societies throughout the world.[19] We must, therefore, be prepared to demonstrate what was specifically Confucian about Chinese and Korean factions or else seek another way to explain that particular phenomenon. This is true not only for factionalism, but potentially for almost any idea or practice that we now describe as Confucian. Otherwise we cannot escape from the set of discursive practices that use a vaguely conceived "Confucianism" to essentialize East Asia, either as an exoticized other in the West or as an ineffable universality that elides significant spatial and temporal variations, variations which were often reflective of differing social circumstances, in the East.[20]

The question of a Confucian civil society in Chosŏn dynasty Korea

Scholars seeking to apply the notion of civil society in non-Western contexts tend to present it somewhat unproblematically as a "public" space more or less autonomous from the state in which "private" individuals articulate their interests and formulate and pursue their collective goals. In fact, however, "civil society" in the West is a highly contested concept with a variety of conflicting interpretations. Furthermore, the various versions of civil society are embedded in specific historical conditions in ways that raise questions about their applicability of the concept to premodern and non-Western societies.

Public and private, **Kong** *and* **Sa**

Conceptualizations of civil society in the West almost always hinge on the distinction between public and private. But this distinction, too, is the subject of no small degree of controversy. Although there are several competing notions of public versus private in Western scholarship, here I will briefly discuss two of the more prevalent ones in order to demonstrate the complexity of the issue and to provide a kind of baseline for my examination of the question of public versus private in the Chosŏn period (1392–1910).

The first, which we might call the classical liberal-economist view and which still dominates debates on political policy in the United States among other countries, tends to depict public and private in terms of the distinction between the administrative state and the market economy or between state and society, society being defined as made up of "rational" individuals entering into voluntary contractual associations to pursue their self-interest.

A second notion of public and private, which has been advanced largely by social historians and anthropologists, stresses the close relationship between the administrative state and the market economy and the way in which the impersonal relations of both impinge upon individual autonomy. Advocates of this view, therefore, consider the public to consist of both the state and the market economy and contend that the rapid expansion of this realm in modern times has produced the private as an intensely emotional and intimate domain of family and friends characterized by particularistic ties of attachment which serves as a refuge against the selfish individualism and impersonality of the public realm.[21]

Although they vary in their definition of what is public and what is private, these conceptualizations both have as their point of departure the rise of the market economy. Here I am referring not simply to the development of a flourishing commercial economy, which can be found at many times and in many places throughout history, but rather to what Polanyi has shown to be the rise of the market economy in Europe as a paradigm for the workings of society.[22] This is true whether it is the liberal-economists' positive assessment of the market economy itself as constituting the private, or the more negative assessment of the market economy as the driving force behind the expansion of an ever more intrusive public realm. Thus not only is the public–private binary problematic in its definitions, but its emergence as an instrument of social analysis is historically specific to the rise of the capitalist economy in modern Western Europe.

Turning now to the case of premodern Korea, the Western terms "public" and "private" seem to have had Chosŏn equivalents in the terms *"kong"* and *"sa."* To my knowledge, we have yet to see a substantial study of the usage and meaning of these terms in the Chosŏn. But we do have some recent scholarship on *"gong"*(kong) and *"si"*(sa) in premodern China that raises some serious questions about the equivalence of Eastern and Western ideas of public and private.

Mizoguchi Yuzo, who has recently published a book devoted to the analysis of *gong* and *si* in China, argues that whereas the Western notion of "public" is that of an autonomous "public" space, the Chinese notion of *gong* is that of a partnership between elites and the court.[23] One can perhaps argue for some degree of similarity between the Chinese concept of *gong* and that of Western social historians' concept of a public realm made up of close cooperative relationships between the state and the market economy, but that interpretation leaves little hope for civil society, or *gong*, as the seedbed for democratic politics.

Benjamin Elman has noted another crucial problem in the comparison of Western and Chinese concepts of public and private. Whereas modern Western notions of public all relegate kinship and family ties to the private realm, Chinese rulers and their Confucian officials saw instead the convergence of kinship ties and state interests and considered lineages and families to be part of the public domain. Also, whereas political parties are considered to be public in the West, gentry political associations (*dang*) based on non-kinship ties were defined as private and as a threat to the state.[24] In effect, what we have here is the exact opposite of Western notions of public and private.

Furthermore, it is important to note that *gong* and *si* have certain normative connotations: *gong* is often used to mean fair and impartial, while *si* is used to mean selfish and egotistic. Thus when the Chinese were terming gentry political associations as private, they were also condemning them as organizations of men with selfish purposes inimical to the good of society as a whole.

I have, however, already cautioned against the tendency to treat Confucianism in East Asia as an undifferentiated tradition, so it is incumbent on me to explore the notions of *kong* and *sa* in Korea. Unfortunately, there is nothing for Korea like Mizoguchi's study on China. What I propose to do here is to draw on a few secondary studies that have touched tangentially on the issue and on my own knowledge of the use of these terms in Koryŏ and Chosŏn times.

Certainly it would appear that the Koreans shared the Chinese practice of considering lineages and families as part of the public domain. In the early Chosŏn period there was considerable discussion about the close relationship between kinship groups and the state. The prominent mid-fifteenth century scholar-official Yang Sŏngji, for example, wrote with some pride about the role Korea's great hereditary families (*taega sejok*) played in maintaining the country's dynasties.[25] Further evidence of the public nature of lineages can be found in the efforts the Chosŏn court made to compile genealogical information in such publications as the *Sŏnwŏn nok*. Furthermore, as Martina Deuchler has shown, the Chosŏn dynasty engaged in a prolonged legislative effort to restructure the Korean kinship group according to a patrilineal Confucian model.[26] But the Chosŏn state's concern did not stop at the level of the lineage group. Acting in part on the belief, as expressed in the *Greater Learning* (*Daxue*, K. *Taehak*) prescription for cultivated men to regulate the family before ruling the country and pacifying all under heaven, it also sought to intervene in household family relations. Evidence for this exists not only in the way in which, for example, a lack of filial piety was considered a criminal offense, but also in the state's repeated publication of such morals textbooks as the *Samgang haengsilto* (Illustrated Conduct of the Three Bonds), two-thirds of which were devoted to relations between husband and wife and father and son, as well as in the state's policy of rewarding exemplars of such cardinal Confucian virtues as filial piety and chastity.[27] It seems clear, then, that in this crucial area, there was significant divergence between Chosŏn dynasty ideas of public and private and those of the modern West.

One example of apparent equivalence between Western and Korean concepts can be found in the sphere of property ownership, where Koryŏ and Chosŏn era Koreans used such terms as state/publicly owned slave (*kong nobi*) and privately owned slave (*sa nobi*). Another example, which has to do not with ownership but rather with appropriation of resources, can be found in public lands (*kongjŏn*), whose tax receipts went to the state's treasuries, and private lands (*sajŏn*), whose tax receipts went to individuals as prebendal salaries. The paired usage of the terms was not new to the Chosŏn period; it can be found as early as the Koryŏ period (918–1392).

These examples seem to indicate a rather straightforward identification of public (*kong*) with the state and private (*sa*) with families or individuals and thus might be seen as similar to the liberal-economist dichotomy of public administrative state versus private market economy. But these usages of *kong* and *sa* were widely current in Korea at a time when the economy was almost completely agrarian and thus may have had meanings quite different from what public and private meant in the West after the rise of the market economy. On the other hand, however, perhaps we can argue that the agrarian economy of Koryŏ and Chosŏn dynasty Korea, with its concepts of public and private ownership, was quite different from the agrarian economy of premodern Western Europe where such concepts of land tenure as the fief and serfdom may have inhibited the rise of a distinction between public and private ownership. In other words, it may be that the concepts of public and private in Chosŏn era Korea were not contingent on the rise of the market economy in the same way as in Europe.

The problem with this is, as James Palais has pointed out, that although there was private ownership in premodern Korea, there was no strong tradition of the defensibility of that right like that which characterizes modern societies. Instead private property was subject to arbitrary attack and invasion, particularly by the state and its functionaries.[28] One factor behind this may have been the concept that "all land is the king's land" (*wangt'o sasang*), a notion that was generally used to rationalize the collection of land taxes but at the same time also implied that the king had the authority to seize and reallocate landholdings as he saw fit. In this regard, Chosŏn Korea would appear to be similar to the case of late imperial China, where one important motive behind the gentry's quest for office in the imperial bureaucracy appears to have been the need for political connections at the court in order to protect family landholdings.[29]

There are other usages, such as *kongnon*, sometimes translated as "public opinion,"[30] which seem to suggest a broader application of *kong* or public in ways similar to that of Habermas's public sphere. One study of the use of the term *kongnon* during the reign of King Sŏngjong (r. 1469–1494) concludes that *kongnon* at that time was limited to the remonstrance officials and censors of the *Samsa* and thus denoted the opinions of the state's officials, but suggests that in the sixteenth century the concept was expanded to include virtually the whole *yangban* literati class.[31] On the other hand, however, there is evidence from the eighteenth century that *kongnon* was still conceived of in terms of the opinions of the state's officials, and not of a broadly constituted stratum of rural literati. The noted scholar Yu Suwŏn (1694–1755) made a distinction between *kongnon* and *tangnon* (factional opinion) in which he, too, equated *kongnon* with the officials of the *Samsa*.[32] While this is only a contemporary view and does not constitute some sort of definitive statement on the issue, it does raise serious questions about the speculative argument that the usage of *kongnon* expanded to include rural literati in the sixteenth century.

One final note with regard to the issue of public and private terminology has to do with "political parties" or factions (*pungdang*), which are sometimes equated with modern Western political parties.[33] But it was quite common in Korea, as in China, to condemn the *pungdang* as private, selfish organizations. There was in the seventeenth century an effort by certain leaders to justify their factions on the grounds that there were two kinds of factions, those made up of superior men (*kunja*) and those made up of inferior men (*soin*) with the implication that whereas those factions made up of inferior men were private and selfish, those made up of superior men had the public (*kong*) interest at heart.[34] While this may be taken to indicate that a new public sphere-like conceptualization of the *pungdang* was taking shape, it can also be read as a sign that the view of *pungdang* as private and selfish was still so pervasive that *pungdang* leaders had to defend themselves.

At any rate, it is clear that although there may be some areas of overlap between public/private in the West and *kong/sa* in Korea, there are also important areas, such as the family or the political party/*pungdang*, where there are significant divergences. This should remind us to be quite careful of how we use the terms public and private when dealing with the Chosŏn.

Civil society/public sphere

What, then, of the relations between these competing views of public and private and the various conceptualizations of civil society? Let us begin with the social historians. These scholars see civil society as belonging to the public realm. Although they may recognize the links between civil society and the market economy, they do not see civil society and the state in opposition to each other. To the contrary, they tend to lump civil society together with the state in a potentially, if not actually, oppressive public domain. One of the most powerful formulations along these lines has been set forth by Antonio Gramsci. Although Gramsci is careful not to reduce civil society to the economy and to distinguish between civil society and the state, he ultimately sees civil society as a bastion of class hegemony that is ultimately supportive of the state.[35] For these scholars, therefore, the hope of a more democratic politics lies not in realizing the potential of civil society but rather in overcoming it, or in Gramsci's case, restructuring it in such a way that it fuses with the state.[36]

Thus we turn to the liberal-economist view of civil society, much of which can be traced back to the ideas of the Scottish enlightenment, and which dominates political discourse in the United States today. This view, particularly as presented by conservatives in the contemporary U.S., tends to conflate civil society with society at large, society being conceived in terms of the self-regulating market economy. Simply put, the advocates of this approach see civil society/society as the "private sector" in contradistinction with the "public sector" of the administrative state and contend that it is the enlightened self-interest of rational individual actors coming together in the private sector to pursue common purposes against the power of the state that makes democratic politics possible.

The simplistic reductionism of the liberal-economist model has prompted numerous efforts to reformulate the idea of civil society and its relationship to the state. An important point of departure for many of these efforts has been Hegel's formulation of civil society as a space of self-interested individualism, competition, and contractual relationships based on the market and juxtaposed to both state and family. But perhaps the most influential of these in recent years has been Jürgen Habermas's concept of the "public sphere." This view has gained great currency in the past decade, in part because, as Craig Calhoun has pointed out, Habermas's book on this issue first became available in English at the time of the collapse of communism and the transition to democracy in Eastern Europe.[37] Furthermore, there have been several efforts to use Habermas to argue for the existence of a "civil society" in late imperial China.[38]

What makes Habermas's formulation so attractive, aside from the timing of its translation into English, is the way in which it seems to offer a way out of the reductionist identification of civil society and market economy. Habermas accepts Hegel's tripartite division of state, civil society, and family, but to that he adds a "public sphere," a realm between the state and civil society where individuals engage in disinterested rational-critical debate that transcends personal or class interests or status claims. This would seem to provide a space for the development of a public discourse, outside the sphere of the state that is not reducible to economic interests. Habermas's conception, however, is not totally free of contradictions. Against the contention that the kind of public sphere he is positing would be absorbed by the state, Habermas argues that the public sphere is created out of civil society, which for Habermas is an essentially bourgeois entity. Thus Habermas's public sphere, to quote Craig Calhoun, "is based (a) on a notion of public good as distinct from private interest, (b) on social institutions (like private property) that empower individuals to participate independently in the public sphere because their livelihoods and access to it are not dependent on political power and patronage, and (c) on forms of private life (notably families) that prepared individuals to act as autonomous, rational-critical subjects in the public sphere."[39] Furthermore, as Bruce Cumings points out in his chapter in this book, for the "early Habermas" the bourgeois public sphere was "limited to a particular epoch, and is not synonymous with the historical development of civil society itself." Thus Habermas's treatment of the public sphere and civil society and its attendant concepts of public and private ultimately hinge, as do those of the liberal-economists and Hegel, on the rise of the market economy, on the rise of the bourgeoisie as self-aware subjects capable of either the rational pursuit of enlightened self-interest or the disinterested rational-critical pursuit of the common good.

To recapitulate, in this section I have sought to problematize the uncritical adoption of the Western concepts of public and private and civil society in two ways. One is by showing the wide disagreement in the West over the meanings and applications of these concepts; the other is by arguing that almost all the widely varying and sometimes contradictory interpretations of these concepts have a common point of departure: the rise of the market economy and bourgeois society in modern Western Europe. The point here is not to privilege the modern Western experience; rather it is to point out that these concepts have the same kind of historical specificity as, say, the terms *yangban* and *sajok* (literati family) in sixteenth- and seventeenth-century Chosŏn dynasty Korea. Just as it might be very misleading to analyze eighteenth-century France in the terms of the Chosŏn dynasty, so might it be – unless we are very critical and self-reflexive – hazardous to analyze the Chosŏn dynasty in the terms of eighteenth-century Europe.

Difficulties in the application of "civil society" to Chosŏn dynasty Korea

Here I would like to engage in a consideration of the possibility of some sort of equivalent to "civil society" or a "public sphere" in the Chosŏn, focusing on three specific issues and institutions that have been put forth in relation to the question of civil society in recent studies: the *sŏwŏn* or "private academies," the *sarim* or "rusticated literati/backwoods literati," and the issue of "orthodoxy."

The sŏwŏn *or "private academies"*

The *sŏwŏn*, or "private academies" that existed widely in Korea during the late Chosŏn period have been cited by Cho Hein as one of the intermediary institutions that made up civil society,[40] but they have also been suggested by JaHyun Haboush to have been an institutional location that may have constituted in itself a public sphere.[41]

According to Haboush, the *sŏwŏn* were sites of contestation for power and influence between the state and local elites as *sŏwŏn* scholars grew increasingly independent of the state, devised ways to communicate with students and scholars at other academies throughout the entire country, and engaged in a discourse that ranged from the scholarly and intellectual to social and political matters and at times exerted influence on the decision-making processes of government. Haboush is clearly sensitive to the substantial differences between the European bourgeoisie and the Chosŏn scholar but notes also the variances in the ways that civil societies developed in different countries in the West and contends that a flexible use of categories and terminologies from the West may offer a way to conceptualize certain Chosŏn historical phenomena. In effect, she suggests that the community of *sŏwŏn* scholars can be seen as a public sphere in that they were private individuals who came together as a "reasoning public" which formulated public opinion through scholarly organizations largely autonomous of state control.[42]

One of the key points of Haboush's argument is that with the passage of time, the local *yangban* who were the scholars and students of the *sŏwŏn* became less dependent on the state for their status privileges, relying instead on social and familial networks and symbolic behavior.[43] It seems to me, however, that the issue is more complex than that. One could, of course, argue that the strong sense of ascriptive social status may have meant that *yangban* status was in effect independent of the state. But in the Chosŏn period, a lineage group's claim to *yangban* status hinged, at a minimum, on having a forebear who had either attained high office in the dynastic government or passed the government's civil service examination.[44] Thus even though many of the local *yangban* of the late Chosŏn may have been several generations removed from actual participation in the state's bureaucracy and may have sought to maintain their position through local social networks and ritual behavior, ultimately – as is suggested by the literal meaning of the term *yangban* as the two branches of government – they owed their status to connections with the state. This aspect, which seems to correlate with the notion of *kong* (*kung*) set forth by Mizoguchi as a sense of partnership between elites and the court, came to play an important role in the spread of the *sŏwŏn*.

A central organizational feature of the *sŏwŏn* was the enshrinement of a noted individual. In most cases, the individual who was enshrined was a native son who had risen to prominence in the dynastic government. The formation of the *sŏwŏn* around a shrine for a high-ranking official seems to me to be an effort by the local *yangban* to affirm their connections with the state, i.e., to reassert their right to membership in the dynasty's political elite. Recent Korean scholarship on the spread of the *sŏwŏn* contends that the local literati established *sŏwŏn* as a means to defend their status against other groups in local society. According to this line of argument, the disruption of rural Korea by the Japanese and Manchu invasions of the late sixteenth and seventeenth centuries and the rise of wealthy peasants and merchants as a result of the development of a commercial economy greatly weakened the position of the literati in local society; the literati response to this threat was to try to enhance their solidarity and maintain distinction between themselves and other social groups through organizations such as the *sŏwŏn*.[45] Whether this was actually the case, or whether the locals were seeking to defend themselves against marginalization by the relative handful of great aristocratic *pŏryŏl* lineages that came to dominate the dynastic government in the mid- and late Chosŏn awaits further investigation. But at any rate, it seems likely that the *sŏwŏn* came into being not as a space for local literati to aggregate their private interests against the power of the state but rather as a vehicle for local *yangban* to reassert their claim to membership in the state's political elite, either *vis-à-vis* competing groups in the countryside or *vis-à-vis* the *pŏryŏl* in the capital. This, it seems to me, should raise serious questions about the efforts to portray the *sŏwŏn* as equivalent to Habermas's notion of a public sphere.

The "backwoods literati" or "scholars in the wilderness"

In advancing his idea of a Chosŏn dynasty Confucian version of civil society, Cho Hein places great emphasis on a social group he terms the "backwoods literati" or *sarim*, which he defines as Confucian literati who went out to the countryside (or, in his terms, the "wilderness" (*ya*)) in order to protect the people from possible abuses by the state. It was these people whom Cho believes formed the *sŏwŏn* and other locally based intermediary institutions that constituted civil society in the Chosŏn.[46]

Here Cho appears to be engaging in a more-or-less literal translation of the term *sarim*: *sa* meaning literati and *rim* meaning forest, or "backwoods." Thus for Cho the term *sarim* means literati living out in the woods, i.e., out in the countryside away from the capital. This understanding of *sarim* is not without precedent. Indeed, for quite some time it has been standard practice to describe the *sarim* as locally based medium and small landlords engaged in political struggle with capital-based merit subjects. In recent years, however, this view of the *sarim* as a distinct social class has been largely discredited by the research of Ed Wagner and Chŏng Tuhŭi, whose examinations of the social origins of the men known as *sarim* during the late fifteenth and early sixteenth centuries have shown them to come from largely the same background as the meritorious elite (*hun'gu*) who were their political opponents.[47] From this perspective, then, the *rim* in *sarim* does not signify a rural mode of existence, but rather simply indicates the "ranks" of the literati in much the same way as it is used in *yurim* to indicate the community or ranks of Confucians. In short it is historically inaccurate to depict the *sarim* as a class of provincially based landlord literati who fulfilled a specialized role as the protectors of rural society against the central state.

Nonetheless, the historical sources for the early Chosŏn period do distinguish between *sarim* and meritorious elite. If the two groups came from similar social backgrounds, then we need to ask on what basis they were distinguished. One possible answer is provided by Kim Ch'ungnyŏl, who notes that there was a tension in Confucianism between the ideal of serving as officials in the king's government, which inevitably involved compromises with social and political realities, and the ideal of preserving one's moral integrity. According to Kim, the *sarim* were those men who chose to preserve their moral integrity, refused to serve in government (or if they were called to serve, rigidly refused to compromise their ideals for the sake of political expediency), and set themselves up as what Kim calls "judges of history" (*yŏksa ŭi simp'an*), routinely criticizing the conduct of government (and the conduct of the government's officials).[48] Thus what Kim offers is a philosophical and ethical basis for a *sarim* scholarly community that conceived of its *raison d'être* to be its role in holding the state to the highest standards of moral conduct and, because of the Mencian emphasis on the welfare of the people, protecting the people against possible abuses by the government.

If the problems attendant in the effort by Cho Hein and other scholars to argue for the existence of a discrete and autonomous social group in the rural literati/ *sarim* make it difficult for us to accept the idea that there was something equivalent to civil society/public sphere in the Chosŏn, then perhaps Kim Ch'ungnyŏl's positing of an independent ethical basis for a *sarim* community might, if we are willing to scrap the basic Western premise of social differentiation and economic interests as the foundation of civil society, allow us to imagine the existence of a public space in which independent and disinterested individuals devoted themselves to advancing the common good. But, it seems to me, without some grounding in social processes which break down the hierarchical status groups or estates of premodern society and thus yield the notion of some sort of fundamental equality that is so crucial to Habermas's formulation, we cannot link this type of public space with the rise of democracy.[49] Nonetheless, Kim's ideas on the ethical independence of the *sarim* bring us to the next issue I wish to examine, the question of orthodoxy.

The problem of "orthodoxy"

One of the central issues in the debate between Cho Hein and David Steinberg on the possibility of civil society in the Chosŏn is the question of orthodoxy. Steinberg makes a number of very well taken points against Cho's conceptualization of the institutions of civil society in Korea, such as his rejection of Cho's idea that the "checks and balances" of the Chosŏn court were an important feature of civil society. But the crux of Steinberg's argument is that a key feature of civil society and modern democracy is pluralism and that the existence in Chosŏn Korea of a strong Confucian orthodoxy prevented the development of pluralism and thus effectively precluded the possibility of civil society.[50] Cho refutes Steinberg by arguing that pluralism and orthodoxy are not necessarily in opposition, that pluralism grows out of orthodoxy and by contending that Westerners who advocate "Western Pluralism" over "Eastern Orthodoxy" are actually imposing a Western orthodoxy that is intolerant of other, Eastern views.[51] While I sense a certain sophistry in Cho's arguments, nonetheless I, too, am uncomfortable with an interpretation that gives primary agency to a "Confucian orthodoxy."

In the first part of this chapter, I devoted several pages to a discussion of the wide variety of modern understandings of Confucianism, to the complexity and richness of the Confucian intellectual tradition, and to the difficulties inherent in trying to come up with an inclusive and comprehensive definition of Confucianism. In another forum, I have also argued against the tendency to see Ch'eng-Chu Learning as state orthodoxy in the early Chosŏn, contending instead that fifteenth-century Korean literati learning consisted of a coexisting and commingling Ch'eng-Chu Learning, Ancient Style (*komun*) Learning, and T'ang-style belletrist syncretism.[52] At this time, there seems to be little reason to question the idea that Ch'eng-Chu Learning rose to dominance in the sixteenth century and after, accompanied by much discussion over "orthodoxy" (*chŏngt'ong*, "the correct transmission of the Way"). But, as Michael Kalton has noted, this did not necessarily mean that there was a single, established orthodoxy; rather there was a multiplicity of individuals and groups each asserting that he or it alone had received "the correct transmission of the Way."[53]

One can argue, of course, that King Sukchong's early-eighteenth-century intervention in favor of the Westerners of Song Shiyŏl (whose insistence that Chu Hsi could not be wrong makes him a key figure for those who argue for rigid orthodoxy) against the Southerners of Yun Hyu and Ch'oe Sŏkchŏng meant state sanction of Song Shiyŏl's version as official orthodoxy. Or one can, as Steinberg does, point to the late-eighteenth- and nineteenth-century persecution of Catholics as evidence of intolerant orthodoxy. One might ask, however, how this was different from state-supported persecution of religious minorities in early modern England and France, countries that presumably were developing civil societies.

Also, there is the plethora of scholarship on the so-called "Practical Learning" of the late Chosŏn which, while sometimes suspect for its equating of "Practical Learning" with early modern Western thought, nonetheless has demonstrated that scholars who continued to engage in *Cheng-Zhu* Learning moral and metaphysical discourse advanced a wide variety of solutions, some quite radical, for the political, social, and economic ills of their time.

Thus though I am in basic sympathy with Steinberg's concerns about pluralism and human rights in modern Korea, I am just as uncomfortable with his description of "Confucian" orthodoxy inhibiting the rise of civil society in the Chosŏn as I am with Cho Hein's contention that Confucianism produced civil society and contained the seeds of a modern democracy that finally flourished in Korea in the late twentieth century. It seems to me that the best way to establish the possibility of some sort of Korean equivalent to "civil society" or the "public sphere" is to demonstrate that there was in the Chosŏn some process of social differentiation analogous to that which took place with the rise of the market economy in Western Europe, a process that both leveled status differences and provided individuals with independent livelihoods that were not dependent on political power and patronage. The arguments advanced by South Korean internal development theorists regarding the "dissolution of the feudal system" and the "sprouts of capitalism" in the seventeenth and eighteenth centuries notwithstanding, I am not sure that any such process began in Korea until after the opening of the country to the outside world in the late nineteenth century. To the contrary, as James Palais has argued, the Chosŏn appears to have been a state and society dominated by an aristocratic landlord class, the central *yangban* or *pŏryŏl,* until after Korea was forced open in 1876.[54]

Conclusion

As Cho Hein and others have pointed out, while there are elements of the Confucian tradition that work against democratic civil society, there are also aspects of Confucianism that help to reinforce civil society, including a concept of limited government, an emphasis on civility, and a tradition of civilian – rather than military – rule. These points are not without merit, but I think it important to heed Mary Elizabeth Berry's warning about mistaking variable attributes for systems.[55] It is one thing to say that there are elements of the Confucian tradition, however it may be defined, that are not incompatible with democracy; it is quite another to claim, as Cho does, that Confucianism in Korea was on an historical trajectory that would have produced, had it not been for Japanese intervention, a modern democratic system.[56]

Bruce Cumings, on the other hand, suggests that even in the West there were multiple paths towards democracy, notes the problematic aspects of the Anglo-American model held up as the norm by many critiques of East Asian politics, and argues that East Asian state–society configuration that has emerged in the twentieth century bears close resemblance to one phase of the German experience, i.e., the fused state of the late developing country engaged in a race to catch up with early industrializers. Historians of East Asia are well aware of the way in which the Meiji Japanese oligarchs consciously modeled their system on that of Bismarck's Germany in their rush to create an industrialized nation-state that could compete with the imperial powers of the West. This model of state-led economic development was in turn passed on during the colonial period to the young men who eventually became the South Korean political and social elites after liberation in 1945.[57] To this I would like to add that there was also a certain historical parallel in socio-political structure between Germany and Korea.

Just as the Prussia that became the core of Bismarck's Germany was dominated both politically and socially by an aristocratic landlord class of Junkers, so was late Chosŏn dynasty Korea dominated by its own aristocratic landlord class in the *pŏryŏl yangban*. Thus it seems to me that the particular trajectory South Korea has followed towards democracy can be better explained in terms of the exigencies of late development and historical patterns of socio-economic and political organization than in terms of some sort of congruence between Confucianism and the Enlightenment.

Finally, let me note that one of the underlying issues that has motivated my argumentation throughout this chapter is a concern with the use of historically specific and highly idealized Western models to interpret Korea's past. It is not that I consider the Western experience to be somehow inherently superior to the East Asian or Korean experience, or that Western models represent an advanced level of social and political development to which non-Western societies simply cannot aspire. To the contrary, it is because I feel that the unconditioned, nonreflexive use of Western models privileges the modern Western experience and relegates countries like Korea to a kind of enduring subalternation, not only for the nineteenth and twentieth centuries when Western powers dominated the world, but also (as applied to earlier centuries) retrospectively for an historical era when countries like Korea and China were arguably more "advanced" in many ways than countries of the West.

Notes

1 *Chŏnt'ong kwa hyŏndae*, 1–1 (Summer 1997). This inaugural issue contains articles dealing with such topics as Confucianism and globalization, Confucianism and liberalism, Confucian capitalism, Confucian ethics and modern ethics, and Confucian education and modern education.

2 See Cho Hein, "The Historical Origin of Civil Society in Korea," *Korea Journal* 37, 2 (Summer 1997); Steinberg, David, "Civil Society and Human Rights in Korea," *Korea Journal* 37, 3 (Autumn 1997); and Han Sang-jin, "The Public Sphere and Democracy in Korea: A Debate on Civil Society," *Korea Journal* 37, 4 (Winter 1997).

3 Shin Ch'aeho, "Chosŏn yŏksasang 1,000 nyŏnnae cheil tae sakŏn," originally published in the *Tonga ilbo* in 1925: reprinted in Yi Ki-baek, ed., *Kŭndae Han'guk saron sŏn* (Seoul: Samsŏng munhwa chaedan, 1973), pp. 22–48.

4 See Robinson, Michael E., "National Identity and The Thought of Sin Ch'aeho*: Sadaejuŭi* and *Chuch'e* in History and Politics," *Journal of Korean Studies* 5 (1984), pp. 136–141 for a discussion of Shin's radical turn.

5 *The Korean Repository* II (1895), p. 401.

6 Yi Kwangsu, "Minjok kaejoron," *Kaebyŏk* 3, 5 (May 1922), pp. 44–45.

7 Robinson, "Confucianism in Twentieth Century Korea," pp. 212–214.

8 Park Chung Hee, *Our Nation's Path: Ideology of Social Reconstruction* (Seoul: Donga Publishing Co., 1962), pp. 34–81.

9 This is the main theme of the discussion of Nature and Principle Learning and the peasants in Han'guk yŏksa yŏn'guhoe, ed., *Han'guksa kangŭi* (Seoul: Hanŭl ak'ademi, 1989), pp. 150–168.

10 See, for example, Han Wansang's comments on the way establishment intellectuals even now use the Confucian idea of self-cultivation to deprive the *minjung* of their

rights in "Minjung kwa ŭisikhwa kyoyuk," in Han Wan-sang and Hŏ Pyŏngsŏp, eds, *Han'guk minjung kyoyuk: kŭinyŏm kwa silch'ŏn* (Seoul: Hangminsa, 1985), p. 61.

11 Robinson, "Perceptions of Confucianism," pp. 212–216; Smith, Warren W., *Confucianism in Modern Japan: A Study of Conservatism in Japanese Intellectual History* (Tokyo: Hokuseido, 1959), pp. 171–179.

12 Pak Ŭnshik, "Yugyo kusin non," *Sŏbuk hakhoe wŏlbo* 1, 10 (March 1909).

13 Chŏng Inbo, "Sŏngho saesŏl sŏ" (1929), reprinted in Tonga ilbosa, ed., *Han'guk hyŏndae myŏng nonsŏl chip* (Seoul: *Sindonga* pyŏlch'aek purok, January 1972), pp. 131–135.

14 Ch'ŏn Kwanu, *Han'guksa chae palgyŏn* (Seoul: Ilchogak, 1974), pp. 136–138.

15 Tu Weiming, Milan Hejtmanek, and Alan Wachman, eds., *The Confucian World Observed: A Contemporary Discussion of Confucian Humanism in East Asia* (Honolulu: East-West Center, University of Hawaii, 1992), pp. 97–98.

16 See the dialogue on college education in a "sick society" between Hong and Song Chae, president of Yonsei University, in Hong's *21 segi wa Han'guk chŏnt'ong munhwa* (Seoul: Hyŏndae munhak, 1994), pp. 274–282.

17 Kim Ch'ungnyŏl, "21 segi wa tongyang ch'ŏrhak," in Tonga ilbosa and Jen-min jih-bao, joint eds, *Kongja sasang kwa 21 segi* (Seoul: Tonga ilbosa, 1994), pp. 13–49.

18 Sŏ Kijŏng, *Minjung yugyo sasang* (Seoul: Tosŏch'ulp'an Chosŏn munhwa, 1990). The quotation is from p. 312.

19 Eisenstadt, S.N., *The Political Systems of Empires* (New Brunswick, N.J.: Transaction Publishers, 1993) (originally published in 1963 by the Free Press of Glencoe), pp. 156–171.

20 The multiplicity of "Confucianisms" across space and time in China, Korea, Japan, and Vietnam and the way in which they were rooted in changing political, social, and economic conditions, was the organizing theme of a recent conference "Rethinking Confucianism" held May 31–June 3, 1999, at UCLA.

21 This discussion of public and private has been drawn primarily from Jeff Weintraub, "The Theory and Politics of the Public/Private Distinction," in Weintraub and Krishnan Kumar, eds., *Public and Private in Thought and Practice: Perspectives on a Grand Dichotomy* (Chicago: University of Chicago Press, 1997), pp. 1–42. Weintraub also discusses a third major view, that advanced by feminist scholars. The feminists agree with the social historians in seeing the public realm as being made up of intrusive and impersonal state and market forces. But, rather than seeing the family-centered private domain as a byproduct of the modern expansion of state and economy, the feminists treat the private realm, which they prefer to term the "domestic," as primary and the public realm as secondary. In doing so, they not only shed light on the way in which conventional views of public and private are gendered constructs but also force us to rethink the relationship between macrosocial and microsocial institutions. Indeed, if we accept the idea that the domestic realm is primary and the so-called "public" realm is derivative, the whole public/private dichotomy comes to the brink of collapse.

22 Polanyi, Karl, *The Great Transformation: The Political and Economic Origins of Our Times* (Boston: Beacon Press, 1957). Originally published by Rinehart and Company in 1944.

23 Mizoguchi Yuzo, *Chugoku no ko to shi* (Tokyo: Kembu Press, 1995).

24 Elman, Benjamin, "Imperial Politics and Confucian Societies in Late Imperial China: The Hanlin and Donglin Academies," *Modern China* 15, 4 (1989), pp. 379–418.

25 Yang Sŏngji, *Nuljae chip sokkwŏn* (Seoul: Aseamunhwa sa, 1988) 1:10a.

26 Deuchler, Martina, *The Confucian Transformation of Korea: A Study of Society and Ideology* (Cambridge: Harvard University Press, 1992).

27 See Pak Chu, *Chosŏn sidae ŭi chŏngp'yo chŏngch'aek* (Seoul: Ilchogak, 1990) for a study of Chosŏn court policy of rewarding moral exemplars.

28 Palais, James B., "Land Tenure in Korea: Tenth to Twelfth Centuries," *Journal of Korean Studies* 4 (1982–1983), pp. 187–190.

29 Fei, Hsiao-Tung, "Peasantry and Gentry: An Interpretation of Chinese Social Structure and Its Changes," in Reinhard Bendix, ed., *State and Society* (Berkeley: University of California Press, 1973), pp. 125–139.

30 See, for example, Song Ki Joong (Song Kijung), comp., *Basic Glossary of Korean Studies* (Seoul: Korea Foundation, 1993), p. 19.

31 Nam Chidae, "Chosoŏn Sŏngjongdae ŭi taegan ŏllon," *Han'guk saron* 12 (1985), pp. 106–120.

32 Yu Suwŏn, Usŏ 4:15a. See also the translation in *Saryo ro pon Han'guk munhwasa: Chosŏn hugi p'yŏn* (Seoul: Ilchisa, 1985), p. 88.

33 Cho Hein, "The Historical Origin of Civil Society in Korea," p. 32.

34 See Haboush, JaHyun Kim, *A Heritage of Kings: One Man's Monarchy in the Confucian World* (New York: Columbia University Press, 1988), pp. 119–121.

35 Femia, Joseph V., *Gramsci's Political Thought: Hegemony, Consciousness, and the Revolutionary Process* (Oxford: Clarendon Press, 1981), pp. 23–29.

36 See Bruce Cumings' discussion of Gramsci's view of civil society and the state in his contribution to this volume.

37 Calhoun, Craig, "Nationalism and the Public Sphere," in Weintraub and Kumar, eds, *Public and Private in Thought and Practice*, p. 81.

38 See, for example, Robert Hymes and Conrad Schirokauer, "Introduction," in *Ordering the World: Approaches to State and Society and Sung Dynasty China* (Berkeley: University of California Press, 1993), pp. 51–58.

39 Calhoun, "Nationalism and the Public Sphere," p. 83.

40 Cho Hein, "The Historical Origin of Civil Society in Korea," p. 32.

41 Haboush, JaHyun Kim, "Academies and Civil Society in Chosŏn Korea," in *La société civile face a l'État: dans les traditions chinoise, japonaise, corénne et vietnaménne* (Paris: Ecole française d'extrême-orient, 1994), pp. 381–390.

42 Ibid., p. 381 and p. 389.

43 Ibid., pp. 381–382.

44 Song June-ho (Song Junho) *Chosŏn sahoesa yŏn'gu* (Seoul: Ilchogak, 1987), pp. 36–37.

45 See Yi Haejun, "Chosŏn hugi sŏwŏn yŏn'gu wa hyangch'on sahoesa," *Han'guk saron* 21 (1991), pp. 3–28 for a review of scholarship on *sŏwŏn* and local society.

46 Cho Hein, "The Historical Origin of Civil Society," p. 31.

47 Wagner, Edward W. "Yijo sarim munje e kwanhan chae kŏmt'o," *Chŏnbuk sahak* 4 (1980) and Chŏng Tuhŭi, "Chosŏn Sŏngjongdae ŭi taegan yŏn'gu (Seoul: Han'guk yŏn'guwŏn, 1989).

48 Kim Ch'ungnyŏl, *Koryŏyuhaksa* (Seoul: Koryŏtaehakkyo ch'ulp'anbu, 1990), pp. 248–250.

49 If we accept Kim's formulation of an ethically autonomous *sarim* as equivalent to civil society (a position which Kim himself has never taken), then we can make the same argument for, say, the prophets of Israel or the mullahs of Islam.

50 Steinberg, David, "Civil Society and Human Rights in Korea," pp. 145–154.

51 Cho Hein, "The Historical Origin of Civil Society," p. 37.

52 Duncan, John B., "Confucianism in the Late Koryŏ and Early Chosŏn," *Korean Studies* 18 (1994).

53 Michael Kalton comments on the question of orthodoxy made during the workshop for volume three of the forthcoming *Cambridge History of Korea* at the University of Washington, September 1996.

54 Palais, James B., *Politics and Policy in Traditional Korea* (Cambridge: East Asian Research Center, Harvard University, 1975).

55 Berry, Mary Elizabeth, "Public Life in Authoritarian Japan," *Daedalus* 127, 3 (Summer 1998), p. 138.

56 Cho Hein, "The Historical Origin of Civil Society," p. 35.
57 Eckert, Carter J., *Offspring of Empire: The Koch'ang Kims and the Origins of Korean Capitalism* (Seattle: University of Washington Press, 1992).

3 Civil society and democratization in South Korea

Sunhyuk Kim

Introduction

Analysts of Korean politics have tended to present two different, and to some extent conflicting, interpretations regarding what really caused South Korea's recent democratization since 1987. According to one popular interpretation, it was primarily – if not entirely – due to a series of elite calculations and interactions.[1] The focus of this interpretation is June 29, 1987 on which the chairman of the ruling Democratic Justice Party, Roh Tae Woo, made his eight-point proposal on democratic reform – the "June 29 Declaration." It is still disputable if there existed a real split between the "hardliners" and the "softliners" within the ruling elite.[2] Nevertheless, according to this interpretation, ruling elites predicted that the opposition would be fragmented, and this is why they agreed to adopt a set of democratic reforms including a change to a direct presidential election system.

The other interpretation, which I support and develop in this chapter, puts emphasis on mass mobilization by civil society groups. The central event, according to this interpretation, is not Roh Tae Woo's June 29 Declaration but a series of nationwide anti-government protest demonstrations from approximately June 10 to June 29, 1987 – the "June Popular Uprising." This approach in essence argues that what was crucial for the democratic transition in South Korea in 1987 was the formation of a pro-democracy coalition and an unprecedented level of mass mobilization, which eventually pressured the ruling authoritarian regime to accommodate popular demand for democratic reform.[3]

These two different interpretations of South Korean democratization closely mirror the two dominant paradigms in the existing literature on democratic transition and consolidation. On the one hand, there is an elite-centered paradigm, emphasizing elite strategies and interactions. According to this paradigm, "elite dispositions, calculations, and pacts … largely determine whether or not an opening will occur at all."[4] On the other hand, there is a mass-centered paradigm, accentuating mass mobilization and civil society.[5] According to this paradigm, the choices that civil society groups and mass publics make induce elites to move towards democracy. In general, the elite-centered paradigm is more applicable to "pacted" transitions, whereas the mass-centered paradigm better explains "reformist" or "revolutionary" transitions.[6] In other words, the relative importance of elite vs. mass factors depends, at least in theory, on the specific case and its mode of transition. In practice, however, most cases present mixed pictures. For instance, even with regard to the Spanish case, which is considered to be a classic example of a pacted transition, the two interpretations are still competing and clashing.[7] Therefore, the debate on elites vs. masses is far from being settled.

The main purpose of this chapter is to demonstrate that the mass-centered approach, i.e., the "June Popular Uprising" interpretation, is a more appropriate explanation for the case of South Korean democratization. The mobilization of civil society was extremely important in South Korea's democratic transition. Furthermore, I argue that civil society has been crucial in the politics of democratic consolidation of South Korea too. In the course of this analysis, I first examine the role of civil society groups in the democratic transition during 1984–87. Next, I analyze the role of civil society groups in the politics of democratic consolidation since 1988 to the present. I then conclude with a few theoretical reflections on the debate about elites vs. masses and on the implications of active civil society for further democratic consolidation in South Korea.

Civil society and the democratic transition, 1984–87

Severe state repression of civil society characterized the first four years (1980–83) of the Chun Doo Hwan regime. Following the violent suppression of the pro-democracy movement in Kwangju in May 1980, the authoritarian regime implemented a series of coercive campaigns to "cleanse (*chŏnghwa*)" the entire society, purging or arresting thousands of public officials, politicians, professors, teachers, pastors, journalists, and students on various charges of corruption, instigation, and organization of anti-government demonstrations, and attempts at insurrection. Meanwhile, a legislature *pro tempore*, the Legislative Council for National Security passed numerous anti-democratic laws, curtailing political competition, restricting basic democratic freedoms, establishing an elaborate system of press censorship, and suppressing the labor movement.

Starting in late 1983, however, Chun's suppression of civil society significantly abated. The authoritarian regime decided to liberalize the polity, allowing anti-government university professors and students to return to their schools, withdrawing the military police from university campuses, pardoning or rehabilitating political prisoners, and lifting the ban on political activities of hundreds of former politicians. What the government intended through these liberalization measures was to make the ruling Democratic Justice Party popular and therefore electorally competitive. The consequence of the liberalization, however, was quite different from what the regime expected – it resulted, in fact, in "the resurrection of civil society."[8] Various groups in South Korean civil society, particularly those movement groups which had been decimated by the authoritarian regime's severe repression between 1980 and 1983, were rapidly resurrected.

First of all, in February and March of 1984, university students, who had just returned to their campuses for the new academic year, restored and reorganized anti-government student groups. In November 1984 students from 42 universities and colleges organized the National Student Coalition for Democracy Struggle (*Chŏnhangnyŏn*). This was the first nationwide student organization since the April Student Uprising that led to the downfall of the Syngman Rhee regime in 1960.

Second, the Korean Council for Labor Welfare (KCLW, *Han'guk nohyŏp*) was organized in March 1984. Composed of various labor unions that had spearheaded anti-Yusin pro-democracy struggles in the 1970s, the KCLW tried to restore and strengthen unity and solidarity among labor movement groups. In April 1984 the *Chŏnggye* apparel labor union, which had been prominent in the labor movement in the 1970s but was dissolved by the authoritarian regime in 1981, was also restored. The KCLW and *Chŏnggye* jointly launched a massive campaign against the arbitrary labor laws enacted by the Legislative Council for National Security. The old student–labor alliance was resurrected, and students actively supported and cooperated with the restored labor unions. In addition, church groups such as the National Catholic Priests' Corps for the Realization of Justice (NCPCRJ, *K'atollik chŏngŭi kuhyŏn chŏn'guk sajedan*) assisted the labor movement, waging a signature campaign for the revision of objectionable labor laws.

Third, and most importantly, the resurrected student groups, youth organizations, labor unions, religious organizations, and other civil society groups were united and coordinated under the unified leadership of a national umbrella organization, the People's Movement Coalition for Democracy and Reunification (PMCDR, *Mint'ongnyŏn*). The PMCDR, established in March 1985, encompassed not only urban labor, landless peasants, and leading intellectuals, but also most of the country's Buddhist, Protestant, and Roman Catholic clergy and lay groups.[9] Unlike numerous national movement associations during the 1970s, this organization was not just a group of dissident dignitaries but was quite reflective of the alliance of students, laborers, and religious leaders.

While various pro-democracy movement groups re-emerged in civil society, a genuine opposition re-emerged in political society.[10] Between 1980 and 1983 there was no real opposition in South Korean politics. Opposition parties such as the Democratic Korea Party (*Minhandang*) and Korean Nationalist Party (*Kungmindang*), created and controlled by the authoritarian regime, had been unable and unwilling to criticize and challenge the political legitimacy of the regime. What the authoritarian regime expected in implementing a series of liberalization measures in 1983–84 was the further fragmentation of the opposition. Contrary to the regime's expectations, however, liberalization resulted in the dramatic resuscitation and expansion of a real opposition. Many of the reinstated opposition politicians formed the New Korea Democratic Party (NKDP, *Sinhan minjudang*) in January 1985, immediately before the National Assembly elections in February.

The politics of authoritarian breakdown and democratic transition began in earnest with the formation of the NKDP and its electoral alignment with civil society groups. Many civil society groups, particularly youth and student organizations, openly supported and vigorously campaigned for the NKDP.

It was the first time since the early 1960s that university students supported a particular political party. The turnout in the National Assembly elections on February 12, 1985 was 84.6 percent, which was the highest since the 1950s. The NKDP emerged as the leading opposition, unexpectedly winning 29.26 percent of the votes, compared with 35.25 percent for the ruling Democratic Justice Party. After the elections, the strategy of the civil society groups and the NKDP was to make the legitimacy question the only and the most important political issue.[11] The coalition between civil society groups and the opposition NKDP outlived the National Assembly elections and later developed into a grand democracy coalition against the authoritarian regime.

Pro-democracy activities by civil society groups in South Korea during 1986–87 primarily took three different forms. First, starting in early 1986, religious activists issued a series of declarations and statements reprimanding the authoritarian regime and demanding an immediate constitutional revision. For instance, Protestant pastors argued in a statement in March 1986 that a new constitution, which would include a direct presidential election system and address basic human rights and economic equality, should be drafted immediately, and the next government should be elected according to the new constitution. Cardinal Kim Su Hwan declared in early March 1986 that "Democratization is the best way to make peace with God. The sooner the constitutional revision, the better."[12] Moreover, beginning with a statement by professors at Korea University on March 28, 1986, 783 professors at 29 colleges and universities nationwide publicly announced "statements on the current situation (*Siguk sŏnŏn*)," which was an organized and peaceful nonconfidence campaign against the authoritarian regime.

Second, the opposition NKDP launched a popular campaign to collect ten million signatures nationwide in support of constitutional revision. The number – ten million – was almost half of the electorate and a quarter of the entire population of South Korea at the time. The campaign started on February 12, 1986, the first anniversary of the 1985 National Assembly elections, and rapidly spread across the country. The "size and ferocity" of the signature drive astonished the authoritarian regime.[13] The police carried out a series of harsh crackdowns on the signature campaign by raiding the NKDP headquarters and the offices of civil society groups and arresting numerous campaign activists. But the regime could not stem the tide of the campaign.

Third, concurrently with the signature campaign, civil society groups and the NKDP jointly sponsored and held a number of mass rallies in support of democratization. The People's Movement Coalition for Democracy and Reunification and the NKDP set up the National Coalition for Democracy Movement (*Min'gungnyŏn*) and coordinated, organized, mobilized, and led mass rallies in major cities of the country – Kwangju on March 30, Chŏngju on April 4, Taegu on April 5, Taejŏn on April 19, Inch'ŏn on May 3, Masan on May 10, and Chŏnju on May 31. Civil society groups and the opposition party were particularly encouraged by the "February Revolution" in the Philippines in which the Marcos regime was at last expelled by the "people's power." The number of participants in these mass rallies exceeded 700,000 in total. Such a level of mass mobilization, except during election campaigns, was the highest since the April Uprising in 1960. The grand democracy coalition of civil society groups and the opposition party succeeded in mobilizing South Koreans from all walks of life – students, workers, peasants, urban service industry employees, religious leaders, and other citizens – under the banner of "Down with the Military Authoritarian Regime and Up with a Democratic Government."

Two events were particularly instrumental in bolstering the power of the pro-democracy coalition and maintaining the high level of mass mobilization. First, at the dawn of 1987, Pak Chong Ch'ŏl, a Seoul National University student, was tortured to death during a police interrogation. The police initially announced that Pak had died of a heart attack. On May 18, however, the National Catholic Priests' Corps for the Realization of Justice (NCPCRJ) disclosed that Pak died of police torture and that the police and the regime had attempted to conceal the fact. Pak Chong Ch'ŏl's torture death and the revelation of the regime's conspiracy to cover up the crime put the authoritarian regime and the ruling party on the defensive and dramatically augmented the position and power of the pro-democracy coalition.

Second, Chun Doo Hwan declared on April 13, 1987 that he could no longer tolerate wasteful discussions on constitutional revision. This unilateral decision to terminate the public discussions on constitutional revision intensified mass mobilization. University professors initiated a public statement campaign, criticizing and opposing Chun's decision. Artists, novelists, writers, and actors followed suit. Religious leaders and priests waged a series of hunger strikes. Cardinal Kim Su Hwan and many religious organizations including the NCPCRJ, the National Council of Protestant Pastors for Justice and Peace, and the Korean Christian Council (*Han'guk kidokkyo hyŏbŭihoe*) also expressed their strong opposition to the decision. Violent anti-government protests by students, labor unions, and other civil society groups spread across the country, and tens of thousands of South Koreans in major cities demonstrated against the decision.

In May 1987 civil society groups established the National Movement Head-quarter for Democratic Constitution (NMHDC, *Kungmin undong ponbu*). This organization, consisting of the People's Movement Coalition for Democracy and Reunification and 25 other major civil society groups, covered all major sectoral groups and geographical areas. Organizing and coordinating local branches throughout the country, the NMHDC mobilized a series of massive pro-democracy demonstrations against the authoritarian regime in June 1987. The mobilization escalated particularly after Yi Han Yŏl, a Yonsei University student, was hit by tear gas bomb fragments on June 9 and critically injured. On June 10 the NMHDC organized the "Uprising Rally to Defeat the April 13 Decision and to End Dictatorship". On June 26 it held the "Peace Parade" in which one million people participated nationwide. Not only the pro-democracy movement groups but also many middle-class citizens participated in these mass rallies. Pak Chong Ch'ŏl's torture death and Yi Han Yŏl's injury (and later death) particularly angered middle-class citizens, because these two incidents most vividly demonstrated the immoral, illegitimate, violent, and repressive nature of the authoritarian regime.

Just like the death of high school student Kim Chu Yŏl in 1960 and the death of a female labor striker, Kim Kyŏng Suk, in 1979, the deaths of Pak Chong Ch'ŏl and Yi Han Yŏl brought to the minds of ordinary citizens the image of "democratic martyr," which has been a recurrent theme in the checkered history of South Korean democratization.

Confronted with unprecedented mass protests and mobilization, on June 29, 1987, the authoritarian regime finally announced dramatic and unexpected concessions to the demands of civil society groups and the opposition party, adopting a direct presidential election system.

Civil society and the democratic consolidation, 1988–

Perhaps ironically, the presidential elections in 1987 – the result of intense popular pressure – left civil society in South Korea marginalized and fragmented. First, once the authoritarian regime agreed to carry out a set of democratic reforms including direct presidential elections, the focus of the transitional politics rapidly shifted to the "founding elections" – the presidential elections in December 1987 and the National Assembly elections in April 1988. As the founding elections were nearing, South Korean politics increasingly revolved around party politics and electoral competitions in political society. Civil society and mass mobilization became incrementally marginal. Second, after trying in vain to remedy the fatal split between the two opposition leaders, Kim Young Sam and Kim Dae Jung, civil society groups took different positions on whom to support for the upcoming presidential elections. When the presidential elections ended with the ruling party's victory, civil society groups were left deeply fragmented as a result.

However, after the inauguration of Roh Tae Woo, civil society groups remobilized themselves and resumed their pro-democracy campaign with a vigor comparable to or even stronger than that during the 1985–87 period. One of the most important reasons why civil society groups could resume their movement for democratic reform relatively quickly was the continuity of the Roh regime with the previous authoritarian regime. Roh himself did not appear to represent a clear break with the past. He could be seen as just another general-turned-president. Being a close friend of Chun Doo Hwan and deeply involved in the military coup of 1979–80 and the subsequent consolidation of the authoritarian political system, Roh had been groomed and eventually anointed as an official successor to Chun until the last minute, when the ruling bloc decided to yield to popular pressure by proclaiming the June 29 democratization package. Roh was the greatest beneficiary of the past authoritarian regime and therefore extremely constrained in terms of what he could do regarding the liquidation of the authoritarian past. To most of the movement groups that had led the "June Uprising" in 1987, the Roh regime was viewed as a mere extension of authoritarian rule. Thus civil society groups often pejoratively characterized Roh as "Chun with a wig," likening him to the previous military ruler who was bald. At best, Roh's regime seemed to be a liberalized authoritarianism (*dictablanda*), and the need to continue the pro-democracy struggle appeared vital.[14]

Furthermore, the grand party merger in 1990 offered glaring evidence that the Roh Tae Woo regime was just a continuation of the past authoritarianism and the opposition parties were unreliable. In early 1990, Roh – who, as leader of a minority party, had been seriously concerned about his political vulnerability in the National Assembly since his inauguration – succeeded in merging his ruling Democratic Justice Party with two opposition parties: the Unification Democratic Party led by Kim Young Sam and the New Democratic Republican Party led by Kim Jong Pil. The three were merged into a Democratic Liberal Party (*Minjadang*), a conservative coalition clearly modeled on Japan's long-ruling Liberal Democratic Party, and which left Kim Dae Jung's Democratic Party small and isolated. This was similar to transformism (*trasformismo*) in Italy where in 1876, Agostino de Pretis, the new prime minister, invited the opposition Destra Party to shift to the government majority in exchange for personal benefits, access to state patronage, and the right to local rule. The opposition parties, finding themselves marginalized from power and state spoils, agreed and "transformed" themselves from the opposition into a stable part of the governing majority.[15] Such Korean-style transformism was seen by many civil society groups as a frontal attack on the consolidation of democracy in their country; consequently, civil society groups had no choice but to intensify their pro-democracy movement.

It was ironically the election of Kim Young Sam in 1992, the first genuinely civilian South Korean president in more than three decades, that provided the most serious challenge to civil society and mass mobilization in South Korea. Immediately following his inauguration and particularly in the first two years of his tenure, Kim designed and carried out a series of unprecedented political and socio-economic reforms, waging intensive anti-corruption campaigns, introducing a "real name" bank system, legislating political reform bills, and consolidating the civilian control of the military.[16] Most of all, the Kim government's effort to normalize relations with civil society was limited to not only pro-government or moderate groups but also radical groups in civil society. Kim's soaring popularity left civil society groups, which had been so good at criticizing unpopular governments and so used to the repression by authoritarian regimes, bewildered, demobilized, and demoralized.[17] In a word, civil society groups were no longer able to find a common target. Civil society and mass mobilization appeared largely irrelevant to South Korean politics. Civil society groups, which had weathered such harsh state repression during the previous authoritarian regimes, faced their most serious identity crisis under a democratic government.

Such seeming irrelevance of civil society and mass mobilization to South Korean politics and democracy, however, did not continue very long. Civil society groups remobilized themselves and have played an extremely significant role in the politics of democratic consolidation in South Korea during the Kim Young Sam government, by pressuring the government to break with the authoritarian past, protesting the possible erosion of democracy, and pursuing new movement causes such as environmentalism.[18]

What was particularly instrumental in the resurgence of mass mobilization in South Korea during the Kim Young Sam government was the nationwide controversy during 1994–95 over one of the most difficult yet important issues of the consolidational politics – the "liquidation" of the authoritarian past. Democratic consolidation is "the process in which democracy becomes so broadly and profoundly legitimate among its citizens that it is very unlikely to break down."[19] Without a reasonably clean separation from the previous authoritarian regimes, it is nearly impossible for a new democratic regime to become "broadly and profoundly legitimate." Therefore, how to deal with the authoritarian past becomes extremely crucial in either augmenting or undermining the legitimacy of a fledgling democracy.

The Kim Young Sam government was at best opportunistic regarding the issue of confronting and grappling with the authoritarian past. After a year-long investigation of the military putsch on December 12, 1979 and the Kwangju Massacre in May 1980, the government confirmed in October 1994 that Chun Doo Hwan and Roh Tae Woo were found to have engineered a military revolt. To the chagrin of most South Koreans, however, the Kim government announced in July 1995 that it would not pursue insurrection charges against Chun and Roh, because of the statute of limitations and to avoid damage to "national unity." This announcement gave rise to a series of intense protests by many civil society groups, eventually leading to a national crisis.

Beginning with a protest declaration by the Korea Council of Professors for Democratization (*Min'gyohyŏp*) on August 14, 1995, university professors waged a nationwide signature collection campaign to demand a special law for prosecuting the coup leaders.[20] The disclosure of Roh Tae Woo's corruption scandal by an opposition National Assemblyman in October 1995 dramatically escalated the level of mass mobilization. The "All-nation Emergency Committee on Enacting a Special Law for Punishing the Perpetrators of the May 18 Massacre," established by 297 civil society groups, waged a signature collection campaign in which one million people participated. The Committee also held a "People's Action Day" to call for the imprisonment of Roh, which 10,000 citizens and students attended.[21] Throughout November 1995, thousands of students, workers, movement activists, and ordinary citizens waged street demonstrations in Seoul and other major cities of the country.[22] Yielding to the popular pressure that had engulfed the whole nation for several months, the government finally prosecuted Chun and Roh in early 1996 on multiple charges of bribery, insurrection, and treason. Eventually, both Chun and Roh, on the recommendation of then president-elect Kim Dae Jung, were amnestied and released in December 1997. Nevertheless, the dramatic arrests and imprisonments of the two former general-turned-presidents, which had not been possible without the massive remobilization of civil society groups, immensely contributed to the consolidation of South Korean democracy by unequivocally demonstrating that a military coup would never be tolerated or justified as a viable option in South Korean politics.

Another high tide of civil society activism during the Kim Young Sam government came in late 1996. On December 26, 1996, the ruling New Korea Party (successor to the Democratic Liberal Party) passed several labor-related bills and a reform bill regarding the Agency for National Security Planning (ANSP,

Angibu; renamed National Intelligence Service, *Kukka chŏngbowŏn*, in January 1999). These bills had been intensely debated and contested among South Koreans. Labor unions had opposed the proposed labor reform bills, because the bills, if legislated, would weaken labor unions and facilitate massive layoffs. Civil society groups had also disputed the proposed ANSP reform bill, because the bill would expand the investigative power of the already powerful state agency. Despite these concerns and criticisms from labor unions, civil society groups, and the opposition parties, the ruling party rammed the bills through the National Assembly, at 6 a.m. on December 26, clandestinely and without the presence of opposition legislators. This railroading of the controversial bills profoundly outraged civil society groups and led to a series of anti-government protests. Lawyers and university professors waged sit-ins and street demonstrations, demanding the immediate nullification of the bills passed. Student organizations, comparing the passage of the bills with the notorious legislation of two anti-democratic laws during the Chang Myŏn government in 1961, launched nationwide demonstrations. Labor unions characterized the Kim Young Sam government as a civilian dictatorship and led a series of strikes, including a successful general strike in January 1997, the first such strike since the Republic of Korea was founded in 1948. Catholic churches and organizations including the National Catholic Priests' Corps for the Realization of Justice supported the student demonstrations and labor strikes. Buddhist and protestant organizations also joined the support.[23] Well into mid-March, massive demonstrations and signature collection campaigns by civil society groups and labor strikes created disruption throughout the country. The government was determined to remain uncompromising, yielding nothing to the pressure engendered by such mass mobilization. Despite this, the Kim Young Sam regime ultimately lost the battle. These anti-government protests irrevocably tarnished the regime's previous democratic image, which, combined with the onset of a grave economic crisis in late 1997, made Kim Young Sam the most unpopular president in South Korean history.

Lastly, since the democratic transition in 1987, civil society groups in South Korea have explored and addressed new social issues. Particularly notable is the rapid expansion of the environmental movement in the 1990s. On April 2, 1993, the Korea Federation for Environmental Movement (KFEM), the biggest environmental movement group in South Korean history, was created. The KFEM today has 49 regional offices and more than 80,000 dues-paying members, including many working journalists, lawyers, professors, religious leaders, medical doctors, nurses, social workers, artists, businesspersons, farmers, workers, students, and ordinary citizens. The leadership positions of the KFEM are filled with the new urban middle class. The cadres or activists who carry out everyday duties of the organization are also highly educated and reform-oriented. Since its establishment, the KFEM has concentrated on a number of "focal projects" each year. Focal projects have included, for example, preserving clean water; reducing air pollution; increasing international solidarity in the anti-nuclear movement; expanding the membership and local organizations of the KFEM; enhancing environmental education; computerizing environmental information; waste reduction; diversification of energy sources; promoting environment-friendly local politics; and educating children in environmentalism.[24]

The year 1997 proved a crucial year for South Korea. Beginning with the collapse of one of the *chaebŏl* groups, *Hanbo*, several big business conglomerates became insolvent and fell into court receivership. Foreign banks and investors pulled their funds out of South Korea, quickly leading to a foreign exchange crisis. Despite efforts by the government and the Bank of Korea, the exchange rate and stock market plummeted, placing South Korea virtually on the brink of defaulting on its foreign debt obligations. On December 3, 1997, the International Monetary Fund (IMF) agreed to provide a $57 billion package to South Korea, which was the largest in the IMF's history at that time. Various conditions were attached to the loans, including stringent macro-economic policies, the restructuring of the financial and corporate sectors, and rapid capital and trade liberalization.[25] Since the IMF bailout, South Korea, once touted as one of the "four little dragons" in East Asia, has been undergoing a serious economic restructuring.[26]

On the other hand, for the first time in South Korean history, an opposition candidate, Kim Dae Jung, was elected in the 1997 presidential elections. The fact that the opposition candidate could be elected confirmed that the presidential elections were unprecedentedly free and fair. The victory of the opposition was particularly historic because Kim Dae Jung had long been a strong supporter of democracy and human rights in South Korea.[27] He had been one of the most progressive politicians in South Korean politics and, for that reason, had often been labeled and suppressed as a leftist or a communist sympathizer. More significantly, Kim Dae Jung was based in the Chŏlla region of southwestern Korea, a region that had been systematically discriminated against throughout the entire process of industrialization under the preceding authoritarian regimes.[28] His election to the presidency demonstrated that a genuinely horizontal transfer of power, an important indication of democratic consolidation, had finally occurred in South Korea.[29]

Civil society groups continued to play a pivotal role under the Kim Dae Jung regime. To some extent, the role of civil society and mass mobilization became even more salient and crucial, primarily due to the paralysis and immobilism prevalent within South Korea's political society. From the day of his inauguration, Kim Dae Jung confronted bitter criticism and persistent hostility from the opposition, Grand National Party. The National Assembly, throughout Kim Dae Jung's tenure, was characterized by frequent verbal and physical confrontations, completely lacking all the vital signs and elements of a democratic and mature legislature – communication, partnership, cooperation, compromise, constructive engagement, civility, and so forth. With such a barren and dysfunctional political society, it was once again civil society groups and their mobilization that played crucial roles in setting important national agendas and pressuring the government to carry out reforms.

The activities of civil society groups during the Kim Dae Jung government primarily focused on social reform. That civil society organizations campaigned for social reform was hardly new in South Korea. However, the breadth and vigor of the movement were notable. Civil society groups aimed at a complete transformation and rebirth of entire South Korean society, concurrently calling for political and economic reforms. In pushing for these various reforms, civil society groups also tried to formulate and present viable policy alternatives to the state, forging and nurturing a constructive engagement with the state.

First, mobilization of civil society groups was crucial in transforming the "election climate (*sŏn'gŏ p'ungt'o*)" of South Korea. The movement for fair elections, led by the Citizens' Council for Fair Elections (*Kongsŏnhyŏp*), had contributed considerably to increasing the overall fairness of elections. However, civil society groups realized that ensuring fair elections would not fundamentally change the mentality and behavior of South Korean politicians. Hence, in 2000, they switched to a more aggressive movement to endorse and support specific policies and candidates. On January 13, 2000, about three months before the National Assembly elections, 412 civil society groups, including the People's Solidarity for Participatory Democracy (PSPD, *Ch'amyŏ yŏndae*) and the KFEM, established the Citizens' Solidarity for the General Elections (CSGE, *Ch'ongsŏn yŏndae*). At its inauguration, this organization envisioned two different stages of its movement. The first was to generate a list of politicians who should not be nominated by political parties to run for the National Assembly elections (the *Nakch'ŏn* movement). Second, if some of those "blacklisted" candidates were nominated anyway, the movement was to campaign against their actual elections (the *Naksŏn* movement).

On January 24, the CSGE disclosed a list of 66 politicians who should not be nominated as candidates for the April National Assembly elections. The selection criteria included involvement in previous bribery and corruption scandals, violation of the election laws, lack of legislative activities (e.g., too many absences in national assembly sessions), destruction of constitutional order (e.g., cooperation with Chun Doo Hwan's authoritarian regime in the early 1980s or involvement in military coups), failure or refusal to sign anti-corruption laws, instigation of regionalism, and so on.[30] Various faith-based organizations, including Episcopal, Catholic, Protestant, and Buddhist organizations, publicly expressed their support for the CSGE's *Nakch'ŏn* and *Naksŏn* campaign, stating that they completely endorsed the movement's objective to expel corrupt politicians from the political arena and to restore the people's right of political participation. Furthermore, 232 members of Lawyers for Democracy (*Minbyŏn*) created a legal support team to give legal advice to the CSGE's movement. Participating lawyers stated that the main goal of the *Nakch'ŏn* and *Naksŏn* movement was to protect and enhance people's constitutional right of political participation.

The CSGE announced the final *Naksŏn* list of 86 unfit candidates on April 3. The final list included 64 candidates who had been on the original *Nakch'ŏn* list but were nominated by parties and 22 more candidates selected according to the criteria of anti-human rights backgrounds, tax evasion, inappropriate remarks and behaviors in the national assembly, and so forth. In the national assembly elections held on April 13, 2000, 59 out of 86 candidates listed by the CSGE failed to be elected. In its disintegration ceremony one week after the elections, the CSGE made the self-assessment that its *Nakch'ŏn* and *Naksŏn* movement, in which 975 civil society groups and 1,000 activists participated in one way or another, had significantly contributed to the increase of voters' political consciousness and efficacy, to the emergence of a new generation of young politicians, and to the partial revision of election laws.[31]

Second, many civil society groups during the Kim Dae Jung administration strongly demanded economic reforms, particularly reforms of the *chaebŏl*. It was a widely shared consensus among South Korean civil society groups that, in contrast with the significant progress in political democratization, there had not been any notable progress in economic democratization. Economic democratization had two dimensions: the first with respect to the overall market structure and the second with respect to the internal structure of companies. In terms of the overall market structure, scholars had long pointed out that the enormous power and influence of *chaebŏl* groups had to be reduced to level the economic playing field for all economic actors. In terms of the second dimension, it had long been demanded that the internal structures of all major *chaebŏl* groups were too authoritarian, hindering managerial accountability and transparency.[32] These two issues of economic democratization became particularly prominent after the economic crisis in 1997, because it was believed that lack of progress in economic democratization was the essential cause of the crisis.[33]

Civil society groups in South Korea, especially the PSPD, concentrated on the minority shareholders movement as a specific method of achieving economic democratization. They used lawsuits and physical presence at shareholders' general meetings to promote minority shareholders' rights and to fight against the dominance of *chaebŏl* owners – chairpersons and their families. On December 12, 1997, the PSPD represented 100 minority shareholders of the First Bank (Che'il Bank) in a lawsuit to contest and annul a decision passed at the March 1997 stockholders' general meeting. The Seoul district court made a ruling in favor of the PSPD that it was unlawful for the Bank to ignore the right of expression of the minority shareholders and to proceed with revision of the statutes and election of the board members and auditors without voting.[34] On March 4, 1998, the PSPD submitted a proposal to revise corporate statutes to appoint external auditors, strengthen the power of the board of directors, and prevent internal transfer of funds among *chaebŏl* companies of the same group.[35] On September 10, 1998, the PSPD launched a campaign to acquire ownership of ten shares of stock of each of the five *chaebŏl* group companies: Samsung Electronics, SK Telecom, Daewoo, LG Semiconductors, and Hyundai Heavy Industry. After acquiring the stocks, the PSPD's plan was to inquire about the responsibility of the management and to demand effective *chaebŏl* reform.[36] Chang Ha Sŏng, a Korea University business professor and a leading member of the PSPD, filed class action suits against several *chaebŏl* companies on behalf of minority shareholders, charging them with mismanagement and abuse of power. Since 1999, the PSPD has been tenaciously leading a movement to hold economically powerful actors in South Korea more accountable to the law and the general public.

In the sixteenth presidential elections held on December 19, 2002, South Korean voters elected Roh Moo Hyun as their new president. Roh, who had once been a labor lawyer and human rights activist, was a political novice compared with the three Kims (i.e., Kim Dae Jung, Kim Young Sam, and Kim Jong Pil) and other seasoned party politicians in South Korea. Born in 1946, he represented a new, younger, post-liberation generation. In his political career, Roh had displayed a stubborn maverick style – principled, consistent, and strongly supportive of political and economic reform. Since Roh's election, progressives have entered the political establishment *en masse*. The successful entry of the Korea Democratic Labor Party into the National Assembly in the April 2004 elections marked the culmination of the recent ascendance of progressives in South Korea. Now, progressives, who had spearheaded the pro-democracy movement during the 1980s, are in charge of designing and implementing various crucial democratic reforms. What has been taking place during the current Roh Moo Hyun government is the gradual but unmistakable shift of power from older and conservative to younger and progressive political actors. Government agencies, civil society groups, business firms, and many major social institutions are increasingly occupied and operated by younger and progressive actors.

It is still too early to evaluate the role of civil society during the current Roh government of South Korea. But a few preliminary assessments seem possible and useful. Two elements have been conspicuous about the activities of civil society groups since 2003. First, civil society groups have been gradually expanding their issue area to include foreign policy and international relations. In 2003, for example, civil society groups waged intense nationwide protests against the Roh government's decision to send South Korean soldiers to Iraq to help the United States. The anti-war movement was facilitated by a comprehensive alliance of diverse civil society groups, politicians (especially progressive legislators in the National Assembly), and even some public officials in the government agencies such as the National Human Rights Commission. Furthermore, in waging the anti-war campaign, civil society organizations also explored and employed new movement methods, such as one-person demonstrations, candlelight vigils, lawsuits, and cyber protests.

Another foreign policy issue that has brought about significant civic activism is the South Korean government's agreement with the U.S. to relocate U.S. military bases in the cities north of Seoul such as Tongduch'ŏn and Ŭijŏngbu to those south of Seoul such as P'yŏngt'aek. On March 15, 2005, 606 residents in P'yŏngt'aek and 1,033 other citizens representing various civil society groups filed a lawsuit, arguing that the agreement between the Roh Moo Hyun government of South Korea and the Bush administration about the relocation and expansion of the U.S. military bases would seriously infringe upon their rights to ensure survival and pursue happiness and equality, as well as violating the Republic of Korea's sovereign principle to refuse a war of aggression.[37]

During the past authoritarian period, it was possible for a small group of elites to design and implement foreign policy, completely insulated from the public purview. Foreign policymaking was characterized by secrecy, centralization, top-down nature, and lack of transparency. Now, after the democratic transition, South Korea's foreign policy is increasingly affected and determined by domestic politics. Because foreign policy is immensely consequential in affecting the daily lives of ordinary citizens, it is crucial to promote and institutionalize citizen participation in its making. Democracy is a political system that provides structures and procedures through which sensible foreign policies can be derived and pursued. In a democracy, elites and masses must jointly decide the goals, paths, and orientations of their foreign policies.[38] In this regard, it is a natural and inevitable outcome of the country's democratization that South Korean civil society groups are turning their attention to foreign policy issues.[39]

Second, civil society groups have challenged and opposed state-sponsored large-scale projects. Since 2001, for instance, major civil society groups including the KFEM and the PSPD have been waging protests against the government's Saeman'gŭm reclamation project. The Saeman'gŭm project began in 1991 during the Roh Tae Woo administration to reclaim land and increase water supply in the Kunsan-Pu'an area, North Ch'olla Province. From the outset, however, the project has been intensely contested and challenged by a number of civil society organizations for the possible damage it would cause to the surrounding environment. In response to the protracted and ever-intensifying protest activities by civil society groups, the Seoul administrative court in the end decided on February 4, 2005 that the mega-project, with 85 percent of the construction already completed, should either be cancelled altogether or significantly changed due to its potential environmental, ecological, and financial harm to the region and the residents.[40]

Another state-sponsored mega-project that has been acutely contested, challenged, and opposed by civil society groups in South Korea is the plan to locate and build a nuclear waste dump site. When the county chief of Pu'an, North Ch'olla, without adequate consultation with residents, submitted an application to the Ministry of Commerce, Industry, and Energy in July 2003 to invite a nuclear waste dump site, various environmental groups in the area and the vicinity launched an intensive anti-nuclear campaign against the action. Faced with a series of violent demonstrations by residents and environmental organizations, the plan to locate the nuclear waste site in Pu'an was completely abandoned. The Roh government instead pledged to make the policymaking more transparent and democratic, incorporating sufficient input from the local residents themselves. The site was finally decided through a direct popular referendum in four competing cities in November 2005. As a result of the vote, Kyŏngju was selected as the site for a nuclear recycling center.[41]

Both the Saeman'gŭm and Pu'an incidents demonstrate that civil society groups in South Korea are now focusing their energy more on making the policymaking process more transparent and accessible. State-sponsored mega-projects, which in the past during the authoritarian regimes were carried out without any significant supervision by civil society, are now under the close surveillance and scrutiny of able and vigilant civil society groups and ordinary citizens. As a result, the policymaking process in South Korea is becoming increasingly democratic and accountable.

Conclusion

As far as South Korea is concerned, the answer to the debate on elites vs. masses in the literature on democratization seems clear. As I have shown in this chapter, civil society and its mobilization were crucial in the democratic transition and consolidation of South Korea. Mass-ascendance characterized South Korea's democratic transition. During the transition, it was the resurrection and remobilization of various civil society groups and their grand pro-democracy coalition with the opposition party that ultimately induced the authoritarian ruling regime to agree on a set of democratic reforms. In this respect, during what Rustow calls the "prolonged struggle," critical choices were made among the mass public and in its interaction with elites.[42]

What is even more remarkable in the case of South Korea is the continued importance of civil society and mass mobilization in the period of democratic consolidation. It is generally agreed in the existing literature that civil society is demobilized – and therefore the role of civil society becomes significantly marginalized – in the consolidational phase.[43] As Tarrow observes, "elite choices appear to predominate at the consolidation phase of newly emerging democracies."[44] But in the case of South Korea, even during the democratic consolidation, civil society and mass mobilization have played crucial roles in pressuring the democratic regimes to continue and deepen political, economic, and social reforms and to make the policymaking process more transparent and accessible. Civil society in South Korea, in brief, continues to serve as the main driving force for social transformation. In this regard, Dryzek's observation is perfectly applicable to South Korea: "pressures for greater democracy almost always emanate from oppositional civil society, rarely or never from the state itself."[45] Therefore, in the epic of South Korean democratization, the elites rumble in the wings, if not actively sabotaging the whole drama; the actors on the stage are civil society groups and the mass public.[46]

In the last analysis, however, as Schmitter cautions us, civil society and its continued activism is "not an unmitigated blessing for democracy."[47] In one very crucial aspect, the fundamental political dynamics under both the previous Kim Dae Jung regime and the current Roh Moo Hyun regime are surprisingly similar to those under the previous authoritarian regimes. That is to say, political society is sharply dichotomized between the ruling and the opposition parties, entirely wanting in compromise, cooperation, civility, courtesy, and constructive interactions. Bypassing such a polarized and petrified political society, the principal focus of politics continues to consist in the direct – sometimes conflictual, sometimes cooperative – interactions between the state and civil society. There is nothing intrinsically wrong with this close interaction and engagement between the state and civil society. However, if this direct engagement between the state and civil society keeps on circumventing and ultimately *replaces* party politics, this may pose a threat to the consolidation of South Korean democracy. Virtually all the existing consolidated democracies in the contemporary world are predicated on the balance of two elements – vibrant civil society and functional political society. This balance between a strong civil society and a strong political society serves as an antidote to the abuse of power by the state. Therefore, as long as the imbalance between an energetic civil society and a lethargic political society drags on, South Korean democracy will be most likely to remain uninstitutionalized, unconsolidated, unstable, and fragile.

Notes

1 Ki-yŏng Kwŏn, "Pisa: 6-29 chŏnyaŭi kwŏnbu [Hidden History: The Ruling Elite on the Eve of the June 29 Declaration]," *Wŏlgan Chosŏn* [Chosŏn Monthly] (June 1993): 197–237; Hyug-baeg Im, *Sijang, kukka, minjujuŭi: han'guk minjuhwawa chŏngch'i kyŏngje iron* [The Market, the State, and Democracy: Democratic Transition in South Korea and Theories of Political Economy] (Seoul, Korea: Nanam, 1994), pp. 253–97.

2 See Kyŏng-ryung Sŏng, "Han'guk chŏngch'i minjuhwaŭi sahoejŏk kiwŏn: sahoe undongnonjŏk chŏpkŭn [The Social Origins of South Korean Democratization: A Social Movement Approach]," in Kyungnam University Institute for Far Eastern Studies, ed., *Han'guk chŏngch'i sahoeŭi sae hŭrŭm* [New Currents in South Korean Politics and Society] (Seoul, Korea: Nanam, 1994), pp. 121–3; Tae-hwa Chŏng, "Han'guk minjuhwawa chibae seryŏggŭi kyoch'e [Korean Democratization and Changes in the Ruling Power]," *Tonghyanggwa chŏnmang* [Trends and Prospects] 36 (Winter) (1997), p. 181; Pyŏng-ju Mun, "Han'gugŭi minjujuŭiroŭi ihaengrone taehan kŏmt'o [Review of Theories of Democratic Transition in Korea]," *Tonghyanggwa chŏnmang* [Trends and Prospects] 33 (Spring) (1997), p. 287. Regarding the concepts of "hardliners (*duros*)" and "softliners (*blandos*)," see Guillermo O'Donnell and Philippe C. Schmitter, *Transitions from Authoritarian Rule: Tentative Conclusions about Uncertain Democracies* (Baltimore: Johns Hopkins University Press, 1986), pp. 15–21.

3 Sunhyuk Kim, *The Politics of Democratization in Korea: The Role of Civil Society* (Pittsburgh: University of Pittsburgh Press, 2000); Sunhyuk Kim, "Civil Society in South Korea: From Grand Democracy Movements to Petty Interest Groups?" *Journal of Northeast Asian Studies* 15 (1996): 81–97; Kyŏng-ryung Sŏng, "Social Origins of South Korean Democratization"; Myŏng-sun Sin, "Han'gugesŏŭi simin sahoe hyŏngsŏnggwa minjuhwa kwajŏngesŏŭi yŏkhal [The Formation of Civil Society in South Korea and Its Role in Democratization]," Pyŏng-jun An, ed., *Kukka, Simin sahoe, chŏngch'i minjuhwa* [The State, Civil Society, and Political Democratization] (Seoul, Korea: Hanul, 1995); Jang-jip Choi, "Han'gugŭi minjuhwa: ihaenggwa kaehyŏk [South Korean Democratization: Transition and Reform]," Jang-jip Choi and Hyŏn-jin Im, eds., *Siminsahoeŭi tojŏn: han'guk minjuhwawa kukka, chabon, nodong* [Challenge from Civil Society: State, Capital, and Labor in South Korean Democratization] (Seoul, Korea: Nanam, 1993).

4 O'Donnell and Schmitter, *Transitions from Authoritarian Rule*, p. 48; John Higley and Richard Gunther, eds., *Elites and Democratic Consolidation in Latin American and Southern Europe* (New York: Cambridge University Press, 1992), p. 3.

5 Sidney Tarrow, "Mass Mobilization and Regime Change: Pacts, Reform, and Popular Power in Italy (1918–22) and Spain (1975–78)," in Richard Gunther, P. Nikiforos Diamandouros, and Hans-Jürgen Puhle, eds., *The Politics of Democratic Consolidation: Southern Europe in Comparative Perspective* (Baltimore: Johns

Hopkins University Press, 1995); Jean-François Bayart, "Civil Society in Africa," Patrick Chabal, ed., *Political Domination in Africa: Reflections on the Limits of Power* (Cambridge: Cambridge University Press, 1986); Larry Diamond, ed., *The Democratic Revolution: Struggles for Freedom and Pluralism in the Developing World* (New York: Freedom House, 1992); Doug McAdam, Sidney Tarrow, and Charles Tilly, *Dynamics of Contention* (Cambridge: Cambridge University Press, 2001); David S. Meyer and Sidney Tarrow, eds., *The Social Movement Society: Contentious Politics for a New Century* (New York: Rowman & Littlefield, 1998).

6 Terry Karl, "Dilemmas of Democratization in Latin America," *Comparative Politics* 23 (1990): 1–21. For different typologies, see Scott Mainwaring, *Transitions to Democracy and Democratic Consolidation: Theoretical and Comparative Issues,* Working Paper #130 (Helen Kellog Institute for International Studies, University of Notre Dame, 1989); Gerardo L. Munck and Carol Skalnik Leff, "Modes of Transition and Democratization: South America and Eastern Europe in Comparative Perspective," Lisa Anderson, ed., *Transitions to Democracy* (New York: Columbia University Press, 1999).

7 For an elite-centered explanation, see Donald Share, *The Making of Spanish Democracy* (New York: Praeger, 1986). For a mass-centered explanation, see Joe Foweraker, *Making Democracy in Spain: Grassroots Struggle in the South, 1955–1975* (Cambridge: Cambridge University Press, 1989). See Tarrow, "Mass Mobilization and Regime Change," fn. 15.

8 O'Donnell and Schmitter, *Transitions from Authoritarian Rule,* pp. 48–56.

9 Selig S. Harrison, "Dateline from South Korea: A Divided Seoul," *Foreign Policy* 67 (1987): 154–75.

10 Political society is defined as the "arena in which the polity specifically arranges itself for political contestation to gain control over public power and the state apparatus." It includes "political parties, elections, electoral rules, political leadership, intraparty alliances, and legislatures." Alfred Stepan, *Rethinking Military Politics: Brazil and the Southern Cone* (Princeton, NJ: Princeton University Press, 1988), p. 4.

11 James Cotton, "From Authoritarianism to Democracy in South Korea," *Political Studies* 37 (1989), p. 251.

12 KCSRC (Korean Christian Social Research Center), *Kaehŏn'gwa minjuhwa undong* [Constitutional Revision and Democracy Movement] (Seoul, Korea: Minjungsa, 1986), p. 40.

13 Koon Woo Nam, *South Korean Politics: The Search for Political Consensus and Stability* (Lanham, MD: University Press of America, 1989), p. 302.

14 Sunhyuk Kim, "State and Civil Society in South Korea's Democratic Consolidation: Is the Battle Really Over?" *Asian Survey* 37, 12 (1997): 1135–44.

15 Frances Hagopian, "The Compromised Consolidation: The Political Class in the Brazilian Transition," Scott Mainwaring, Guillermo O'Donnell, and J. Samuel Valenzuela, eds., *Issues in Democratic Consolidation: The New South American Democracies in Comparative Perspective* (Notre Dame, IN: University of Notre Dame Press, 1992), p. 282; Jang-jip Choi, "'Pyŏnhyŏngjuŭi'wa han'gugŭi minjujuŭi [Transformism and South Korean Democracy]," *Sahoe pip'yŏng* [Social Critique] 13 (1995): 187–99.

16 Victor D. Cha, "Politics and Democracy Under the Kim Young Sam Government: Something Old, Something New," *Asian Survey* 33, 9 (1993): 849–63.

17 Mun-hong Song, "Munmin ch'unggyŏk, 'taesasaek'e ppajin chaeya [The Civilian Shock: Dissident Movement in 'Profound Agony']," *Sindonga* [Tonga Monthly] (May 1993): 494–505.

18 For a general overview of state–civil society relations under the Roh Tae Woo and the Kim Young Sam regimes, see Sunhyuk Kim, "State and Civil Society in South Korea's Democratic Consolidation: Is the Battle Really Over?" *Asian Survey* 37, 12 (December 1997): 1135–44.

19 Larry Diamond, "Toward Democratic Consolidation," *Journal of Democracy* 5 (1994), p. 15.
20 *Kwangju ilbo* [Kwangju Daily], August 29, 1995; *Hankyoreh sinmun* [Han'gyŏre Daily], August 30, 1995.
21 *Joongang ilbo* [Chungang Daily], November 2, 1995.
22 *Hankyoreh sinmun* [Han'gyŏre Daily], November 5, 1995.
23 *Hankyoreh sinmun* [Han'gyŏre Daily], January 14, 1997.
24 Regarding the relationship between environmentalism and democratic consolidation in South Korea, see Sunhyuk Kim, "Democratization and Environmentalism: South Korea and Taiwan in Comparative Perspective," *Journal of Asian and African Studies* 35, 3 (2000): 287–302.
25 Peter Beck, "South Korea in 1997," in Korea Economic Institute of America, *Korea's Economy 1998* (Washington, DC: KEIA, 1998), pp. 2–3.
26 Regarding the politics of economic restructuring, see Sunhyuk Kim, "The Politics of Reform in South Korea: The First Year of the Kim Dae Jung Government, 1998–1999," *Asian Perspective* 24, 1 (2000): 163–85.
27 Kim Dae Jung's contribution to democracy and peace in Korea was recognized worldwide with the Nobel Peace Prize he received in December 2000.
28 See Sunhyuk Kim, "Patronage Politics as an Obstacle to Democracy in South Korea," in Howard Handelman and Mark Tessler, eds., *Democracy and Its Limits: Lessons from Asia, Latin America, and the Middle East* (Notre Dame, IN: University of Notre Dame Press, 1999).
29 As already noted above, Kim Young Sam, despite his previous political career as a prominent opposition leader, ran as a ruling party candidate in the 1992 presidential elections, after his party had merged with Roh Tae Woo's party in 1990 through a type of Korean transformism.
30 *Chosŏn ilbo* [Chosun Daily], January 25, 2000.
31 *Chosŏn ilbo* [Chosun Daily], April 21, 2000.
32 Eun Mee Kim, "Reforming the *Chaebol*," in *Institutional Reform and Democratic Consolidation in Korea*, ed. Larry Diamond and Doh Chull Shin (Stanford, CA: Hoover Institution Press, 2000).
33 Sunhyuk Kim, "The Political Origins of South Korea's Economic Crisis: Is Democratization to Blame?" *Democratization* 7 (2000): 81–103.
34 *Chosŏn ilbo* [Chosun Daily], December 13, 1997.
35 *Chosŏn ilbo* [Chosun Daily], March 5, 1998.
36 *Chosŏn ilbo* [Chosun Daily], September 10, 1998.
37 *Yonhap News*, March 15, 2005.
38 Bruce Russett, *Controlling the Sword: The Democratic Governance of National Security* (Cambridge, MA: Harvard University Press, 1990).
39 Katharine H.S. Moon, "Korean Nationalism, Anti-Americanism, and Democratic Consolidation," in *Korea's Democratization*, ed. Samuel S. Kim (Cambridge: Cambridge University Press, 2003).
40 *Yonhap News*, February 4, 2005.
41 *Hankyoreh sinmun* [Han'gyŏre Daily], November 2, 2005.
42 Dankwart Rustow, "Transitions to Democracy: Toward a Dynamic Model," *Comparative Politics* 2 (1970): 337–63; Tarrow, "Mass Mobilization and Regime Change," p. 207.
43 Steven Fish, "Rethinking Civil Society: Russia's Fourth Transition," *Journal of Democracy* 5 (1994), p. 34.
44 Tarrow, "Mass Mobilization and Regime Change," p. 207.
45 John S. Dryzek, "Political Institution and the Dynamics of Democratization," *American Political Science Review* 90 (1996), p. 476.
46 Tarrow, "Mass Mobilization and Regime Change," p. 205.

47 Philippe C. Schmitter, "Civil Society East and West," in Larry Diamond, Marc F. Plattner, Yun-han Chu, and Hung-mao Tien, eds., *Consolidating the Third Wave Democracies: Themes and Perspectives* (Baltimore: Johns Hopkins University Press, 1997).

4 Engendering civil society

The role of the labor movement

Hagen Koo

Much of the literature on civil society assigns a prominent role to the middle classes in nurturing and sustaining civil society. There are, of course, good reasons for this emphasis on the middle class. Historically, the development of active civic organizations and a public sphere outside the control of the state came with the expansion of the market economy and the middle classes. And it is the middle classes that are most likely to possess the kinds of interests, inclinations, and cultural attributes – such as moderation, tolerance for different opinions, liberalism, and communicative skills – which are necessary for maintaining a viable civil society. Furthermore, in many societies it is the middle classes that have played a pivotal role in bringing about democracy and defending it against potential threats.

The recent experience of democratization and the civil society movement in South Korea fits this general model very nicely. Rapid economic growth based on export-oriented industrialization was accompanied by the rapid expansion of the middle classes, which became increasingly vocal and resistant to the authoritarian regime, and at a particular juncture became mobilized on a large scale to bring about a political breakthrough for democratization. It is widely agreed among observers of South Korean politics that without the growth of sizable middle classes, a smooth transition to democracy might not have been possible.[1] Of particular importance is the mushrooming growth of civic groups or citizens' movement organizations in the wake of the democratic transition in 1987. These new social movements – aimed at promoting distributive justice, a clean environment, gender equality, fair elections, consumer protection, and the like – are predominantly led by middle-class, well-educated citizens. Thus, as elsewhere in the world, it seems to make sense to look at South Korea's present civil society as a natural product of capitalist economic development and of its social concomitant, the expansion of the middle class.

However, this chapter takes issue with privileging the role of the middle classes in the making of South Korean democracy and civil society. Against this prevailing assumption, I argue that democracy and civil society in Korea did not occur as the "natural" outcome of economic growth and the expansion of the middle class, but as a consequence of persistent struggles by students, intellectuals, and workers against successive authoritarian regimes. Here I agree with Bruce

Cumings, who argues in his chapter that the path to democracy in South Korea "was hardly smooth; instead it was filled with decades of torment and turmoil." Those who stress the conflictual aspect of South Korea's transition to democracy, like Cumings, Lee, and Kim in this volume, tend to give prominence to the role of students and dissident intellectuals. The aim of my chapter is, however, to draw attention to another important agent of democratization, and another pillar of civil society: the working class. My major argument here is that spirited working-class struggles under harsh authoritarian regimes played a critical role in bringing about both democratic transition and the expansion of civil society. This is not to argue that the working class alone played such a role. Rather, it was the close interaction between the grassroots labor movement and the student-led democracy movement that enhanced the power of social movements against the authoritarian state, and eventually led to the ending of the military regime. And it is through involvement in labor struggles, directly or indirectly, that many students and intellectuals acquired critical consciousness and later became leaders of the civil society movement. Those who are actively involved in the post-1987 citizens' movements do not represent ordinary middle-class citizens, but those who had experienced the political and social movements of the pre-1987 period.

The purpose of this chapter, then, is to describe the development of the South Korean labor movement since the 1970s, paying special attention to its relationships with other social movements and with its contribution to the development of civil society. As the South Korean labor movement developed from an extremely weak and vulnerable situation in the early 1970s to a relatively powerful and autonomous force in the late 1990s, its relationships with other social movements changed significantly, as did its position in civil society. Although there is already a great deal of scholarship on the Korean labor movement and the various other social and political movements, few studies have given focused attention to the relationships between labor and the other movements, and to their joint contributions to the development of South Korea's civil society.[2] This chapter aims to fill this void in the literature.

For the purpose of this analysis, it seems useful to divide the recent history of the South Korean labor movement into three periods: (1) the period of authoritarian industrialization (1960s to 1987); (2) the period of democratic transition (1987–1996); and (3) the era of globalization and economic crisis (1997 to the present). In the first period, that of authoritarian industrialization, labor struggles in the labor-intensive export industries received much organizational support · from church organizations and students as well as ideological support from the *minjung* (people's) movement. During this period, industrial workers were generally viewed within such intellectual-led organizations and movements as helpless victims of exploitation and repression, and thus as a target for outside support and assistance. Consequently, workers occupied only a marginal position within the larger movement for democracy.

In the second period, however, the volcanic eruption of labor unrest after the 1987 political liberalization brought the Korean labor movement to an entirely different plane and modified its relationship with the civil society movement. The labor movement no longer required outside assistance to be viable, and its position within civil society had improved remarkably. However, a sudden growth in the organizational strength of labor and the aggressive collective actions of labor led to a noticeable change in the attitudes of the middle classes toward the labor movement, causing a delicate tension and competitive relationship between the labor movement and the middle-class-led civil society movement. During the 1990s, the labor movement grew steadily as an independent movement of its own, focusing on developing its national organization.

The third, current period is characterized by a new pattern of worker struggles against the forces that threaten their job security. The massive nationwide protest against the passage of new labor laws in the winter of 1996–1997 signaled the beginning of this new era, followed by a grave economic crisis that suddenly hit the nation at the end of 1997. This period has been greatly shaped by the structural pressure of globalization, and workers confront not just their own employers and the state, but also the forces of global capital. In this new era of labor market flexibility and growing job insecurity, labor unions have taken on a new role of defending not just blue-collar industrial workers, but the entire working people, including white-collar professionals. The political and social status of national unions has thus improved significantly, and so has their position in the civil society. Ironically, however, the same structural forces threaten the future of the Korean labor movement by forcing it to become a narrowly focused economic unionism, concerned with immediate job problems for union members rather than with broader social issues. Increasingly, broad community issues are taken up by the active citizens' movement.

The period of authoritarian industrialization (1961–1987)

Export-oriented industrialization in South Korea began in the early 1960s, but active labor resistance did not occur until the early 1970s. The working conditions in the export manufacturing industries were extremely poor and dehumanizing, but the first generation of factory workers, most of whom came from poverty-stricken farming families, endured the poor working conditions quietly and worked hard to produce Korea's rapid industrial growth. Labor volatility began to increase gradually from the late 1960s. These labor conflicts occurred mainly in the form of spontaneous and unorganized protests, as desperate individual actions against intolerable work conditions or against mistreatment by employers and managers. One of these desperate worker protests had a special significance for the development of the South Korean labor movement since the 1970s: the self-immolation of a garment factory worker, named Chŏn T'ae-il, in November 1970. A young tailor, Chŏn had been protesting against the inhumane work conditions in a garment district in Seoul where hundreds of young women worked under severely exploitative conditions. In a desperate attempt to bring this injustice to the attention of society, Chŏn decided to sacrifice his own life. On November 13, during a street protest with his fellow workers at Pyŏnghwa garment district, Chŏn poured gasoline over his body and set himself on fire.

This tragic event provided the first occasion to bring labor issues to the attention of broader society, and to link the intellectual community with workers suffering under the shadow of economic growth. From the mid-1970s, the highly politicized intellectual community began to be connected to the shopfloor resistance movement. Two non-labor social groups played a particularly important role in supporting grassroots labor struggles. The first was the church organizations, influenced by progressive theological orientations similar to Latin America's liberation theology (see Donald N. Clark's chapter in this volume). These Christian organizations took advantage of their international networks and their relatively secure political and ideological position in society to provide guidance and shelter for labor activists. They also ran workers' night schools and organized small-group activities where workers had opportunities to share their experiences with one another, and to develop a sense of identity and solidarity among themselves. Union consciousness was first born through these activities, and so was the first group of grassroots union activists, the majority of whom were women workers employed in the garment, textile, and electronics industries. These women led the grassroots labor movement from the late 1970s to the early 1980s.

Entering the 1980s, church influence on the labor movement declined considerably, as labor leaders gradually became disenchanted with the church leaders' mild approach to labor struggles. They realized that in the face of the determined efforts of the Chun regime to pulverize the democratic union movement, church organizations were of little help and church leaders' humanitarian orientation looked a little too meek and passive to represent workers' recent experiences with the repressive regime. By the early 1980s, there were a large number of workers who had been fired and blacklisted because of their involvement in the 1970s' democratic union movement. As these workers were blocked from gainful employment by the government, they had little choice but to become professional labor activists. These "outside" (*chaeya*) labor activists played an instrumental role in connecting unionists across firms and linking them to dissident political communities. They organized mass demonstrations demanding the revision of labor laws and the abolition of the blacklist. The consequence of hard-line labor repression during the Chun regime was, therefore, the ever enlarging circles of *sŏnjin nodongja* (workers with advanced consciousness), who had acquired years of experience in the democratic union movement and, through this experience, a high level of class consciousness. With the growth of grassroots labor activists, both inside and outside the industrial arena, the labor movement gradually overcame the need to depend on outside organizations, especially church organizations.

The growth of class-conscious labor activists and grassroots organizations, however, did not lead the South Korean labor movement to develop in complete autonomy. On the contrary, Korean working-class struggles became more intimately enmeshed in the larger political struggles against the authoritarian state. Increasingly, however, the workers' ties with outside agencies were not necessarily the result of the weakness of the workers' organizations or their inability to defend themselves, but because of their very strength and strategic value as other anti-government opposition groups began to recognize. Although still beset by internal organizational difficulties and workplace conditions that stifled their interest articulation beyond immediate economic circumstances, the number of factory workers had grown to three million by the early 1980s and constituted the largest occupational group in South Korea, possessing huge potential power. The concentration of these workers in a few industrial centers and the slow improvement of their working conditions in a rapidly growing economy, along with the rapidly growing class awareness among workers, suggested that the industrial proletariat was destined to become a major social force in the evolution of the new industrial society.

Those who recognized this potential most clearly were student activists. Although students began to be involved in labor affairs from the 1970s, their direct involvement in the labor movement had been relatively insignificant until the early 1980s. However, the bitter experiences of struggle around the Chun Doo Hwan coup and the Kwangju Incident in 1979–1980, and the harsh political repression of the Chun regime, led activist students to view labor mobilization as an important new strategy for the anti-authoritarian, democratic movement. During the first three years of Chun's rule, when political opposition was not tolerated, the student movement adopted labor praxis (*hyŏnjangron*) as its major strategy of political struggle. The goal of labor praxis was for students to enter the industrial arena by becoming factory workers, trying to promote class consciousness among workers and help them organize unions. Their ultimate goal was to lead the workers in a joint struggle to end military rule and radically transform Korean society. A large number of students dropped out of college and became workers during this period. The development of the labor movement in the 1980s was intimately connected to the role of these "students-turned-workers," whom the government labeled "disguised workers."

Under the new strategy of labor–student alliance (*nohak yŏndae*), a large number of students carried their political convictions into the factories in the first half of the 1980s. Some dropped out of college, some graduated, and some were expelled from their schools for being involved in illegal anti-government demonstrations. The largest number of them entered factories between 1983 and 1986, each year numbering several hundred. Ogle estimates that there were about three thousand or more "student-turned-workers" in the mid-1980s.[3] They were mostly employed in medium-sized manufacturing firms located in major industrial centers around metropolitan Seoul, Inchon and Pup'yŏng (west of Seoul), and Anyang (south of Seoul). Very few of them went to heavy industrial belts in the southern part of the country, like Ulsan, Masan, and Changwŏn.

The close interconnections that developed between labor and students was to a great extent the product of the state's repressive approach to labor control. From Park's Yushin period (1972–1979) to the end of the Chun era (1980–1987), the state's consistent policy was to forestall the emergence of any independent union movement outside the government-controlled union structure, and to prevent the development of any connections between labor and opposition movements. Thus, any sign of organized resistance was ruthlessly repressed, allowing no channel for the release of the mounting tensions and resentments on the shop floor. The Korean state's labor control had been more repressive than corporatist, more direct and physical than bureaucratic or ideological, and more blatantly anti-labor than subtle and disguised. Workers who participated in labor disputes rarely failed to confront state repression and see the true nature of the relationship between capital and state power. The authoritarian state's attempt to remove the "impure elements" from the labor arena, by having activist workers fired and blacklisted for industrial employment, had an ironic consequence of strengthening worker-student ties and fostering wide clandestine networks of labor activists, church leaders, and dissident intellectuals. A critical role of the labor movement in South Korea's democratization and civil society movement can, therefore, be found in its role of fostering these interconnected networks of movement groups throughout the 1980s.

The period of democratic transition (1987–1996)

The summer of 1987 marks the most critical moment in the South Korean labor movement. In the three months following the downfall of the Chun regime in the face of enormous popular protest in June 1987, an unprecedented level of labor conflicts swept across the country, paralyzing industrial production at virtually all large manufacturing firms. From July to September in 1987, some 3,311 incidents of labor conflict occurred in South Korea, virtually all of which involved strike actions or violent demonstrations. The amount of labor unrest that occurred during this summer exceeded the total number of labor disputes that had occurred during the previous two decades under the Park and Chun regimes. The total number of workers who participated in these labor actions is estimated to be 1.2 million – representing more than a third of the regularly employed workers in enterprises with ten or more workers.

The democratic transition in 1987 was clearly not the making of the labor movement alone. The main actors, as in most other previous political upheavals in Korea, were students, who had fought for democratization tenaciously throughout the 1970s and 1980s. But the success of the student-led democratization struggle in June 1987 owed much to the participation of a large number of citizens, including white-collar workers, small business owners, poor urban residents, and industrial workers. As street protests escalated across the country, several white-collar unions which had been recently formed began to participate in the democratization movement. In May and June, many white-collar workers employed in banks and other financial institutions in downtown Seoul were seen joining students' street demonstrations during their lunch breaks.

The role of the industrial workers in this struggle for democracy, however, is not so clear. Many analysts believe that the role of the industrial workers and labor unions was minimal. One indication of labor's marginal role in the democratization movement is that labor leaders comprised a tiny fraction within the grand national coalition of the democratization movements which led the civil protests against the Chun regime in Spring 1987; of the total of 2,200 founding members of the grand coalition, there were only 37 labor representatives. Unions played no particular role during the June civil uprising, and there is no evidence of any organized participation of factory workers in street demonstrations, although many workers participated in protests as individuals.

Other analysts, however, stress a more important role played by the industrial workers in Korea's democratic transition. They point out that a large number of wage workers, more than middle-class citizens, in fact participated in street demonstrations during June.[5] But more important than actual participation by industrial workers is the potential threat of their mass participation. Jang Jip Choi suggests that the Chun regime's calculated move toward political liberalization was influenced by the very real possibility of thousands and thousands of factory workers pouring onto the streets.[6] Another analyst also argues that "The main reason why the ruling bloc hurried to announce the democratization plan at the end of June when the civil uprising began to spread to the working class was because they could not underestimate the potential threatening power of the labor movement."[7]

As soon as the Chun regime announced its plan for political liberalization, however, industrial labor became mobilized on a large scale. A wave of violent labor conflicts erupted within two weeks of Roh Tae Woo's June 29 announcement. A series of strikes began in the manufacturing industry and rapidly spread to mining, transportation, the dockyards, and the service sector. Interestingly, the strike wave started not in Seoul or in its surrounding region where labor activism had developed previously, but in a southern industrial city, Ulsan, where there had hardly been any labor unrest thus far. This labor unrest quickly spread to other major industrial centers in the southern coastal region – including Pusan, Changwŏn, and Masan – and by mid-August, the strike wave had reached the Seoul area, where small-scale light manufacturing industries were concentrated.

The "Great Workers' Struggle" of 1987 brought the democratic union movement to yet another plane. The level of union organization showed a quantum jump between 1987 and 1988. Within a year of the workers' uprising, as many as 4,000 new unions were formed, and some 700,000 workers joined unions anew. The number of unions, which was 2,675 at the end of 1986, jumped to 6,164 by the end of 1988. Thus, by early 1989 more than a half of the existing unions had been organized since the Great Workers' Struggle in 1987. Correspondingly, during this period the number of unionized workers increased from slightly over one million to 1.7 million.

The significance of the 1987–1988 struggle, however, lay not just in the dramatic growth in the level of union organization. The struggle also brought a significant shift in the main actors of the South Korean labor movement. As noted above, the major site of intense labor struggles in 1987 and 1988 was not small-scale enterprises but large-scale firms in heavy and chemical industries. This also meant a shift in the sex composition of the main actors of the labor movement, from female to male workers. Virtually overnight, male semi-skilled workers in heavy and chemical industries emerged on the forefront of the labor movement, pushing aside female workers who had led the struggle for the "democratic union movement" in the 1970s through the early 1980s.

One striking development in the workers' movement after the mid-1980s was its autonomy: the struggle was made by the workers themselves, with very little help from church organizations or students, although the political opening was provided by the students. It is important to stress that the Great Workers' Struggle occurred without the initiation, leadership, or active support from the intellectual and religious communities that had played such a critical role in the pre-1987 labor movement. In particular, students-turned-workers played no significant role in the labor struggles that began in Ulsan, largely because most of them had been working in the Seoul region before 1987 and very few of them had been able to enter large-scale firms in southern industrial cities.

Undoubtedly, the 1987 explosion of labor militancy was a major turning point in the South Korean working-class movement. It brought the industrial workers to the center stage of the movement for democracy. No longer was the labor movement an appendage to the popular *minjung* movement, and no longer were workers dependent upon the ideological and organizational leadership provided by the intellectual community. The collective power of labor, as demonstrated in the Great Workers' Struggle of 1987–1988, confirmed a vital role to be played by the working class in the struggle for political and social democracy. Now the new leaders of the Korean working-class movement were the skilled and semi-skilled workers employed in the core sectors of Korean manufacturing industries, the same type of workers who have been the mainstay of the working-class movements in all other industrial societies.

Along with the aggressive union movement among blue-collar workers, a significant development also occurred in the white-collar union movement. In addition to financial workers, who had been organized earlier, white-collar and professional workers employed in the media, hospitals, printing industry, and government-sponsored research institutes also succeeded in organizing unions. The active white-collar movement during this period was derived primarily from two sources. One was the deteriorating job market conditions among the routine white-collar workers. With the rapid increase of lower-level white-collar workers in the process of industrial deepening, and with the continuous introduction of automation and rationalization processes into clerical work, white-collar work in Korea had become increasingly proletarianized, in terms of both the nature of work and economic status. Particularly hurt by this proletarianization of white-collar work were those employed in the financial sector, especially those with no college degrees who were faced with bleak promotion prospects. As their working conditions became increasingly routinized and their economic status marginalized, Korean clerical workers began to develop the same collective responses as their counterparts in advanced industrial societies did. They realized that unions were the best means for fighting against their deteriorating work conditions.

In South Korea, however, the white-collar union movement represented more than a narrow economic unionism. Equally important, or possibly more important, was the political nature of the movement. Aggressive unionization struggles among media workers, teachers, researchers at government-sponsored institutes, and printing industry employees were also a reaction to the lack of democracy in Korean workplaces and to the state's political and ideological control over intellectual production. It was not just blue-collar workers, but also white-collar workers who suffered from the highly authoritarian culture in Korean work organizations. Long hours of work, arbitrary assignments, irrational work procedures, the lack of a voice, and generally poor industrial relations characterized work situations equally for blue-collar and white-collar workers.[8] Moreover, journalists, teachers, and researchers were subjected to the state's ideological control over their work and were often forced to produce state-dictated materials. Although ideological control over intellectual work had always been present in Korea since the colonial period, a new generation of intellectuals who had gone to college during the highly politicized decade of the 1980s reacted to it quite differently. They brought the culture of student activism to their occupational world and were keen to make their workplaces more democratic and humane. The active white-collar union movement thus became another pillar of the Korean "democratic union movement" beginning in the late 1980s.[9]

The ascent of organized labor through the Great Workers' Struggle in 1987, however, brought important changes in the relationships between the labor movement and other social movements, and between the working class and the middle class. Prior to the political liberalization in 1987, the Korean middle classes had held a generally favorable attitude toward the labor movement as well as toward the student movement. This was because the middle classes had a strong desire for political freedom and participation, and had been extremely discontented with the harsh authoritarianism and human rights abuses by the military regime. As mentioned above, they had also been highly sympathetic toward the plight of the working class and had given strong emotional support to their struggles for justice. Such a progressive political orientation was stronger among the college-educated new middle-class people than among the petty bourgeoisie, but even the latter had been highly critical of the government's oppression of workers' rights and union activities.

The huge explosion of labor militancy in the 1980s and the growing power of organized labor in the early 1990s, however, brought a noticeable change in the middle-class attitudes toward the labor movement. Surveys conducted in 1989 indicate that a majority of middle-class respondents had critical attitudes toward labor strikes, especially toward what appeared to be excessively aggressive and violent strikes led by the independent union leadership. They were also in favor of strong government intervention to control labor unrest.[10]

This new conservative tendency among many middle-class people during this period seems to have derived from two sources. One was the activation of their class interest, especially their economic interest in maintaining a stable capitalist order. The assertion of this economic class interest was particularly strong among small businessmen, whose businesses were seriously affected by the prolonged labor unrest. But no less important seems to be the deep-seated status consciousness among the white-collar workers toward the manual workers. Between 1987

1990, wages for blue-collar workers rose an average of about 20 percent, siderably narrowing the gap with white-collar wages. Furthermore, unions de a pointed attack on the wide status differentials that existed between blue-collar and white-collar workers. Such a change would have activated the latent interest among the middle class in the status quo in the distributive system.[11]

It is, however, not just a change in their class situation that affected the political attitudes of the middle classes. Equally important was the ideological campaign by the state and capital through the government-controlled mass media. The mass media had shown a somewhat neutral stance toward the post-1987 aggressive labor movement at the initial stage but had gradually shifted to an unfriendly and hostile posture. They tended to portray strikes generally as "violent," "radical," or "irresponsible," and defined the workers' demands for wage hikes as "selfish" behavior intended to maximize private gains in the midst of national economic troubles. The public was led to believe that the nation's current economic slump was primarily due to the continuous labor unrest, and that lest unions restrain themselves their irresponsible actions would cause Korea to lose its competitive edge in the world market.

Another significant development that appeared during the Roh Tae Woo period (1988–1992) was the rise of the middle-class-led social movements, and a corresponding decline in the trade union movement. The political atmosphere during this period of democratic transition was congenial to a mushrooming growth of new social movements, including the environmental, consumer, anti-nuclear, feminist, and civil consciousness movements, among others. The general thrust of these new social movements was to downplay the significance of class conflict and to highlight broader social issues concerning distribution, environment, gender inequality, consumption, and civic morality. These new civil society movements were, by and large, led by the middle-class activists, and their major constituencies were also from the middle class.[12]

One organization, the Citizens' Coalition for Economic Justice (CCEJ), was of particular importance because of its phenomenal success and because it was quite characteristic of the new type of social movements that became popular during the 1990s. Founded in July 1989 by some five hundred professionals (professors, church leaders, lawyers, doctors, writers, journalists, and the like), the CCEJ took "injustice" in wealth formation and income distribution as its main target of activity. In particular, it focused its civil campaigns on the issues of unearned income, real estate speculation, and inadequate financial and tax systems. From the outset, the Citizens' Coalition proclaimed that it would be committed to a peaceful, non-violent civil movement, a "non-political" movement in which "both the haves and the have-nots can participate."[13] Within three years of its inception, CCEJ membership grew from 500 to 7,000, and by 1993 it had a number of regional chapters and its own research institutes, and published a bi-monthly magazine. Furthermore, its scope of activities expanded continuously to include agricultural issues, environmental issues, and even labor issues.

In many ways, the new social movements that have arisen since the late 1980s could be considered to be an extension of, rather than a break with, the previous democratic movement. Although the main issues of these social movements are no longer political democracy, the concern with social democracy and economic justice are on the main agenda of these new movements. The leadership of the new social movements was predominantly composed of former student activists, progressive church leaders, and liberal intellectuals. The political socialization they received through their participation in the labor movement and the *minjung* movement in the 1980s provided a major impetus for their active engagement in the new social movements.

Notwithstanding this continuity in the leadership, the rise of the new social movement entailed a significant change in the politics of the middle-class intelligentsia. For these new social movements were now primarily represented by middle-class members, and their leadership consciously distanced itself from the labor movement and from the radical *minjung* movement. The separation of the new social movements from the labor movement was, perhaps, the most significant development of the social movements of the 1990s. The social movements that had existed earlier in the 1980s, such as the environmental and urban housing movements, had been closely allied with labor and student activism, and they had been all united under the same ideological banner of *minjung*. But in the 1990s, tension and competition appeared between the two types of movements, eventually leading to a clear separation of the two. With this bifurcation of social movements, the labor movement and the *minjung* movement declined noticeably, whereas the new social movements grew significantly. It seems thus clear that there existed more than an accidental relationship between the decline and isolation of the labor movement and the success of new social movements.

The era of globalization (1997–)

As if the history of the Korean labor movement evolves on a ten-year cycle, the year 1997 saw another gigantic eruption of labor struggles. Starting from the last days of 1996 through the first three weeks of 1997, large-scale labor strikes broke out in protest against the passage of new labor laws by the National Assembly on December 26, 1996. This explosion of labor militancy resembled the Great Workers' Struggle in 1987, but unlike the event of ten years before, the nationwide strike in the winter of 1996–1997 (hereafter, for the sake of convenience called the January 1997 strike) was not a spontaneous and unorganized explosion of labor conflicts during a time of political transition. Rather, it was a well-organized strike orchestrated by the national union leadership. This was the first general strike South Korea had seen since the Republic of Korea was founded in 1948, and the first massive-scale labor mobilization over legal and institutional matters.

The new laws were designed to give more power to employers to lay off workers and to hire temporary workers and strike replacements, while postponing the right for multiple unions for another few years. The laws had been railroaded through the National Assembly at the crack of dawn by the ruling party, without the presence of opposition party legislators. Immediately after the passage of these laws, the still-illegal national union, the Korean Confederation of Trade Unions

(KCTU), called a general strike. In response, hundreds of thousands of workers walked out, paralyzing production in the automobile industry, shipyards, and practically all large-scale manufacturing firms. The strike also disrupted services in many hospital wards, public transportation, and television news broadcasting.

The 1997 strike generated enormous support from various groups in Korean society as well as from several international organizations including the ILO, OECD, and the International Confederation of Free Trade Unions (ICFTU).[14] Despite the unfavorable seasonal factors involving the New Year holidays and cold weather, the three-week-long strike maintained a consistently high level of worker participation and also a surprisingly high level of public support. The strike ended in late January when the government reluctantly agreed to rescind the controversial labor laws for revision.

The main reason for the successful mobilization of workers against the labor legislation was that it addressed the vital economic issues that were of serious concern for the great majority of people in South Korea at the time. As the South Korean economy continued to falter in a brutally competitive global economy, and as Korean employers sought various ways to reduce their labor costs, a long tradition of lifetime employment became seriously strained, and the threat of layoffs became a reality to many workers for the first time. Threatened by unemployment were not just factory workers but also many white-collar workers, and middle-level managers. From the mid-1990s, newspaper articles and television dramas were filled with stories of "honorary retirees"– people induced, or often forced, to retire early in return for a generous severance package. Controversy over the labor law revision greatly intensified public anxiety over job security, since the new labor law would enable companies to lay off workers more easily and even without severance pay.

Job security had a special social meaning in a society where workers had been expected to devote themselves wholly to the company in return for long-term job security. Laying off workers because of a company's temporary financial difficulty is widely considered unfair and morally unjust, because such behavior violates the important social value of reciprocity that has been at the base of institutional practice in Korean companies. Furthermore, in a society with virtually no social safety net outside of the family, losing one's job is likely to mean losing the only source of one's livelihood as well as a major basis of one's social identification.

When the January 1997 strike ended, however, the actual gains for the workers turned out to be modest. The new laws enacted on March 10 were only moderately different from the earlier controversial laws. Like the earlier laws, they retained the employers' layoff right, to be exercised after two years' deferment. The "no work, no pay" rule and no payment to full-time union leaders were also written in the new laws, as well as the flexible workday policy aimed to reduce real wages. Therefore, employers have succeeded in strengthening their power in the labor market, while workers have lost legal protection against layoffs and job instability. In return, organized labor obtained the immediate authorization for the KCTU and the right to form multiple unions at the industry level (but not at the workshop level until the year 2002). The new laws, however, continue to forbid unions among schoolteachers and public servants.[15]

Despite its rather unimpressive result, the January 1997 strike was undoubtedly a groundbreaking labor struggle in several respects. First, it was a highly organized protest on a national scale. Unlike previous waves of labor unrest in South Korea, that had usually erupted during periods of political turmoil with no organization or coherent leadership, the January 1997 strike was well organized and orchestrated by the two national centers of unions, the newly formed Korean Confederation of Trade Unions (KCTU) and the older and more moderate Federation of Korean Trade Unions (FKTU). From the beginning of the strike to the end, these two national centers cooperated closely and employed a rather sophisticated and flexible strategy of strike mobilization and propaganda campaigns to create the first successful general strike in nearly 50 years. Second, the January 1997 strike was a struggle not for immediate economic concerns but for broader institutional reform. It was the first time in the history of the Korean labor movement that workers were mobilized on such a massive scale for the purpose of institutional and legal reform, and were able to demonstrate strong class solidarity across firms, industries, and regions. It was a political struggle rather than an economic one, and the main object of the struggle was the state rather than individual capitalists. Third, the 1997 strike demonstrated that organized labor had emerged as a leading force, or as "a new social power," in the social and economic movements for a democratic society. As one Korean labor expert observes, "For the first time in Korean history, the success of a general strike proves that the Korean labor movement is able to present itself as a significant political and social entity representing working people."[16] Furthermore, the strike demonstrated that the position of the industrial workers in civil society had improved significantly. Whereas in previous periods, industrial workers occupied a marginal place in the civil society, through the 1997 struggle workers have emerged as a major champion for the rest of society. Another Korean labor analyst argues, "by exercising its national leadership over other popular forces in democratic struggles, the Korean working class for the first time went beyond the expression of narrow 'corporate' interests and began to function as a kind of 'hegemonic' class, whose class interests were perceived as representing the interests of the people in general."[17]

All these positive assessments of the current state of South Korean labor were, however, put in great doubt a few months later by another historic event that hit the South Korean economy unexpectedly and plunged it into a deep recession. The South Korean economy, which had grown sluggishly in the mid-1990s, began to show serious symptoms of weakness with export decline, frequent business failures, credit crunches, and a sharp increase of unemployment. Even many of the large conglomerates of *chaebŏl*, which used to be the last to suffer economic downturns, collapsed, causing a great sense of uncertainty about the Korean industrial structure and financial system. Then came the explosion. In November 1997, the Kim Young Sam government revealed the grave financial situation of the South Korean economy and requested the IMF for a rescue loan. The worst economic crisis since the Korean War thus arrived in South Korea like thunder in the night, giving no warning and no time for preparation. The IMF's $57 billion bailout fund was accompanied by a stringent financial and restructuring program. The impact of the financial crisis was devastating to Koreans, causing rising unemployment, business failures, sharply reduced incomes, homelessness, family breakdown, and a host of other problems.

Following the IMF bailout, Korean labor became the focus of attention from all sides – from the Korean government, from the business community, and from international lending institutions and prospective investors. All parties seemed to agree that labor held the key to overcoming the current economic crisis. The IMF-mandated economic restructuring inevitably necessitated large-scale layoffs in order to carry out extensive corporate restructuring though bankruptcies, mergers, and acquisitions, as well as to induce foreign equity investments. Thus, the success of structural adjustment under the IMF regime depended, to a great extent, on making Korean labor accept their sacrifices without causing much industrial or social instability. Maintaining industrial peace in the process of economic restructuring was thus defined as a major task for the newly elected president, Kim Dae Jung. One reason why the international business community welcomed his election was because he was believed to be the best person to deal with unions, due to his longstanding ties with labor and the popular sectors.

One of the first things that president-elect Kim Dae Jung did was to form a labor–management–government tripartite body, along the social corporatist model. The Labor–Management–Government Tripartite Council (*No-Sa-Chŏng*) was formed on January 14, 1998. On January 20, the Tripartite Council issued the first labor-management-government joint communiqué, in which the three parties agreed on the basic principle of fairly sharing the pain and burden of economic restructuring. Business promised to pursue active structural adjustments and do its best to prevent indiscreet layoffs and unfair labor practices, labor pledged to make every effort to raise productivity and the firm's competitiveness and to cooperate with management in readjusting wage and working hours in order to minimize layoffs, while the government promised to make efforts to increase corporate transparency and competitiveness as well as to protect basic labor rights and develop a comprehensive social security program. After arduous negotiations, the Labor–Management–Government council produced a historic Tripartite Accord on February 6. In addition to the reiteration of the basic agreements announced in the early joint communiqué, the Accord included an agreement on the necessity of redundancy layoffs in the case of an emergency affecting the company, something that unions had steadfastly refused to accept. In compensation, the Accord endorsed collective bargaining rights among schoolteachers and civil servants as well as civil rights for unions to participate in political activities.

The Tripartite Accord was welcomed and praised both inside and outside the country as a historic compromise. But workers were very unhappy about accepting the redundancy clause in the Accord. Subsequently, the discontented members of the KCTU voted out their incumbent union leaders and elected the hard-line leader of the Hyundai Heavy Industry union as their new president. Lee Kap-Yong, the new KCTU president, pledged to fight for the nullification of the provisions on redundancy layoffs and on hiring substitute workers for strikers. Under his leadership, the KCTU organized new strikes, boycotted the Tripartite Council meetings, and finally decided in February 1999 to leave the Council, claiming that the Council functioned merely as a vehicle for passing all the burden of economic restructuring to the workers.

Thus, we can see that the 1997 financial crisis brought ironic consequences to Korean labor. The crisis devastated the lives and destroyed the livelihoods of many Korean workers, but at the same time it helped elevate the political and social status of organized labor. The establishment of the Tripartite Council under the direct authority of the President signified the first moment in Korean history that labor was officially invited into a national decision-making body. For Korea's organized labor, which had never been included in the dominant political coalition or decision-making process, this was not a minor achievement. But an irony of the empowerment of Korean labor at this juncture is that, with their enhanced status and power, union leadership was faced with the task of accepting changes that would seriously impair and destabilize workers' labor market position. With the political inclusion that labor had so long fought for, labor leaders were now required to pacify their workers and to cooperate to maintain industrial peace for economic restructuring. Thus, the current trend of the Korean labor movement converges to the common situation in other advanced economies. As Hyman describes, "In most countries the economic climate restricted the scope for substantive achievements. Unions had to settle increasingly for procedural and symbolic outcomes, while often being expected to perform a restraining and disciplining role."[18] South Korea is no exception to this general pattern.

Nevertheless, the political inclusion of labor in the new corporatist framework succeeded in maintaining a relatively high level of industrial stability in recent years in the midst of the mounting problems of unemployment and unfair labor practices in the industrial arena. Overt labor conflicts were restricted more or less to large-scale firms where there existed strong unions, and the focal point of conflict was the issue of redundancy layoffs. Workers in smaller firms, especially in the labor-intensive sector, were unable to resist corporate restructuring or plant relocation. Strong unions were concentrated in large conglomerate firms, but the rest of the unions were mostly very small and fragile and could easily disappear with the collapses of their companies. As the effects of the economic crisis on jobs became more deeply felt, most unions became preoccupied with the immediate problems of protecting jobs and preventing wage cuts for their own members and could ill afford to concern themselves with broader issues pertaining to other workers.

Thus, the general trend in the Korean labor movement in the second half of the 1990s was to develop into economic unionism rather than into social unionism, confining its primary concern to workplace issues among union members. The failure of the labor movement to address broader community issues opened the door for the blossoming of citizens' movements after the democratic transition. These civic movements were led by progressive intellectuals, many of whom had been active in the labor movement during the pre-1987 period.[19] This led to the separation of the working-class movement and the middle-class-led social movements in the 1990s, further restricting the scope of the labor movement.

Internal differentiation of the working class

A distinct characteristic of the Korean working class until the mid-1980s was its homogeneity, both in terms of socio-demographic characteristics and market positions. The great majority of the working class were semi-skilled workers engaged in the mass production system under what might be called "peripheral Fordism." Not only was there little differentiation in terms of skills, as well as ages and family background, there were also few differences in terms of wages, job security, or welfare benefits. Wage differentials between large-scale and smaller-scale firms were very modest, and so were the differentials between unionized and non-unionized workers.[20] Working conditions were uniformly poor and hazardous across industries and across firms of various sizes. In many of these aspects, the Korean factory workers constituted a very homogeneous working class, close to the ideal type of the industrial proletariat.

But after the 1980s, the South Korean economy began to move beyond peripheral Fordism. Led by the *chaebŏl*, large-scale manufacturing firms strove hard to move up the technological ladder in world production in order to overcome the sandwich position between advanced industrial economies and the new tiers of export economies. Escalating wage costs and the growing power of trade unions in Korea were major contributing factors to the capitalists' endeavor to move beyond the low-wage-based mass production system. The general strike in the winter of 1996–1997 occurred in this context, as Korean capitalists tried to restructure the legal framework to be more compatible with the post-Fordist regime of capital accumulation.

Even before this legal battle, Korean capitalists had actively sought to increase flexibility in the utilization of the labor force. Since the mid-1980s, subcontract production increased fast in Korean manufacturing, as large-scale firms farmed out an increasing proportion of their production process to external and internal subcontract units in order to save labor costs as well as to discourage union formation. In the 1990s, large firms in both manufacturing and service industries employed a strategy of reducing regular employees and hiring instead a large number of temporary, part-time, and home workers. The financial crisis in 1997 accelerated this trend. Thus, the internal structure of the Korean working class began to converge on the common pattern in the advanced industrial societies, with the overall improvement of the working-class material conditions, as indicated by their wage improvement and life-style change, and increasing disaggregation of the working class by a polarizing labor market structure.

The internal differentiation of the Korean working class in recent years occurred along several dimensions. First, significant differences in job and wage conditions appeared between employees at large firms and those at small and medium-sized enterprises. Since the late 1980s, workers at large firms, especially in the *chaebŏl*, have obtained a substantially higher level of wage increase than those working in small factories, resulting in widening economic gaps between the two categories of workers. In 1980, the average wage for workers employed in small firms with 10–29 workers was 92.9 percent of the average wage at large firms (hiring 500 or more workers), but the ratio decreased to 87.5 percent in 1987 and to 72.3 percent in 1997.[21] Greater economic disparities between small and large firms developed in the provision of various company welfare measures. There is no comparison between large *chaebŏl* and smaller firms in terms of the extent and quality of company welfare offered to the regular employees. While this difference had existed to a certain extent before 1987, the disparity greatly increased thenceforth as large-scale firms tried to buy labor cooperation and company loyalty by offering generous welfare services to their workers. Employees of large firms in the heavy and chemical industries enjoy a variety of company welfare services, including housing subsidy, commuter bus, medical insurance, children's tuition support, funeral expenses, and a variety of other family-related supports. Whereas large-scale firms in core industries combined better wages and generous company welfare to tame their workforce, small firms in the competitive sector continued to rely on old methods of wage minimization or decided to transfer their plants to less developed economies in their search for lower wages.

Another critical axis of cleavage within the working class, that has become more important in recent years, is between those who are regularly employed and protected by legal contract and/or by unions and those whose employment status is irregular, unstable, and easily disposable. This is a well-known problem of core–periphery, formal–informal, or insider–outsider division of the labor force in advanced industrial societies.[22] In South Korea, this dual labor market problem had not been really serious until 1987, partly because of a generation of continuous employment thanks to rapid economic growth, and partly because of no pressing need for capital to hire many workers of a temporary status because regular employees did not enjoy much bargaining power either.

One of the most significant changes that has occurred in the Korean labor market in recent years is the rapid growth of temporary and irregular workers. The labor statistics indicate that between 1988 and 1997, the number of full-time employees increased from 5,348,000 to 7,133,000 (3.3 percent annual increase), while temporary workers increased from 2,766,000 to 4,204,000 (4.8 percent annual increase).[23] The growth of irregular workers increased more sharply in the latter half of the 1990s, especially after the financial crisis in 1997. It is estimated that in 1999 more than half of all employed workers (about 52 percent) were either temporary or daily workers.[24] Most likely, the actual size of the workforce in unstable jobs was larger than this, because government labor statistics exclude those employed in tiny enterprises with less than five employees. Also, many workers who were classified as employed full time may be in short-term contract positions.

Not surprisingly, women were the main victims of this flexibilization strategy. In 1999, regular employees constituted only 31 percent of the female labor force, while 69 percent among the male labor force were regular employees.[25] With a severe labor shortage occurring in the labor-intensive sector since the late 1980s, a large number of married women were encouraged to enter the labor force, but a majority of them found themselves working in temporary, part-time, or dispatched positions. The impact of the financial crisis in 1997 was much harsher on the female labor force. In most firms, women were the first to be laid off, and this was particularly the case for white-collar workers. Blue-collar women also suffered severely, because many of their employers (most of whom were in the competitive sector) did not survive the financial crisis or had to scale down their business operations.

The development of such a structural cleavage within the working class inevitably exerted a dampening effect on the Korean labor movement. As noted previously, an important structural source of the rapid growth of the Korean labor movement was the homogeneity of the working class – predominantly semi-skilled, low paid, unprotected, and suffering the same social degradation. Worker solidarity was much easier to achieve under such a condition of high structural homogeneity, especially because of their high geographic concentration. But such structural conditions no longer prevailed. As one labor scholar argues, "Workers, who were comrades in the past struggle, become more self-interested competitors in the intensified market competition. Divided workers with pragmatic concerns took the place of working-class solidarity in the early phase of democratic consolidation in Korea."[26] Increasingly, differential market positions began to be reflected in union orientations. Unions representing the privileged core workers became increasingly pragmatic and trade-unionist, while the KCTU representing peripheral workers adhered to political unionism. Thus, the general trend of the Korean union movement in the late 1990s was to become more pragmatic and inwardly oriented within the confines of enterprise unionism. This tendency was stronger in unionism at *chaebŏl*-level firms.

However, there also occurred a counter movement to this trend. The devastating impact of the economic crisis in 1997–1998 triggered novel efforts to organize vulnerable workers and defend their interests. There were efforts to organize temporary and part-time workers in the construction industry, and in the sales and service sectors. Although it is too early to predict the outcome at the present time, many attempts were undertaken to organize temporary workers into unions. The KCTU also adopted an official policy to increase unionization among temporary workers and the unemployed. In recent years, a majority of labor disputes have been protests against employers' attempts to maintain a flexible labor market.

Another important development in the late 1990s was the attempt among female workers to organize their own unions apart from the male-dominated unions. In the 1990s, feminist consciousness had grown noticeably among women activists. Within the KCTU and the FKTU, women unionists demanded a greater voice by women and secured greater women's representation in the leadership positions within the organizations. Yet, many women found the changes too slow and felt the need to organize women's own unions outside the male-dominated union structure. In early 1999, they organized women's trade unions in nine geographical regions, made of both regular and temporary or part-time workers across industrial and occupational categories. In the same year, these nine regional unions formed a national umbrella organization, the National Federation of Women's Trade Unions. The dominant orientation of the women's unions is well expressed in the inaugural statement of the Seoul Women's Trade Union: "We organized women's trade unions in order to achieve women's rights with the power of women workers. Despite the fact that a large number of women workers have been laid off and pushed into temporary jobs with no rights, the existing unions are losing their ability to fight back. Also, the patriarchal hierarchy within the present unions became an obstacle to organizing women workers."[27]

Given that a majority of women workers are temporary, part-time, or subcontract workers, women's unions were formed on a regional basis, including diverse categories of workers, and addressing not only employment issues but also other feminist issues like gender discrimination at work, sexual harassment, or the lack of child-care services. Thus, from the beginning, the women's trade union movement revealed the character of social unionism more than the male-dominated conventional unions. The future of the women's trade union movement at the present time is very uncertain, but it showed some promise of stimulating the Korean labor movement to broaden its constituencies and community concerns. So, it is possible that female workers can make a unique contribution in linking workplace struggles and community issues, thereby broadening the Korean labor movement toward social unionism.[28]

Conclusion

Until the democratic transition began in 1987, civil society in South Korea had developed in active opposition to the authoritarian state. Harsh authoritarian rule under the Park and Chun regimes allowed very little space for the activities of autonomous civic organizations or independent trade unions. Nonetheless, a vigorous opposition movement and grassroots union movement occurred outside the legal and institutional arena. Expelled from the legitimate political space by extremely repressive and exclusionary state policies, the two movements had been pulled together by their common opposition to the authoritarian state. South Korea's civil society grew out of the close interaction between these two movements, both of which were the products of the state's exclusionary approach to civil society.

But the relationship between the democracy movement and the labor movement has changed over time, as the latter has grown out of its marginal and dependent status to become a vigorous, independent social force. If the grassroots labor movement in the 1970s depended heavily on church organizations for moral and organizational support, in the 1980s it was the student labor activists who played the critical role in helping workers organize unions and develop broader networks of worker solidarity across firms. Workers also received much-needed ideological and organizational support from the *minjung* movement. During this authoritarian period, industrial workers occupied a marginal position within the broad alliances for democracy and civil society.

After the watershed explosion of labor unrest in 1987, the union movement has established itself as a truly independent movement without need of external assistance for leadership or organization. Trade unionism has been brought inside the institutional arena, and collective bargaining has become a well-accepted industrial practice. However, the sudden growth in the power of organized labor, and the aggressive union efforts to increase wages in a sluggish economy, led to a noticeable change in middle-class attitudes toward the labor movement. While the majority of the new middle class had been supportive of labor struggles during the authoritarian period, their attitude became generally unfriendly and critical toward what they now perceived to be an aggressive and selfish labor movement. Furthermore, new cleavages and tensions appeared between the labor movement and the new social movements which began to proliferate after the democratic transition. Although the labor movement has gained a larger space and organizational influence within civil society, it has lost much of its moral authority, as workers have been increasingly viewed as selfishly pursuing their own group interests at the expense of other groups or the society as a whole.

The January 1997 general strike against the newly revised labor laws, however, brought moral authority back to South Korea's union movement. By fighting for job security, which was of vital concern to all categories of workers, the labor movement has established itself as a social force that fights for the general interest of the whole society rather than just for the interest of blue-collar wage workers. The ability of the national union centers to mobilize a huge number of workers and citizens to block the legal measures that would rob them of job security played a critical role in establishing a dominant position for labor unions within the civil society. This status was short-lived, however, as the financial crisis that hit the South Korean economy in late 1997 brought new troubles to Korean trade unionism. The crisis created mounting problems of unemployment, job insecurity, and wage losses, forcing unions to become primarily concerned with protecting their own workers and to abandon larger issues of economic restructuring and democratic reforms. At the current stage, there is a clear danger of Korean trade unionism becoming narrowly focused, inwardly oriented, and defensive. Under such circumstances, the position of the labor movement in the civil society may also become narrowed and weakened. But, of course, it is still too early to predict how the relationship between the labor movement and civil society will evolve through this economic crisis and afterwards.

Notes

1 Doh C. Shin, *Mass Politics and Culture in Democratizing Korea* (Cambridge and New York: Cambridge University Press, 1999); Larry Diamond and Byung-Kook Kim, *Consolidating Democracy in South Korea* (Boulder: Lynne Rienner, 2000).
2 One nice exception is Yin-Wah Chu, "Labor and Democratization in South Korea and Taiwan," *Journal of Contemporary Asia* 28: 2 (1998): 185–202. An important study that stresses the role of the working class, instead of that of the middle class, in democratization is: Dietrich Rueschemeyer, Evelyne Stephens, and John Stephens, *Capitalist Development and Democracy* (Chicago: University of Chicago, 1992).

3 George Ogle, *South Korea: Dissent within the Economic Miracle* (London: Zed Books, 1990), p. 99.
4 *Joong-ang Daily News*, July 7, 1987.
5 For example, laborers comprised the largest proportion of the people who were arrested during this period, although many of them might be construction workers or casual laborers. See Young-soo Kim, Han'guk nodongja kyekŭp chŏngchi undong [The Political Movement of the Korean Working Class] (Seoul: Hyŏnjangesŏmiraerŭl, 1999), p. 207.
6 Jang Jip Choi, "The Working Class Movement and the State in Transition to Democracy: The Case of South Korea," paper presented at the conference on East Asian Labor in Comparative Perspective, University of California, Berkeley, 1993.
7 Joong-Ki Roh, "Kukka ŭi nodong tongje chŏnryak'e kwanhan yŏngu: 1987–1992" [A Study on the State's Strategy of Labor Control: 1987–1992], Ph.D. dissertation in sociology, Seoul National University, 1995, p. 81.
8 Choong Soon Kim, *The Culture of Korean Industry: An Ethnography of Poongsan Corporation* (Tucson: University of Arizona Press, 1992); Roger Janelli and Dawnhee Yim, *Making Capitalism: The Social and Cultural Construction of a South Korean Conglomerate* (Stanford, CA: Stanford University Press, 1993).
9 For a good English source on the white-collar union movement in South Korea, see Doowon Suh, "From Individual Welfare to Social Change: The Expanding Goals of Korean White-Collar Labor Unions, 1987–1995," Ph.D. Dissertation, Department of Sociology, University of Chicago, 1998.
10 Dong-A Research Institute, "Current Political Attitudes of the Koreans" [in Korean], Monthly Dari (February, 1990): 272–298; Korean Institute of Labor Studies, *A Study of Workers' Attitudes about Labor Problems and Labor Relations* [in Korean] (Seoul: KILS, 1990). For a similar view on the shifting attitude among the middle classes, see John Kie-Chiang Oh, *Korean Politics* (Ithaca, NY: Cornell University Press, 1999), pp. 114–116.
11 For more detailed discussion on this issue, see Hagen Koo, "Middle Classes, Democratization, and Class Formation: The Case of South Korea," *Theory and Society* 20 (August 1991): 485–509.
12 On the development of citizens' movements in the 1990s, see Sunhyuk Kim, *The Politics of Democratization in Korea: The Role of Civil Society* (Philadelphia: Temple University Press, 2000); Hyuk-rae Kim, "The State and Civil Society in Transition: The Role of Non-governmental Organizations in South Korea," *Pacific Review* 13: 4 (2000): 595–613; Hee-Yeon Cho, "Democratic Transition and Social Movements in Korea," paper presented at the conference on Democracy and Social Contention in South Korea, Center for Korean Studies, University of Hawaii, December 1997.
13 Kyung-suk Suh, "Kyŏngsilryŏn 3-nyŏnŭi pyŏngkawa pansŏng" [The Evaluation and Reflection on the Three Years of the Citizens' Coalition for Economic Justice], Sahoe Pyŏngron (1992), pp. 192–202.
14 Hochul Sonn, "The 'Late Blooming' of the South Korean Labor Movement," *Monthly Review* 49 (July-August, 1997): 117–128; Yong Cheol Kim, "Industrial Reform and Labor Backlash in South Korea: Genesis, Escalation, and Termination of the 1997 General Strike," *Asian Survey* 38: 12 (December, 1998): 1,142–1,160.
15 See Yong Cheol Kim, "Industrial Reform" for more detail.
16 Chang-Hee Lee, "New Unionism and the Transformation of the Korean Industrial Relations System," *Economic and Industrial Democracy* 19 (1998), p. 371.
17 Sonn, "The 'Late Blooming,'" pp. 127–128.
18 Richard Hyman, "Trade Unions and the Disaggregation of the Working Class," pp. 150–168 in *The Future of Labour Movements*, edited by Marino Regini (Newbury Park, CA: Sage, 1992), p. 157.
19 Sunhyuk Kim, *The Politics of Democratization*.

20　Ho-keun Song, *Han'guk ŭi nodong chŏngchi wa sijang* [Labor Politics and Market in Korea] (Seoul: Nanam, 1991), pp. 107–136; Hyung-ki Kim, *Han'guk ŭi tokchŏm chabon kwa imkŭm nodong* [Monopoly Capital and Wage Labor in South Korea] (Seoul: Kachi, 1988), pp. 378–417.

21　KOILAF, *Labor Relations in Korea* (Seoul: Korea International Labour Foundation, 1999), p. 133.

22　For excellent discussion of this issue, see Hyman, "Trade Unions".

23　KOILAF, *Labour Relations*, p. 41.

24　Pulanjŏng nodong yŏngu moim, *Sinjayu chuŭiwa nodong wiki: pulanjŏng nodong yŏngu* [Neoliberalism and the Crisis of Labor: A Study of the Unstable Labor Force] (Seoul: Muhwa Kwahaksa, 2000), p. 43.

25　Ibid., p. 47.

26　Ho Keun Song, *Yŏlin sijang, tatchin chŏngchi* [Open Market, Closed Politics] (Seoul: Nanam, 1994), p. 16.

27　*Pulanjŏng nodong*, p. 270.

28　Gay Seidman suggests that in Brazil women's involvement in the union movement contributed to linking workplace issues to community issues, thereby promoting social unionism rather than economic unionism. See Seidman, *Manufacturing Militance: Worker's Movements in Brazil and South Africa, 1970–1985* (Berkeley: University of California Press, 1994).

5   The South Korean student movement

Undongkwŏn as a counterpublic sphere

Namhee Lee

The historical emergence of *undongkwŏn*

In the late 1980s, the South Korean student movement was considered one of the most important political actors next to the military. In 1986, a government official privately remarked that South Korea seemed to be "at the brink of choosing either a military republic or a student republic."[1] Leaders of national student organizations such as the National Students' Alliance (*Chonhangnyŏn*, organized in 1985) and the National University Students' Committee (*Chondaehyŏp*, organized in 1987) were portrayed as "heroes" and as "the year's most important persons" by the mass media.[2] Without the persistence and sacrifice of the students, South Korea would not have achieved the level of democracy nor seen the rise of civil society which occurred in the 1990s.[3]

Students won accolades by being widely recognized as "a force of conscience" (*yangsim seryŏk*); much like former East European dissidents, they were "morally superior" because they spoke what was in everybody's mind, without considering the consequences.[4] In the 1970s, when the draconian Yushin measures of Park Chung Hee kept everyone silent, students dared to speak even if it was in whispers. In the 1980s, as the Kwangju Uprising interjected a revolutionary fervor in the social movement at large in seeking to build a "scientific" and "*minjung*-oriented society," as opposed to being merely anti-government, the student movement was at the forefront of this new development, providing theoretical articulation, intellectual vigor, and physical force. It was also through their great sacrifice that the students profoundly changed the landscape of social activism; many lost their lives, many more were expelled or quit school, and an unprecedented number of students changed their life-course to become factory workers.[5]

Claiming themselves to be a voice of conscience and the true representative of the *minjung* (common people), the students "presented the issues" to society. All of the major political, social, economic, and cultural issues confronting Korean society, from the regime's political legitimacy, questions of distributive justice, the truth of the Kwangju Uprising, to reunification, have been persistently articulated and presented by students as public and legitimate. In other words, students defined the grounds and conditions of the social and political discourse in South Korea in the 1980s.

Through this process emerged one of the paradigmatic terms of the 1980s' *minjung* movement, *undongkwŏn*. Literally meaning "the movement sphere," *undongkwŏn* refers to both an individual activist and the *minjung* movement itself as a whole. The frequent invocation of this term both inside and outside of the *undongkwŏn* implicitly acknowledged the existence of a separate but parallel "counterpublic sphere" in which values and attitudes different from the public at large resided.

The regime (and media) portrayed *undongkwŏn* both as "marginal" and "insignificant" but it also branded it a menacing "pro-communist force" (*yonggong seryŏk*), potentially the most dangerous element in South Korean society at the time. Within the *minjung* movement, the meanings and implications of the term shifted uneasily between empowering and delimiting. The array of *undongkwŏn*'s self-descriptions betray their own fluctuating self-identities: *abang* (friend), *hwaldongga* (activist), *hyŏgmyŏngga* (revolutionary), *inja* (cell), *int* (intelligentsia), *hakppiri* (a disparaging and disapproving reference to intellectuals), and *mŏngmul* (literally "ink-water," used in a similar context as *hakppiri*), to name just a few.[6] As aspiring revolutionaries, *undongkwŏn* individuals often used self-deprecating terms such as *hakppiri* and *mŏngmul* to chastise themselves for falling short of their ideals.

By the mid-1980s, *undongkwŏn* was neither marginal nor only for the extraordinary. *Undongkwŏn* had become truly "massified" (*taejunghwa*); when the Seoul National University (SNU) students initiated boycotts of exams in 1984, almost 90 percent of the student body participated. Students did not confine their activism to individual campuses: a nationwide network of students, cutting across gender, regions, and schools, was mobilized for protests. In May 1985, 30,000 students from 80 universities protested with the same slogans and same demands in the Kwangju Uprising.

The *undongkwŏn*'s zeitgeist is embodied in the students' persistent and almost incantatory invocation of *minjung*, history, and subjectivity. These three concepts defined and constituted the South Korean democratization movement of the 1980s, of which the student movement was a significant, and to a large degree a leading, force. With their intimate and detailed knowledge of modern history, students delineated "lessons," "tasks," "obstacles," and "conclusions" for the present and future society. The movement hailed *minjung*, the common people, as the true subject of historical development. Its capacity for social change entitled it to play the role of charting the future democratic society.

Through harnessing the historically and socially ambiguous notion of *minjung* into a strong conception of historical agency, students projected a community of "intersubjective" *minjung*. Their *minjung* discourse involved and presumed the counter-image of others: the military dictatorship, conglomerates, and foreign powers. This combination of the exaltation of the *minjung* and the othering of the three forces gave rise in the 1980s to an unprecedented politicization of the students and the society. Everywhere new political symbolism and language such as the "Three *Min* Movement" (Democracy, Nationalism, and People), were created, imposed, and enforced. Traditional cultural practices, such as situational plays (*madang gŭk*), mask dances (*t'alch'um*), and four-instrument musical troupes (*p'ungmul*), were reinvented and reinvested with new meanings. From the vocabulary of daily life to modes of dress to interpersonal relationships, efforts were put into making a *minjung* out of factory workers, farmers, ordinary citizens, and most of all, the students themselves. From these multifarious practices, the repertoire of the student movement of the 1980s was fashioned.

The counterpublic sphere and the student movement

While the term *undongkwŏn* had variegated and conflicting receptions in Korean society, it nevertheless came to embody the 1980s *minjung* movement's ideals, yearnings, and hopes, as well as its shortcomings. Informed by the multiple meanings, implications, and potentialities, this chapter conceptualizes *undongkwŏn* as a "counterpublic sphere," a sphere in which students mapped out their oppositional and alternative positions against the dominant culture and value system. "Counterpublic sphere" is a term proposed by feminist scholars critically and creatively appropriating Jurgen Habermas's notion of "public sphere." Although Habermas's notion of "public sphere" has been criticized for being Eurocentric and insensitive to gender, his public sphere as a normative category offers possibilities for multiple and contestatory constructions. A public sphere as "an institutionalized arena of discursive interaction" is not only about an already established "public agenda" delivered through "rational and critical discourse." It is also about the parallel discursive processes that often challenge the established public agenda. This process gives rise to what Nancy Fraser terms "subaltern counterpublics" in which "members of subordinated social groups invent and circulate counterdiscourses to formulate oppositional interpretations of their identities, interests, and needs."[8] For example, the U.S. feminist movement has a variegated array of journals, bookstores, publishing companies, film and video distribution networks, lecture series, research centers, academic programs, conferences, conventions, festivals, and local meeting places. In these counterpublic spheres, feminists have invented new terms for describing social reality, including "sexism," "the double shift," and "sexual harassment," among others. These newly invented terms have been crucial in redefining and reframing the needs and identities of women.[9]

My use of counterpublic sphere is similar in spirit. But there is another element in Habermas's notion of public sphere that also resonates with the South Korean student movement. That is, the Habermasian public sphere, both as conceptual construction and as historical account, is integral to the development of civil society, broadly understood as a realm separate from the state (and economy). The concept and categories of civil society have become central in articulating some of the social movements that projected their vision broadly as "liberalization and democratization," such as Poland's Solidarity, France's "second left," Germany's Greens, and Latin America's new democratic left.[10] It is widely recognized that the student movement is the most significant contributing force to the "revival" of civil society in South Korea.[11]

Habermas's notion of public sphere was also a critique of the category of bourgeois society and was concerned with "the element of truth and emancipatory potential." I propose to think of *undongkwŏn* as that sphere in which truth and emancipation was the ultimate aim, despite its own "ideological misrepresentation and contradictions."[12] Truth and emancipation in the case of the *minjung* project was not limited to simply building Western liberal democracy but included creating a community in which human potential is fully realized and in which there is economic, as well as political, equality, as Bruce Cumings argues.[13] The counterpublic sphere of the *minjung* movement is therefore a sphere in which *minjung* practitioners articulate not only oppositional interpretations of their identities, interests, and needs but also envision an emancipatory program for the whole society.

The South Korean university student movement of the 1970s to the 1980s encapsulates the moment of a counterpublic as a counterdiscourse to the dominant ideology of the state, not so much by restructuring the students' own identity but by restructuring the "public agenda." In the process, all of the major political, social, economic, and cultural issues confronting Korean society at the time, including the regime's political legitimacy, questions of distributive justice, the truth of the Kwangju Uprising, and reunification, were debated vociferously in public.

The student movement also illustrates much of the basic strategies of a counterpublic sphere: how its projected visions, possibilities, and potentialities are constituted, organized, and articulated. In other words, the analysis of the student movement shows the ways in which *undongkwŏn* constituted itself as *undongkwŏn*, the discursive strategies that define *undongkwŏn*'s shared visions, languages, codes, and images, and the ways in which this counterpublic sphere relates to the process of larger societal transformation.

A discourse of moral privilege and the informal institutions of *undongkwŏn*

As much as South Korean intellectuals and university students agonized over their shifting roles in a rapidly changing society, it was the very pace of such change, and the political repression that accompanied it, that made it possible for them to retain their traditional relations to the larger society. Compared with their counterparts elsewhere in Asia such as Taiwan, Singapore, and Hong Kong, South Korean university students and intellectuals have been regarded as having higher social importance and relevance. In Taiwan, Singapore, and Hong Kong, post-colonial developments had largely broken the traditional roles of intellectuals vis-à-vis the state and society.[14] In Taiwan, for example, the role of intellectuals was weakened after the Kuomintang takeover "via a land reform that undermined their traditional economic base and (by compensating dispossessed landlords with stock in nascent industries) converted the intellectuals themselves into members of the bourgeoisie."[15] In contrast, in South Korea, the post-colonial authoritarian rule had the effect of strengthening and intensifying the traditional role of intellectuals within the society. This was partly due to the fact that South Korea's industrialization was conceived and implemented by military dictators who pushed the speed of development at the expense of distributive justice.[16] The resulting dislocation and disintegration had the effect of pushing the intellectuals to retain, until the 1980s, the traditional role of Chosŏn's Sŏnggyun'gwan students and memorial-writing scholars, in spite of their growing numbers and, thus, relatively reduced status in society – their proletarianization, if you will.[17]

The process of the student movement constructing its own identity as countervailing and oppositional to the state was a practice that was embedded in the traditional role of intellectuals, a long tradition of social criticism. I characterize this practice as "a discourse of moral privilege." In what follows, I argue that moral privilege discourse and informal institutions of the movement enabled students to structure their movement as a counterpublic sphere. In the students' moral discourse, the dichotomic vision of the world as *abang* (friends) and *t'abang* (enemies) was crucial. In this vision, the *minjung* was projected as a true intersubjective agency, and the military dictatorship, conglomerates, and foreign powers as not only anti-*minjung* but also as anti-national and anti-democratic. The strategy of exalting the *minjung* while othering and even at times demonizing the three other forces was a powerful discursive process constituting *undongkwŏn* as a counterpublic sphere.

In this public sphere, the discourse of moral privilege created a realm in which previously "unpublic" issues were reconstituted as public; issues that had been monopolized by the state or considered too threatening by society at large, such as the legitimacy of the state, distributive justice, welfare, and reunification. Existing concepts and terms, such as *minjung* (people), *minju* (democracy), *minjok* (nation), and *t'ongil* (reunification), were reinvested with new meanings and charged with emancipatory possibilities. Different and alternative meanings were given to certain historical moments, such as the Cheju People's Uprising and the Kwangju People's Uprising. Individuals whose acts were previously cast in historically ambiguous shades were elevated to positions of *yŏlsa* (patriot) or *minju-t'usa* (fighter for democracy) as in the case of Chŏn Tae-il, Kim Se-jin, and Yi Han-yŏl.[18]

South Korean students were not unique in their claim to be the moral voice and conscience of their nation and people. Numerous accounts of the Tiananmen protest described the Chinese students' cause and rhetorical construction as moral and moralist.[19] In Europe and in the United States as well, the 1960s' New Left was a moralist critique of contemporary society.[20] In fact, moral protest was difficult to distinguish from elitist attitude. During the Tiananmen protest, the Chinese students saw their own politics as "selflessly pure" and that of peasants and workers as motivated by "crass materialism."[21] The New Left German students' call for fundamental change was not altogether separate from their fear of "relative loss of class position" that was associated with the decline of the new intellectual elite in West Germany.[22]

In South Korea's case, the discourse of moral privilege was injected with urgency by the distinctive historical experience of Korea: its colonial past and the divided state. To the students of the 1970s and 1980s, the responsibility of discovering past history, previously perceived to have been buried (as the history of armed struggle, for example) or distorted (as the history of the nationalist movement, for example), the act of re-reading and reinterpreting the past history became an integral part of the movement. With the production of a historiography of *minjung*, which aimed towards an "authentic" representation of the Korean people, they received an intellectual affirmation of their claims.

The discourse of moral privilege was therefore embedded in the society's perception of the role of intellectuals and the intellectuals' own sense of historical destiny. Accompanying the discourse were several informal institutions that made the student movement politically effective and organizationally sustainable. These are interpersonal networks created out of the close bond between *sŏnbae* and *hubae* (one's senior and junior in school, respectively), and variegated networks formed out of an institutional and cultural milieu, such as study groups and extracurricular activities. Ever since the modern educational system was introduced in Korea, these informal networks have constituted the core of university life. These were also vital in sustaining the student movement as a counterpublic sphere.

Nexus of upperclass–lowerclass

The first of these informal institutions to consider is the nexus of upperclass–lowerclass (*sŏnbae–hubae*). *Sŏnbae–hubae* ties remain one of the most important types of "social capital" in South Korea, where age and hierarchical relationships are very much operational and school and regional ties remain instrumental,[23] very much as in Japan's *sempai* relationships. The degree of intimacy and meaningfulness of *sŏnbae–hubae* ties varied considerably for each individual. For *undongkwŏn* in the 1970s when university circles were driven underground, *sŏnbae–hubae* ties were the gateway to the movement; it was usually with *sŏnbae*'s introduction to an underground circle that one began the process of becoming an *undongkwŏn*. In the 1980s, *sŏnbae* was a critical and in some cases determining factor in an *undongkwŏn* individual's ideological orientations, so much so that in the mid-1980s, "If the *sŏnbae* was NL (National Liberation, one of the major ideological groups in the mid-1980s), then the *hubae* was also NL."[24] An underground circle was called a "family" and their aggregate was called a "house"[25] until the mid-1980s.

It is, however, misleading to present *sŏnbae–hubae* relations as strictly hierarchical or unilateral; for if *sŏnbae* was the moral guide, counselor, and a model to be emulated, *hubae* is someone *sŏnbae* feels responsible for, creating a certain reciprocal relationship between them.[26] It was often the sense of commitment to his *hubae* that pushed a *sŏnbae* to engage in an act that he or she might not have otherwise engaged in, especially if he is the one who guided numerous seminars through which the *hubae*'s previous ambivalent position with respect to the movement was clarified and commitment solidified. It was not unusual to find an *undongkwŏn* who stayed in the movement for the sense of responsibility toward his *sŏnbae* or *hubae*.

The case of one male student from Korea University, Ch'oe In-ch'ŏl, illustrates the point. Having entered Korea University in 1982, Ch'oe In-ch'ŏl spent the first six months of his freshman year socializing with his *sŏnbae*s, attending not a single class but mostly hanging around, drinking, agonizing over politics, and learning movement songs. One of his *sŏnbae*s, as he was being dragged away by police, exhorted Ch'oe to carry on the movement. Although his fellow classmates were dropping out of the movement one by one and his parents were appealing to him to concentrate on his studies, as he was the only hope for the family, Ch'oe was driven by what his *sŏnbae* had told him and what he had promised his *sŏnbae*.[27]

*Sŏnbae*s were also responsible for a gradual crumbling of Ch'oe In-ch'ŏl's deeply embedded anti-communism. Ch'oe was initially greatly confused when his *sŏnbae*s talked freely of the armed guerrilla movements in the Chiri Mountains in the 1940s and 1950s, a taboo subject at the time. The apparent pro-North Korean sentiments expressed by his *sŏnbae* – "If we get kicked out from school, we'll carry on the guerrilla movement; we'll call North Korea for help" – made him confused and anxious but also put a few cracks in his anti-Communist beliefs.[28]

Sŏnbae–hubae ties can lead individuals to danger and suffering. Throughout the post-1945 period, numerous people were arrested, tortured, and imprisoned, solely because of their personal ties to a *sŏnbae* or a *hubae* who was implicated as "anti-state". Pak Wŏn-sik was implicated in the 1982 case of Pusan USIS arson. He was severely tortured and sentenced to a seven-year prison term. Although he helped to distribute the pamphlets before the time of arson on the behest of his *sŏnbae*, Mun Pu-sik, he had not been aware of the plan for arson.[29] Kim Nam-ju served 15 years in prison for his membership in the "South Korean Liberation Front" (Namminjŏn). He had joined the organization without asking many detailed questions; it was enough that the other members were *sŏnbae*s or colleagues whom he could trust.[30]

Circulation of texts

Along with the *sŏnbae–hubae* nexus, another crucial informal institution of the student movement was the circulation of printed materials such as banned literature, pamphlets, underground newsletters, diaries of symbolic figures such as Chŏn-Tae-il, and appeals written by imprisoned students.[31] Underground newsletters and pamphlets were often directed to both *undongkwŏn* and the general public. Those designated for *undongkwŏn* provided analyses of the current political situation and guiding principles for future action. In the absence of an open and public channel of communication among *undongkwŏn*, the circulation of underground materials and banned literature became the main medium of communication and the sustaining force of the movement. For this reason, duplication and distribution of underground literature constituted an integral part of activism.

It is possible to postulate that from the late 1970s to mid-1980s, the mode of the movement became as important as the content. *Undongkwŏn*'s major ideological developments were sometimes determined by certain pamphlets. The so-called

"Murim-Hangnim Debate," which set off the major debate in 1981 on the future of the student movement, was sparked by the appearance of the pamphlet entitled "Declaration of Anti-Imperialist and Anti-Fascist Struggle." Another well-known debate on the direction and goal of the movement initiated at the beginning of 1985 was known as the "Flag and Anti-Flag Debate," from the pamphlet of the same name.

The circulation of texts contributed to a remarkable degree of homogeneity within the movement in terms of issues, attitudes, ethos, and cultural markers. In what one former student termed "The Era of Great Circulation of Texts,"[32] there were many original theoretical texts (*wŏnsŏ*) that became the "text" for the movement. It was as if there was a correspondence course on the student movement and every *undongkwŏn* took it. In the early 1970s, such texts were only available in their original languages or in (often crude) Japanese translation. Most of these were also on the government's banned lists, which partly contributed to their "mythical" quality.

Before the ban was briefly lifted in 1983, the possession of books such as E.H. Carr's *What Is History* and Mao's *On Contradiction* was a violation of the National Security Law that could carry a minimum one-year prison term.[33] Obtaining and reading these texts took tremendous effort; many students taught themselves German and Japanese. One student remembered reading aloud the Korean translations of Lenin and Marx in the hope of understanding them better.[34]

The student movement culture was essentially a literati culture in which reading Kant's *Critique of Pure Reason* was thought requisite, although "few did and many just pretended to have read it." Once a theoretical text (usually from the West) was introduced into the network of underground (and later open) circulation, it took less than a month for *undongkwŏn* to have at least a shaky command of it. Among an array of variations of "isms" that were introduced and soon became out of fashion – few "isms" lasted for more than six months[35] – Leninism and Marxism took a special hold of the students, starting from the early 1980s.

The "texts" in the early to mid-1980s were Lenin's *What Is To Be Done?* and Marx's *Capital*. These were pored over and memorized for the urgency and imminence of the "battle" to be waged. Kim Su-kyŏng, class of 1983, felt that Lenin's *What Is To Be Done?* was really "our" story: "It almost felt as if Lenin wrote the book based on the reality of South Korea of 1983." She also remarked on her reading of *Capital*: "[The description in the] *Capital* was so real that I could hear my heart palpitate; the part on England's industrial development was so similar to South Korea's that I wanted to put exclamation marks on every single word."[36] Students compared the maturity of their own movement with corresponding developments in the Russian revolution.

What was available and distributed within the *undongkwŏn* at the time was limited to translated materials; hence, what students had access to was extremely truncated Marxism and Leninism, which one scholar called "pamphlet Marxism."[37] South Korean scholar Chŏng Un-yŏng examined the state of translation and publication of Marxist literature in the late 1980s and concluded that the priority of translation was given to those texts believed to be more relevant to the present needs of the social movement.[38] Indeed, Lenin became the "absolute science" for many activists. Little effort was made to analyze, criticize, or debate his writings; rather, they were simply to be absorbed. According to one former *undongkwŏn* student, "Theories defined reality, and reality was redefined according to Marxism and Leninism."[39]

The partial lift on the ban following the liberalization policy in 1983 and the spread of copy machines made possible the wide and rapid dissemination of various texts.[40] Many former activists became publishers, editors, writers, and translators who helped to spread the texts. At least 16 publishing houses were reportedly established by these former activists in the early 1980s; by 1987, the number had increased to 24.[41] These publishers were devoted exclusively to the publication of "ideological literature" such as classical works on socialism, and writings on the nature of world capitalism and the Korean economy, workers' and peasants' movements, and Korean politics and history.

Circles and seminars

If the circulation of texts mapped the topography of issues for the *undongkwŏn*, then the accompanying circulation of reading lists (*k'ŏri*, from the English word "curriculum") and *ssŏkkŭls* (extracurricular clubs of mostly academic nature, from the English word "circle," hereafter circle) disseminated these issues as public knowledge within the *undongkwŏn*. Throughout the history of the Korean student movement, circles were a crucial medium. Politically conscious and eager minds usually gathered in circles and gradually transformed them into a nursery for movement activities. These circles go back to the late 1950s, when a few study groups with limited membership were the only alternatives to the state-sponsored student organizations. In Seoul National University, for example, the New Progressive Club (*Shinjin-hoe*) consisted primarily of students in the political science department, with its membership not exceeding 15 at any given time during its existence (1956–60).[42] The state's intelligence network always linked the existence of circles, both underground and open, to the outbreak of campus demonstrations.[43] During the protest against the Normalization Treaty in 1964, many of these circle members were active leaders. The members of the "Society and Law" circle in the Department of Law at SNU and "Studies on Comparative Nationalism" in the Department of Sociology were main leaders in the organization of the "National Democratic Youth and Student Federation" (*Minch'ŏnghangnyŏn*) in the early 1970s, as I discuss later.

With the 1983 liberalization policy, which I discuss in more detail later, circle activities became open and legitimate. These circles conducted seminars at every level and at every available forum: underground, open, during their activism in factories (known as *konghwal*), in farming villages (known as *nonghwal*), and in slum areas. Intensive seminars called "Membership Training" (MT) were conducted during vacations and holidays. A newspaper article claimed that in

1986, there were 72 *undongkwŏn* circles in 22 universities in the Seoul area alone, which was an increase from the previous year's 51 circles in 19 universities.[44] Students replaced their regular classes with seminars, often attending school only for the purpose of carrying out their assigned movement activities. Seminars were grueling but intellectually challenging and exhilarating, especially for first-year students.

Many former activists recalled that they read a tremendous amount in the study groups. For example, one student recollected that in his second year in college (1983), his readings covered dependency theory, liberation theology, and Euro-communism, in addition to analyses of the current political situation, cases of revolutionary movements in other countries (such as Russia, China, the Philippines, Bolivia, Cuba, Nicaragua, and the Anti-Fascist People's Front during World War II), philosophy, political economy, and theories of social movements.[45] Another student remarked, "Seminars offered an opportunity to travel to all historical eras and countries" by virtue of offering a curriculum on economic history, capitalism, and world revolutionary movements.[46]

Historical evolution of the *undongkwŏn*

If the discourse of moral privilege and informal institutions were discursive practices that generated and constituted *undongkwŏn* as a counterpublic, how does one actually become *undongkwŏn*? What are the ways in which ordinary students enter into the realm of the movement and remain active in the movement? While there were basic patterns that persisted throughout the period that I am discussing, there were also considerable differences between time periods. In the following, I break down the discussion into three historical time periods: the "era of yearning for democracy" from the early 1970s to the mid-1970s, the "era of Emergency Measure Number Nine" from the mid-1970s to the late 1970s, and the "era of liberalization" from the mid-1980s to the late 1980s.

Throughout the 1970s and until the mid-1980s, university life for the majority of students was disappointing.[47] Before entering college, students usually deferred everything, from the pursuit of lofty ideas such as freedom, justice, truth, and true learning, to the more mundane desires such as one's own clothing and hair styles.[48] Most students did not choose their majors based on their interests or aptitudes but based on what was most likely to get them in, due to complex application procedures. Most students did not know what to expect from their own area of study. Students had a vague notion that college was going to be romantic, carefree, and vibrant.

What greeted these incoming students in common was the poor quality of courses, which in some cases were no different in content from high school courses, the ubiquitous presence of state agents known as *kigwanwŏn*, and scenes of *sŏnbaes* and classmates involved in heated discussions one day and dragged away by riot soldiers the next. For many who became involved in the movement, *sŏnbaes* provided much more in the way of intellectual stimulation and genuine human relationships than the academic courses or professors. Gradually, these students were introduced to various circles and immersed in a series of seminars offered by circles. This "qualitatively different" organizational life, coupled with the eye-opening experiences of working in a slum, farming village, or factory for the first time in their lives, or attending the trial of someone they knew, all became transformative and often determining experiences that led many to the path of *undongkwŏn*.

The "era of yearning for democracy," early 1970s

The experience of Kim Pyŏng-gon points to the intersection among *sŏnbae*s, circles, and the path to movement activism in the early 1970s.[49] When Kim Pyŏng-gon was introduced to a circle in his first year at SNU in 1970 (through an older alumni from his high school who was attending the same university as Kim), he was not aware that the circle was one of the oldest at SNU and that he was soon to be involved in the student movement. He liked the circle members and the issues they discussed. His movement life began from the first semester, as he began reading social theories and immersing himself in fact-finding research on the living conditions of factory workers and the slum dwellers. Even then, he did not have clear ideas about what he was to do or the nature of the circle. After witnessing the "too cruel" reality of the workers' situations and the slums, he developed a vague idea that the student movement was to change the existing injustice and inequality in society.

In the early 1970s, the university circles were the most important bases for the movement; their activities, however, were mostly academic in nature. Kim Pyŏng-gon's circle held a seminar once a week; the reading list was limited to what could be purchased at bookstores, as the elaborate system of underground copying of banned literature was not in place then. What most attracted the circle members was the social gatherings called "after-hours," however. Seminar participants would gather in a nearby tavern to carry on the discussion, often joined by *sŏnbae*s of the circle dating back to the 1960s. One former circle member recalled an all-night discussion on the issue of whether "the history's motor is elite or minjung" or whether "the priority of the movement should be placed on [individual] freedom or [social] equality."

Elite universities' circles had well-established routines and protocols. The circle that Kim Pyŏng-gon belonged to held an initiation ceremony for new members in a remote campground in the outskirts of Seoul. Present at the ceremony were Kim's immediate *sŏnbae*s and those who graduated several years earlier in the 1960s. The ceremony started with each new member's "report" on his life history, worldviews, political views, and future plans. This "report" was then followed by *sŏnbae*s' comments, with more discussions, songs, and drinking; barrels of *makkŏli* (unrefined rice wine) and cigarettes were essential in these gatherings. The rather intensely personal yet at the same time intensely group-oriented experience was for some students "the beginning of the new world, which was full of wonder and fear, and yet the world to which one could not say no."

When Park Chung Hee announced the Garrison Decree in 1971, all universities were closed and circles became illegal. Most of Kim Pyŏng-gon's circle members were forcibly inducted into the army,[50] and the circle meetings continued at a great risk, often at remote places away from the reach of police. Students devised intricate ways of arranging their rendezvous *à la* James Bond, with their communications cryptic and filled with codes. For example, if one mentioned at the end of a meeting the number 135, it meant that the next meeting place would be somewhere around the terminal of the bus number 135. Upon arriving there, one of them would shout, "West," and the meeting would take place at the first restaurant on the west side of the terminal. Meetings in coffee houses also became both necessary and popular. The court record of the Minch'ŏnghangnyŏn case in which Kim Pyŏng-gon was later implicated shows that his group met, in the space of two weeks, no fewer than 63 times in 43 different coffee houses.[51]

Campus demonstrations

Student demonstrations during the early 1970s were brief affairs. Once a decision to demonstrate was made, usually by someone who had a link with a dissident organization, one or two in the group, be it an underground seminar or school circle, were assigned to work on a manifesto or a statement, which was copied manually using stencil paper and a mimeograph. On the designated day, students gathered in a lecture room, read manifestoes or statements, and marched around the campus. Venturing into the streets outside the campus gate was to wait until the late 1970s. At SNU, large numbers of students participated in demonstrations in the early 1970s. Students would scrum[52] together, circle around the campus a few times, and then advance towards the point where the riot police waited. They would exchange tear gas and rocks, after which the students headed back to campus, where female students waited with buckets of water to wash the tear gas off their faces.[53]

Prior to Park Chung Hee's declaration of Yushin in 1972, student protest was limited to major universities located in Seoul such as SNU, Korea University, and Yonsei University, as well as some of the major provincial universities such as Chŏnnam University. Given that elite universities tended to have long-standing traditions of well-established circles and that protest organizers were mostly circle members, it is not surprising that elite universities dominated the student movement in the early 1970s.

The romantic aura that is generally associated with the 1970s student movement in South Korea was brief and confined to the pre-1975 era; that is, before the declaration of Emergency Declaration Number Nine in 1975. Before 1975, the student movement mainly consisted of participating in campus demonstrations and circles, requiring only a sense of justice and youthful ardor. Students and society at large considered participation in a campus demonstration as a natural phenomenon, almost a required course in the humanities. It was not unusual to find students playing cards between demonstrations. The campus demonstrations were not ritualized in the sense of having repertoires, as in the case of the 1980s. Before

1975 there were no particular "movement songs," essential to the repertoire of the student movement in the 1980s; the protesting students sang a mixture of folk songs, *pponggjak*,[54] and pop songs, with no apparent tension or irony. There was a sense of humor in the student protest as well. One slogan during this time read, "The United States should supply Kleenex instead of tear gas."[55]

The "era of Emergency Number Nine," 1975–79

With the promulgation of the Emergency Measure Number Nine in 1975, however, the romantic era of the student movement came to an end, and what South Korean sociologist Cho Hŭi-yŏn called the "era of determination" arrived.[56] The Yushin Constitution of 1972 had effectively removed any remnants of democracy in South Korea, but it was the issuance of the emergency measures that truly inaugurated the culture of terror in university campuses. From January 1974 to March 1975, a total of nine emergency measures were issued. They made it illegal to criticize the Yushin constitution (Number Two and Three), made it illegal to join a specific organization deemed anti-state (Number Four), and made it possible for the military to occupy universities (Number Seven).[57] The most severe and sweeping of all was the infamous Emergency Decree Number Nine. Spurred by the fall of Saigon and announced in the midst of Park's "national security offensive,"[58] Emergency Measure Number Nine prohibited "any criticism of the constitution, any political activity by students, or any public presentation or statement describing or discussing any act which might violate the decree." As Hart-Landsberg observed, "given the scope of Emergency Decree 9, Park had no need for further decrees."[59] Emergency Decree Number Nine was indeed a declaration of war on the Korean people.[60]

With Emergency Number Nine, the government re-established the National Student Defense Corps (*Hakdo Hogukdan*) which was abolished in the aftermath of the 1960 April 19th Uprising, forcibly dissolved the existing autonomous student organizations, revised the student regulations, making it difficult to reinstate the dismissed students, legalized the occupation of security agents (known as *kigwanwŏn*) and military in the university campus, extended students' military training, curtailed various extracurricular activities, and introduced the system of re-appointment for faculty members, terminating the tenure system.

The Emergency Decrees intruded upon every aspect of students' lives. A play by SNU students was cancelled, for the Ministry of Culture and Information would not issue the necessary permit to stage the play.[61] Ewha Women's University students were forced by the school to perform the May Queen pageant, which they had earlier voted not to, to express their solidarity with the Tongil Textile women workers. In 1979, the Yŏngnam University folklore research team's mask-dance performance landed its main leaders one-year sentences each for violating Emergency Decree Number Nine. A Seoul student's letter to a friend at Pusan University regarding an upcoming demonstration was intercepted by police and the student was sentenced to two years in prison for violating Decree Number Nine. Students who were alleged to have planned a demonstration were forced to submit a letter of withdrawal from school even though the planned demonstration failed to take place; students were threatened for attending certain churches where pastors were known to have progressive leanings. A fourth-year Kungmin University student was stopped and handed over to security agents by the members of the National Student Defense Corps when he tried to distribute pamphlets on campus. The students felt that they were "suffocating" and their campuses being "raped."

Chŏn Sang-in, a student belonging to a class of 1980, thus summed up his and his classmates' experience during the era of Yushin:

> What awaited [us] at the university was the romance of death. The campus was owned by *cchapsae* (plain-clothed security agents). Notions of justice, peace, and patriotism cried silently in streets and one's boarding house. Faced with the glittering knife of Decree Number Nine, the spirit of youth was like an egg hitting the rock. Even friendship was rare and confidential. While the society indulged in revelry by the sudden economic prosperity, the first of its kind since Tangun, people were internally hungry for love and attachment.[62]

In this atmosphere, any gesture of opposition or resistance was indiscriminately punished with imprisonment, dismissal, or suspension from school. Involvement in the movement required "a resolute sense of sacrifice and dedication." The demarcation between the *undongkwŏn* and non-*undongkwŏn* emerged during this time (although the term itself began to be used widely from the 1980s). The number of protesting students decreased but the content of the protest took on a sense of urgency, and underground seminars began to emerge in earnest. Campus demonstrations required careful planning and a soul-searching decision as to who would be ready to go to prison in the event that those involved were arrested. The issue of whether one was ready to go to prison was equally pressing as how to attract fellow students during the brief precious moments before one was dragged away by security agents. It was in this atmosphere that the students resorted to what one observer called "kamikaze tactics": school buildings' fire alarms were pulled; military training sessions were seized for distribution of pamphlets; mask-dance performances were often a prelude to street demonstrations.[63] What was called a "five-minute strategy" allowed for the heavily human-flanked student leader to distribute the pamphlet or spread out the banner shortly before the advancement of security agents or police.[64] Outside university campuses, students also raided movie theaters with pamphlets.[65]

Students' mode of resistance also changed as the state's mode of control and suppression changed. Before 1975, the Park regime's control of resistance was through framing students' protest as a large-scale organizational attempt to overthrow the regime and handing out heavy sentences, thereby "warning" the public about the danger of opposition. This effected a certain public recognition and created larger-than-life public images for the individuals implicated. During the emergency measure era, however, the regime's strategy changed to the concealment of resistance. Emergency Decree Number Nine blockaded any media coverage of dissident activities. Students were driven underground, and they worked in "shadows," nameless and hidden.[66]

In this atmosphere, university campuses were thick with an air of gloom, defeatism, and grim determination. The activism consisted of finding a few like-minded fellow classmates and studying together in underground circles in a secretive and even conspiratorial atmosphere. The simple act of reading certain books was courting danger with possible prison terms. Seemingly innocuous names such as *Utopia* betray the efforts to conceal the nature of these circles. The state of affairs at universities nevertheless attracted the sensitive and socially conscious to the movement. In a widely quoted and celebrated (within the *undongkwŏn* initially and in the larger society later) "Statement of Appeal" (*hangso iyusŏ*),[67] Yu Si-min, a student leader at SNU, writes how within six months of entering the prestigious SNU in 1979 he came to stray from his goal of becoming a judge. His journey from a hopeful and unsuspecting 19-year-old, a model student and a bookworm, to a "problem student" and "violent criminal," epitomized one of the typical ways through which an ordinary student came to be one of the *undongkwŏn* in the late 1970s.

As he was leaving home for Seoul to enter the university, Yu felt on his back the proud and hopeful gaze of his mother standing at the village corner. Upon graduation from university, he was going to become a judge "to pay back my parents who, raising six children, could not afford good food or clothing all their lives, and because I was sure that becoming a judge was not a bad thing."[68] This was not a flight of fancy. A judge is one of the most prestigious and sought-after occupations in South Korea even well into the 1990s. SNU had been a bastion of judges and top bureaucrats. If a student from SNU was on trial, it was entirely possible for everyone involved (the defendant, the defense lawyer, the prosecutor, and the judge) to be SNU graduates.[69] A scholarship student, Yu began his gradual awakening soon after entering the university:

> As the greenery of the spring and acacia flowers seemed to explode against the warmth of the May sun, I saw a female classmate being dragged away by her hair. I desperately tried to wipe the tears that kept on rolling down, the tears from the tear gas that I tasted for the first time. I was watching all this time from the corner of the student hall, where no one could see me, unable to breathe and overcome with fear. Since that day, gradually, things began to have a different meaning for me. I became embarrassed that our monthly expense for room and board was more than what a sixteen-year-old female worker could earn in a month, working over sixty hours or more a week. From time to time, as I drank beer with friends or had a date with a pretty girl, I would be suddenly struck by the pang of conscience as if I was caught doing something wrong. Perhaps these were all symptoms that I was to be a "delinquent" student (*munje haksaeng*). And that very winter, as I watched my respected *sŏnbae* coming out of the "sacred court" as "criminals," I finally erased in my head, after much agony, the image of myself as a judge sitting on the bench with dignity and authority.[70]

Elected in his sophomore year as a representative of his department, which made Yu an official troublemaker from the school's point of view, he started throwing stones in campus demonstrations. During the brief moment of breathing space called the Spring of Seoul in May 1980 (following the assassination of Park Chung Hee in the previous year), Yu plunged himself into reviving autonomous student organizations and was arrested on May 17th in the wave of arrests that followed the Kwangju Uprising. He was soon forcibly conscripted into the army: "As I was getting my hair cut in a unknown village the night before I was to enter the army, I realized that the fact that I was still alive was no longer a blessing but an insult." His father died of a shock while he was in the army.[71]

After his three-year stint in the army, Yu returned to the university in May 1984, and in August, he became the president of the "Committee of Reinstated Students." He was arrested again within two weeks because of the "fake student" (*p'ŭrakch'i*) incident,[72] dismissed from school, and was sent to prison for a year and a half. As he started his prison term, his neighbors collected money to send to him – he had been known as a filial son, having helped his mother run the family store throughout high school.

Although Yu did not state this in his Statement of Appeal, it was most likely that he was first introduced to an underground circle upon entering the university, that the *sŏnbae* whom he watched in the courtroom probably belonged to the same circle, and that he had shared with his circle members the sudden attacks of conscience that he felt during a date. The informal institutions of the student movement were operating in full gear, even as the harsh conditions outside pushed them deep underground. It is Yu's class and its immediate predecessors, the generation of Emergency Number Nine, who paved the way for what was to come in the 1980s in the larger democratization movement.

The "era of liberalization," 1984–88

The death of Park Chung Hee in 1979 meant the end of the Yushin era and all of its absurdities and political terror.[73] If the Yushin period was the "Frozen Republic," the new era was the "Spring of Seoul." The students relished their sense of relief by openly calling the dead dictator "rogue" and "scoundrel."[74] The end of the authoritarian regime also opened a floodgate of democratic yearnings in all sectors of the society, from miners to factory workers to university students. The students also greeted the Spring of Seoul with an exuberant display of energy, enthusiasm, and hopefulness. An array of academic and cultural activities sprang forth, from the exhilarating *madang-gŭk* (mask-dance drama) performances, to wall newspapers (*taejabo*), and circle activities.[75]

All the euphoria generated from the newly found freedom and the hopes for immediate democratization were met with the Kwangju People's Uprising, as I discuss elsewhere.[76] In the aftermath of Kwangju, most student leaders were in hiding or in jail, or in some cases in the infamous purification camps. The still surviving few clandestine circles sustained themselves by circulating crudely mimeographed underground newsletters or foreign journal articles with the censor's marker obscuring half of their contents.

Student activism revived with a series of so-called "Campus Autonomy" measures in December 1983 (which became effective mostly in 1985), which fostered what later came to be called the "renaissance" of the student movement. As a result of these measures, the once-menacing presence of *kigwanwŏn* disappeared, the dismissed students and professors returned to the campus, the state-controlled National Student Defense Corps was dissolved, and the effort to revive the autonomous student organizations spread like wildfire. With the revival of autonomous student organizations, nationwide university organizations such as the National Students' Alliance in April 1985 became possible.

More significantly, the student movement's locus of activism moved from underground cells to *hakhoe* (students' academic-oriented groups affiliated with departments). What was once the domain of the underground circle comprising a small number of like-minded people became open, legitimate, and public. Organized at the divisional and the departmental levels, the open and public nature of *hakhoe* also generated a tremendous outpouring of academic circles, publications, and seminars. In the post-liberalization period, "every student became a movement activist," as one journalist commented.[77] In April 1983, Yun Kil-jung, son of the then chair of the National Assembly, headed a demonstration at SNU. In 1984, when SNU student leaders initiated boycotting exams, more than half of the student body participated.[78] When the student government president at Korea University paraded in the campus dressed in traditional Korean clothing with the slogan "Whatever kind of oppression, let's destroy it and obtain democracy," the quadrangle of the campus was filled with 3,000 cheering students.[79]

The songs favored by the students also reflected these changes. In the beginning of the 1980s, march songs, short and mostly in a minor key, were popular. Most were about "death" and "sacrifice"; comrades and friends have gone, people have fallen, and the ground was soaked with blood. Gradually, Kwangju and its failure were overcome in the songs emerging from the mid-1980s. From 1985, melodic and lyrical songs became popular. If marching songs were appropriate for demonstrations and rallies, lyrical songs indicated that the student movement's focus had moved from rallies and demonstrations to the everyday lives of students.[80] The widespread popularity of these songs was also due to university singing groups, which began to emerge in 1984 and which constituted an active part of the student movement throughout the 1980s.[81]

In sum, the liberalization policy brought several significant changes to the landscape of the student movement. First, the student movement became popularized, no longer dominated by the elite (such as SNU, Yonsei, or Korea University) or by the traditionally known as "movement-prone" universities (such as Chŏnnam University in Kwangju). Nationwide organizations mobilized the students, cutting across region, school prestige, and gender. Second, the quantitative expansion of the student movement brought cultural changes within it. The secretive and conspiratorial culture of the 1970s and early 1980s in which circle members and leaders were pre-selected and groomed gave way to open and more democratic ways. The movement was not, and could not be, monopolized by a few selective or courageous students. Anyone could join a circle without the introduction of a *sŏnbae* or a classmate. There was also a dazzling array of circle activities to choose from, from traditional four-instrument groups (*p'ungmul*) to "*minjung* comic clubs." This is not to suggest, however, that joining the movement required less determination on the part of students. Until the early 1990s, being an *undongkwŏn* meant facing the possibility of expulsion from school, going to jail, becoming a fugitive, and, for male students, forced induction into the army.

Third, women students became increasingly active in the student movement. In the case of the 1984 occupation of the ruling party's headquarters, for example, 57 of the 264 participants were women. In the case of the 1985 occupation of the United States Information Services in Seoul, 20 of the 73 occupying students were women. A newsjournal article estimated in 1985 that between 20 percent and 30 percent of protestors in co-ed universities were women.[82] In 1985, women accounted for 26 percent (22,000) of university students dismissed for political activities.[83]

Fourth, the student movement as a whole became more ideologically oriented on the one hand, and became more factional and divisive on the other; in fact, these two tendencies were mutually reinforcing. The mid-1980s witnessed a great wave of ideological debates within the larger *minjung* movement, and the movement as a whole was divided into two ideological camps, between the group seeking to emulate North Korea's *chuch'e* ("self-reliance") style revolution and the group advocating an orthodox Marxist-Leninist revolution. Various groups came together and fell apart along the "Great Divide." Some of the most regrettable aspects of the student movement also came from this ideological division. Opposing groups thwarted other groups' public gatherings. Physical assault was not uncommon during the brief period between 1985 and 1986, and even the suicides of students were criticized by an opposing group as an "easy way out of the ideological struggle."[84]

Minjung as a metanarrative

If *undongkwŏn* remained marginal in the society at large, it had a privileged and even hegemonic position in a relatively freer university environment from the mid to late 1980s. From around 1982, campus activities led by *undongkwŏn* students were mostly movement-oriented, with emphasis on *minjoksŏng* (nationalistic orientedness), *undongsŏng* (the movement orientedness), and *kŏnjŏnham* (wholesomeness). The once popular "*ssangssang p'ati*" (couples party) and rock concerts disappeared in most university festivals, as the *undongkwŏn* sometimes took on the role of police, trying to get rid of "degenerative" elements in university life.[85] Short skirts for female students were considered too Western and decadent, and playing video games was looked down upon.

Like any emancipatory project, *undongkwŏn*'s effort to construct a new democratic space also established a parallel "new norms and hierarchies." The new order disdained and suppressed what was considered the holdovers from the previously held (capitalistic) worldview, while privileging what was considered *minjung*-orientedness. *Undongkwŏn* students strove to assimilate into the "pure, healthy," and overall "superior" *minjung* culture, and to shed "capitalistic" and bourgeois tendencies, in terms of language, clothing, food, and everyday habits.

"To become like *minjung* unconditionally" (*mujokkŏn minjung kach'i*) was the motto under which *undongkwŏn* attempted to live.[86] They encouraged what they thought were *minjung* qualities such as honesty, simplicity, and ceaseless participation in productive activities. One's self-identity became closely linked with the demands of the movement, and one's life and personality were frequently expressed as "bourgeois-like" (*pijijŏk*), "petit-bourgeois-like" (*p'ŭt'ijŏk*), and "proletariat-like" (*p'it'ijŏk*).[87]

To call someone bourgeois was a tremendous affront. Han Chi-su recollected: "We all unnaturally imitated the life of the poor; we had elevated the poor to the purest symbol of highest morality and there was tremendous pressure to follow them."[88] There was also strong resistance to what was perceived to be "Western." Traditional Korean folk songs and movement songs were preferred over popular rock songs or *ppongjjak*. Learning or giving too much attention to English was looked down upon.[89]

As a "counterpublic sphere," *undongkwŏn* aspired for truth and emancipation. In efforts to construct an alternative democratic space, students tapped into the past, reinventing and reworking the traditional folk culture. By no means unique – students in Paris in 1968 self-consciously acted in the tradition of past revolution – we see that in creating an alternative vision involved mobilizing moral and cultural resources. Students' efforts brought previously unpublic issues into the public domain, especially with their distinctive form of student–labor alliance. At the same time, the visions of the alternative public sphere were fraught with tensions and contradictions. The shared visions, languages, and codes that contested the hegemonic state-licensed worldviews also imposed their own hierarchy of worldviews and value systems.

Epilogue

By the mid-1990s, the South Korean student movement as it was known in the 1980s had become a thing of the past. With the gradual democratic transition and the collapse of the Soviet Union and East European communist countries occurring since the 1990s, the students no longer could or did claim themselves as uniquely endowed with a historical mandate to be a voice of the people or a true representative of the *minjung*. The "civil society" debate which burst on the South Korean intellectual scene from the 1990s[90] seemed to have effectively declared that the South Korean society was no longer susceptible to the kind of "apocalyptic, Jacobin vision of revolution," of which the student movement was to be the vanguard.

The demise of the student movement was accompanied by a palpable diminishment of the intellectual's privileged status as "moral identity, collective intelligence, historical agency, and cultural force."[91] The dominant mode of intellectuals' social participation also changed in the 1990s from "political" to "cultural." The 1980s concern for "theory, praxis, and politics" among intellectuals was replaced with the 1990s celebration of "sensitivity, spontaneity, and consumption." Instead of "arguments and heroic stands" of intellectuals exemplifying the notion of "*chi haeng il ch'i*" (correspondence between knowledge and conduct), now in demand are originality of ideas and the ability to digest imported theories. In place of the political activism of the 1980s, popular culture is regarded as a key domain of resistance, with the emerging category of "cultural critic" elevated to the position of "culture guerrilla."[92]

Those who led the student movement in the 1980s, known as the "386 generation" (coined in the 1990s, this term refers to those who were in their thirties at the time, entered university in the 1980s, and were born in the 1960s), presently occupy important positions in all aspects of public life, from politics to academia to the film industry. The 386 generation is an especially conspicuous political presence: in the general election of April 2004, the previously minor Uri Party won 162 seats in the National Assembly compared with its past 49 seats. A large number of the elected were 386 generation, and at least ten are former presidents and officers of the nationwide organization that has led the student movement since 1987, *Chondaehyŏp* (National Committee of University Student Representatives). The Democratic Labor Party, whose support base is mainly workers and farmers, has emerged as the third largest party in the National Assembly, and most of its representatives are also 386 generation with years of factory work behind them.[93]

Many 386 generation members in the National Assembly also belong to the conservative Grand National Party (*Hannara*), whose leaders, if not the majority of its members, would have been obvious protest targets in the 1980s. A few have found the present South Korean capitalistic system to be sufficiently reformed and have publicly embraced it as a way to bring further equality in South Korean society and in the world. A few have even declared themselves "New Rightists," advocating Thatcher-style leadership in the party. As neoliberalism has become the key economic policy of the Kim Dae Jung and Roh Moo-hyun governments, many of the 386 generation members of the ruling party have succumbed to the logic of neoliberalism. These governments' mantle of higher moral authority, relative to previous regimes, helped vindicate their embrace of neoliberalism.[94]

But *undongkwŏn* individuals by and large profess their continued commitment to progressive agendas, although it is not always clear what this means, given their ever-shifting allegiances and the constantly varying political circumstances. In this chapter, I hope to not only historicize the conditions of the student movement's emergence as a political and social force but also to generate historical praxis. The purpose is not to recuperate the fallen bygone hero, but to give its history the capacity to enable individuals and society "to experience history in an active way, to orient themselves individually and collectively in the present";[95] it is to enable individuals to reconceptualize social relations in an empowering and participatory way.

Notes

1 Robert E. Bedeski, *The Transformation of South Korea* (London: Routledge, 1994), 176.
2 "Tŭkjip: onŭrŭi taehaksaeng, muŏsŭl saengkak hana [Special issue: Today's students, what are they thinking]," *Wŏlgan Chung'ang* (May 1988), 356.
3 See Kyŏngnamdae kŭkdong munje yŏnguso, *Han'guk chŏngch'i, sahoe ŭi hŭrŭm* [New currents in Korean politics and society] (Seoul: Nanam, 1993); Yu P'al-mu and Kim Ho-gi, eds., *Simin sahoewa simin undong* [Civil society and citizens' movements] (Seoul: Hanul, 1995).
4 Vladimir Tismaneanu, *The Crisis of Marxist Ideology in Eastern Europe: The Poverty of Utopia* (London: Routledge, 1988).
5 See Namhee Lee, "Representing the Worker: Worker–Intellectual Alliance of the 1980s in South Korea," *The Journal of Asian Studies* 64:4 (November 2005).
6 Kim Chin-myŏng, "Ônŏ ŭimi ch'egye ŭi pŭnsŏk ŭl t'onghae pon taehaksaeng chŏhang munhwa" [Resistance culture of university students analyzed through language meaning system], *Hyŏn'sang kwa Insik* 12:2 (Summer 1988), 120–1.
7 Jurgen Habermas, *The Structural Transformation of the Public Sphere* (Cambridge, MA: MIT Press, 1989). For a critical assessment of Habermas' notion of public sphere see, among others, Jean Cohen and Andrew Arato, *Civil Society and Political Theory* (Cambridge, MA: MIT Press, 1992); Craig Calhoun, ed., *Habermas and the Public Sphere* (Cambridge, MA: MIT Press, 1996). On the absence of gender in his analyses see, Nancy Fraser, "What's Critical About Critical Theory? The Case of Habermas and Gender," in Seyla Benhabib and Drucilla Cornell, eds., *Feminism as Critique* (Minneapolis, MN: University of Minnesota Press, 1987), 31–55.
8 Fraser, "Rethinking the Public Space," in Calhoun, *Habermas and the Public Sphere*, 123.
9 Ibid.
10 See Cohen and Arato, *Civil Society and Political Theory*, 29–82.
11 Han'guk chŏngch'i, sahoe ŭi hŭrŭm, 48.
12 Calhoun, "Introduction," in Calhoun, *Habermas and the Public Sphere*, 2.
13 See Chapter 1 in this volume.
14 Elizabeth J. Perry, "Casting a Chinese 'Democracy' Movement: The Roles of Students, Workers, and Entrepreneurs," in Jeffrey N. Wasserstrom and Elizabeth J. Perry, eds., *Popular Protest and Political Culture in Modern China* (Boulder, CO: Westview Press, 1992), 154.
15 Ibid. 163.
16 See, among others, Hagen Koo, ed., *State and Society in Contemporary Korea* (Ithaca, NY: Cornell University Press, 1993); Martin Hart-Landsberg, *The Rush to Development: Economic Change and Political Struggle in South Korea* (New York: Monthly Review Press, 1993); George E. Ogle, *South Korea: Dissent Within the Economic Miracle* (Atlantic Highlands, NJ: Zed Books, 1990).
17 A review of essays written in popular magazines between 1954 and 1978 on the role of intellectuals found that 46 percent viewed the primary duty of intellectuals as criticizing government policies or enlightening people, whereas 20 percent expressed the duty as providing state with necessary knowledge. Ho-Ill Lee, "Confucianism and the Market in a Post-Confucian Society: Intellectual Radicalism, Destruction of Cultural Environment and Resistance in South Korea" (PhD Dissertation, University of Oregon, 1995), 45–74.
18 On Chŏn T'ae-il, see Cho Yŏng-rae, *A Single Spark: The Biography of Chun Tae-il*, trans. Chŏn Sun-ok (Seoul: Tolbegae, 2003); Chang Soo Kim, "Marginalization, Development and the Korean Workers' Movement," *AMPO Japan–Asia Quarterly Review* (1977), 20–39; Kim Se-jin was a student at SNU who also immolated himself

in 1986 protesting university students' compulsory military training. Yi Han-yŏl died after being hit by a tear gas canister during the "June Struggle" of 1987.

19 See, for example, Perry, "Casting a Chinese 'Democracy' Movement," 152.

20 In America, the New Left criticized the gap between liberal democracy and social reality, the discrimination against African Americans, the existence of poverty, and American foreign policy, among others. Cyrill Levitt, "The New Left, The New Class and Socialism," *Higher Education* 8 (November 1979), 643–5.

21 Perry, "Casting a Chinese 'Democracy' Movement," 152.

22 Levitt, "The New Left, The New Class and Socialism," 647.

23 See Byeong-chul Park, "Motivational Dynamics of Student Movement Participation" (PhD Dissertation, Syracuse University, 1995).

24 Pak Tong, interview by author, February 12–13, 1993. On the other hand, the absence of *sŏnbae* for those who graduated from newly established high schools allowed them to pursue their activities without much ideological guidance or influence from *sŏnbae*. Sim Sang-jŏng, interview by author, August 3, 2005.

25 Kim Chong-min, interview by author, May 26, 1993.

26 I am indebted to Prof. Kyeong-Hee Choi for pointing out the reciprocal nature of the *sŏnbae–hubae* relationship.

27 Ch'oe In-ch'ŏl, interview by author, February 14, 1993.

28 Ibid.

29 Kim Ŭn-suk, *Pult'anŭn miguk: pumibang ŭi chinsil* [Burning America: The truth of the Pusan USIS arson] (Seoul: Agap'e, 1987), 87–8.

30 "Kongsojang, sowi Namjosŏn Minjok Haebang Chŏnsŏn sakkŏn: Sin Hyang-sik we 18 myŏng" [Written arraignment: The so-called South Korean Liberation Front Incident; Sin Hyang-sik and eighteen individuals], Typescript (December 26, 1979).

31 In a survey entitled "On the Seoul National University Students' Conscientization" conducted in 1986, university students were asked to name the source that influenced them most in their conscientization process; 43.5 percent replied printed materials, whereas 2.6 percent mentioned professors, 26.8 percent fellow students, and 2.2 percent mass media. "Kyosu dŭrŭi komin" [Dilemma of professors], *Wŏlgan Chosŏn* (June 1987), 244.

32 Chŏng Ch'ŏl-yŏng, interview by author, January 14, 1993.

33 It was not until October 1987 that the Ministry of Culture and Information finally relinquished its "right" to examine whether or not a given publication was legal, thereby formally ending the years of peekaboo with students and intellectuals.

34 Kim Su-kyŏng, interview by author, April 2, 1993.

35 Pak Tong, interview.

36 Kim Su-kyŏng, interview.

37 Won-shik Choi, "Rethinking Korean Literary Modernity," *Korea Journal* 35:2 (Winter 1995), 8.

38 Quoted in Chŏng Kwa-ri, "Pŏlgŏsung'i chisikin – han'guk chisikinŭi wisang: ŏjewa onŭl" [Naked intellectual – The state of the Korean intellectual: Yesterday and today], *Munhak kwa sahoe* 28 (Winter 1994), 1421.

39 Chŏng Ch'ŏl-yŏng, interview.

40 In early 1982, the government allowed, for the first time, publications on Marxism and its criticisms, ostensibly to overcome Marxism by making it possible to criticize it. In May 1985, however, the government reversed its previous policy by banning again hundreds of books and pamphlets. A total of 313 titles were banned between May 1 and 10, 1985. By 1987, the number of banned titles reached almost 1,100. For more discussion on the banned literature see Asia Watch, *Human Rights in Korea* (New York: Asia Watch Committee, 1986), 294–301.

41 Lee, "Confucianism and the Market in a Post-Confucian Society," 118–20.

42 The Shinjin-hoe was small and exclusive. An invitation to a prospective member to join the group was made only after a thorough examination of his family background,

school records, ideological orientation, and upon the unanimous consent of existing members. Sung-joo Han, *Failure of Democracy in South Korea* (Berkeley, CA: University of California Press, 1974), 198–9.

43 The state-directed research institutes specializing in monitoring student groups argued for a close connection between underground circles and student protests. According to an internal publication of the "Naewae Research Institute on Policy" on the recent campus protest in 1981, for example, the authors found that the "leaders of the protests have close connections, directly or indirectly, with some left-leaning campus circles whose purposes are to inspire negative and revolutionary thoughts among members." They also pointed to the increasing number of underground pamphlets as a part of the cause for the increased campus unrest. "An analysis of the backgrounds and characteristics of the college students' leftistic movements" [summary in English], *Naewae nonpy'ŏng* 4:1 (1982), 245.

44 *Chung'ang Ilbo*, December 16, 1986.

45 Hŏ In-hoe, interview by author, February 19, 1993.

46 Kim Chong-min, interview.

47 In a 1981 survey on university life conducted in 24 universities in South Korea, for example, 55.3 percent of the students expressed dissatisfaction and 18.6 percent expressed some sort of satisfaction. In terms of education, the majority of students cited poor quality of professors and lectures as reasons for their dissatisfaction, which they believed were too removed from the reality of South Korea. The second most cited reason was a lack of autonomy for students. See Ko Yŏng-bok, "Han'guk taehaksaengŭi uisik kwa inyŏm" [Consciousness and ideology of Korean university students], in *Han'guk sahoe ŭi kujo wa insik* [The structure and understanding of the Korean society] (Seoul: Sahoe munje yŏn'guso, 1991), 300–1.

48 South Korean middle and high school students wore uniforms and short hair until 1983, a practice bequeathed from the colonial period.

49 For the next three paragraphs and quotes, I have relied on Kim Pyŏng-gon ch'umo saŏp'hoe chunbi'wiwŏnhoe, ed., *Ko Kim Pyŏng-gon hoegomunjip: "Yŏnggwang imnida"* [In memory of the late Kim Pyŏng-gon: "I am Honored"] (Seoul: Kŏrŭm, 1992), 46–171.

50 Under the Conscription Law of 1949, all South Korean males, except for those considered "physically or socially undesirable" for military service, were required to serve in the military for three years. Protesting male students faced a forcible draft into the army, sometimes without a prior notification. Once conscripted, they were subjected to a "re-education" program and were forced to make detailed reports of their friends' and classmates' activities. Seven students died in 1986 while undergoing this program. See *Korea Communiqué* (May 1986), 5–6.

51 "Che ilsim sosong kirok: Minju Ch'ŏngnyŏn Haksaeng Yŏnmaeng" [The record of the first trial: The case of the "National Democratic Youth and Student Federation"], Typescript, n.d.

52 This term originated from rugby, but it was popularly used in South Korea to refer to the formation of line-up during a demonstration. Students would link arms together or put their arms on the next person's shoulder, making a chain-like line. Each line would consist of several students.

53 Participants of circle activities, as well as demonstrations, were mostly men in the 1970s. In the 1980s, as the movement became more widespread, women began to take more active roles in the movement. Female students at women's universities tended to be more active than those at co-ed universities, and leaders of the student movement in co-ed universities were mostly men until the mid-1980s.

54 *Ppongjjak* is "an onomatopoeic Korean term used to describe a common genre of pop music characterized by 4/2 beat and a highly repetitive structure." It is similar to *enka*, a Japanese song genre with a populist appeal, which Marilyn Ivy describes as the following: "[E]nka remains the outdated sonic preserve of the masses – downtrodden

office workers, factory laborers, farmers. Much like country and western music (to which it is often compared), enka encompasses a universe of sentiment outside the bounds of cosmopolitan pretensions." Ivy, *Discourses of the Vanishing: Modernity, Phantasm, Japan* (Chicago: University of Chicago Press, 1995), 225. *Ppongjjak*'s mass appeal was as extensive in South Korea, including among university students. From around the mid-1980s, however, *undongkwŏn* students began to shun *ppongjjak* as an imported genre and un-*minjung*-like. On relationship between *ppongjjak* and folksongs, see Ch'ang-Nam Kim, "The Spirit of Folksongs and Realism in Song," *Korea Journal* 27:3 (March 1987), 33–6.

55   Quoted in Yi Yŏng-mi, "Norae ŭi sahoesa" [Social history of songs], unpublished paper delivered at a public lecture, Seoul, South Korea (April 21, 1993).

56   Cho Hŭi-yŏn, "Minch'ŏng sidae, 'kinjo' sidae ŭi hyŏngsŏng kwa chŏngch'i kaehyŏk chŏnmang" [Formation of the eras of the "Democratic Youth League" and the "Emergency Measures" and prospect for political reform], *Yŏksa pip'yŏng* 30 (Fall 1995), 112.

57   Emergencies Number One and Two were issued on January 8, 1974, stipulating that whoever criticized or opposed the Yushin Constitution was subjected to a 15-year prison term. Emergency Number Three was issued under the pretext of stabilizing citizens' lives, providing tax exemption to the low-income. Emergency Number Seven was issued immediately after a particularly large-scale demonstration at Korea University on April 8, 1975; with this decree, the government closed the University. Yi Chae-o, *Haebang hu han'guk haksaeng undongsa* [History of the post-liberation student movement] (Hyŏngsŏngsa, 1984), 276–83.

58   South Korea was gripped with heightened anti-communism after the fall of Saigon in 1975; textbooks of all levels were revised extensively and anti-Communist rallies took place daily, sponsored by both the government and religious groups. See "Kyogwasŏ e 'Yushin' naeyong ppaegiro" [Plan to excise "Yushin" in textbooks], *Sindong'a* (February 1980), 278; "Pan'gong ŭn taehoe esŏ undong ŭro" [Anti-communism, from rallies to social movement], *Sindong'a* (July 1975), 389.

59   Hart-Landsberg, *Rush to Development*, 198.

60   For example, Park Chung Hee declared on July 16, 1974, "What we are faced with today is not merely a situation of semi-war but rather a situation of war." Quoted in Im Hŏn-yŏng, "74-nyŏn munin kanch'ŏpdan sakkŏnŭi silsang" [The reality of the spy case of the Men of Letters in 1974], *Yŏksa pip'yŏng* 11 (Winter 1990), 301.

61   See "Taehaksaeng kwa chonggyogye ŭi temo sat'ae" [Protest by university students and religious groups], *Sindong'a* (November 1974), 217. All of the quotes and references in this paragraph are from KSCF (Korean Student Christian Federation), "70-nyŏndae huban ŭi haksaeng undong," [The student movement of the late 1970s] (KSCF, 1984), 73–168.

62   Chŏn Sang-in, "Nŏdo 58-nyŏn kaettinya? 58-nyŏnsaeng ŭi sahoehak, " [You, too, are born in 1958 and in the Year of the Dog? The sociology of those born in 1958], *Sisa Chŏnŏl* [*Sisa Journal*], February 10 and 17 1993.

63   KSCF, "70-nyŏndae huban ŭi haksaeng undong," 129–32.

64   Sŏ Chung-sŏk, "3-sŏn kaehŏn pandae, minch'ŏnghangnyŏn t'ujaeng, panyusin t'ujaeng" [Opposition to the Constitutional Amendment for a third presidential term, struggle of the National Democratic Youth and Student Federation, and the struggle against Yushin], *Yŏksa pip'yŏng* (Summer 1988, Inaugural issue), 60.

65   See Sin Chun-yŏng, "80-nyŏndae haksaeng undong yasa: 10.26 esŏ murim kkaji" [Unofficial history of the student movement of the 1980s 1: From October 26th to the incident of Murim], *Mal* (February 1990), 171.

66   Cho, "Minch'ŏng sidae, 'kinjo' sidae," 113.

67   Having circulated as a pamphlet for many years, this "Statement" is now available in Chi Sŭng-ho, *Yu Si-min ŭl mannada* [Meeting with Yu Si-min] (Seoul: Puklain, 2005).

68 Quoted in Hwang Ŭi-bong, *80-nyŏndae ŭi haksaeng undong* [The student movement of the 1980s] (Seoul: Yejogak, 1985), 176.

69 For example, 14 of 24 government ministers in 1987 graduated from SNU (eight from Law Department). Most of the vice ministers were also from SNU. "Kungnip Sŏul Taehakgyo rŭl haebuhanda" [Dissecting the Seoul National University], *Wŏlgan Chosŏn* (January 1987), 326.

70 Quoted in Hwang, *80-nyŏndae ŭi haksaeng undong*, 167–8.

71 "Kusok haksaeng kwa kŭ kajokdŭl" [Imprisoned students and their families], *Sindong'a* (November 1985), 352.

72 Ibid. In September 1984, SNU students discovered a number of "fake students" whom they accused of being informants for the security agency. Having been detained for a few days by students, these "fake students" later charged the students with beatings and other abuses. This incident led to the dismissal of all the students involved, police occupation of the campus, and the subsequent SNU students' campus-wide boycott of exams. "Hagwŏn, 'chayulhwa' esŏ 'hagwŏnbŏp kkaji" [From the "Campus Liberalization" to the "Campus Stabilization Law"], *Sindong'a* (September 1985), 258.

73 The death of Park was a particular shock to middle and high school students, whose education was immersed in Yushin ideology. Kwŏn In-suk, who was a sophomore in high school at the time, describes her own reaction as the following: "[Park's death] was also a big shock to me. My middle and high school teachers had consistently praised the Yushin Constitution as the Korean style indigenous democracy, and I'd even told my friends that Park should be the president as long as he lived. I cried as if my own parent had passed away … But when newspapers began to criticize Yushin Constitution that it was for prolonging his rule and that it was achieved through perverted means … I felt like one of the Hitler's Youth Group who was duped … It was hard to swallow the betrayal and anger against adults who had fed lies to the young." "Tanwŏnsŏ" [Petition], in Han'guk kidokkyo kyohoe hyŏbŭihoe inkkwŏn wiwŏnhoe (NCCK), ed., *Uridŭlŭi ttal Kwŏn yang* [Our daughter, Miss Kwŏn] (Seoul: NCCK, 1987), 175.

74 Students freely changed the lyrics of the then popular song, "The person at the time" (Kŭttae kŭsaram). The singer, Sim Su-bong, was present at the scene of Park's assassination, adding poignancy and irony. The students' changed lyrics went: "I think of that rogue when I hear 'Yushin.' He always liked the Emergency Measures ... He got shot in the Kungjŏngdang [Presidential palace] one day … by the most trusted [Kim] Chae-gyu … mumbling 'I'm ok,' he dropped his head, that scoundrel."

75 In the case of Korea University, for example, 80 new circles registered, including the "Folklore Research group," which had been banned in the previous semester. In addition, students' magazines and newspapers were published literally overnight. "Kyŏkdonghanŭn hagwŏnga," [University campuses in turbulence], *Sindong'a* (June, 1980), 248–9.

76 Namhee Lee, "The Making of Minjung: The South Korean Democratization Movement" (Unpublished book manuscript, 2005), Chap. 1.

77 "81-hakbŏn undongkwŏn ch'ulsin ŭi 11-nyŏn dwi," [Eleven years later: what happened to the undongkwŏn who entered university in 1981] *Wŏlgan Chosŏn* [*Monthly Korea*] (August 1992), 238.

78 Ibid., 239.

79 "Kusok haksaeng kwa kŭ kajokdŭl," 341.

80 Yi Yŏng-mi, "Noraero pon 80-nyŏndae haksaeng undong" [The 1980s student movement seen through songs], *Mal* 42 (December 1989), 167.

81 SNU's "Meari" group, for example, was founded in 1977, and has been a part of the student movement at SNU. By the mid-1980s, almost all universities had their own singing groups as a part of the student movement.

82 "Chŏn'ghangnyŏn, sammint'u wa mimunhwawŏn sakkŏn" [The National Students' Alliance, The Three Min Struggle Committee, and the occupation of the USIS], *Sindong'a* (July 1985), 475–6.

83 *Chung'ang Ilbo*, September 4, 1986.

84 Sin Chun-yŏng, "80-nyŏndae haksaeng undong yasa 5: Minmint'u wa chamint'u" [Unofficial history of the 1980s student movement, Part 5: Minmint'u and Chamint'u], *Mal* (July 1990), 180.

85 Ch'oe In-ch'ŏl, interview. "University Festivals" were especially popular since the 1960 April 19th Uprising, as the newly organized autonomous student groups were in charge. Widely regarded as an essence of university experience, its activities included academic symposia, athletic competition, and masquerade procession. From 1975, the National Student Defense Corps became its main organizer in each campus. Rock concerts and "couple party" (*ssangssang p'ati*) were prominent features of these festivals in the 1970s.

86 Han Chi-su, interview by author, February 27, 1993.

87 Kim Chin-myŏng, "Ŏnŏ ŭimi ch'egye ŭi punsŏk ŭl t'onghae pon taehaksaeng chŏhang munhwa" [Resistance culture of university students analyzed through language meaning system], *Hyŏnsang kwa insik* [Phenomenon and epistemology] 12:2 (Summer 1988), 130.

88 Han Chi-su, interview.

89 "81-hakbŏn undongkwŏn ch'ulsin ŭi 11-nyŏn dwi," 242.

90 See Sunhyuk Kim, "Civil Society in South Korea: From Grand Democracy Movements to Petty Interest groups?" *Journal of Northeast Asian Studies* (Summer 1996), 96.

91 Gloria Davies, ed., *Voicing Concerns: Contemporary Chinese Critical Inquiry* (Lanham, MD: Rowman & Littlefield, 2001), 18.

92 Sin Hyŏn-jun, "Sahŏe kwahak ŭi wigi?: Pop'yŏnjŏk sahŏe pyŏnhyŏk ironi chŏngondwen sidae ŭi 'taeanjŏkin' chŏngch'ijŏk silch'ŏn ŭi mosaek" [Crisis of social science? In search of 'alternative' political praxis in an era of the end of the universal social theory], in Hyŏndae Sasang p'yŏnjipbu, ed., *Chisikin rip'ot'ŭ 1* [Report on intellectuals 1] (Minŭmsa, 1998), 11.

93 No Hoe-ch'an and Sim Sang-jŏng, two of the well-known members of the Party, started working in a factory when they were university students.

94 Sim Sang-jŏng, interview with author, August 3, 2005.

95 Rosalind O'Hanlon and David Washbrook, "After Orientalism: Culture, Criticism, and Politics in the Third World," *Comparative Studies in Society and History* 34:1 (January 1992), 153.

6   Women and civil society in South Korea[1]

Seungsook Moon

Introduction

Since the spread of popular protests against authoritarian regimes in Asia and other parts of the world in the 1970s and 1980s, there has been a growing interest in the study of civil society as a vehicle of democratization and a counterweight to the repressive state and the totalizing market (Silliman and Noble 1998; White 1996; Koo 1993; Cohen and Arato 1992; Gold 1990; Keane 1988). However, as recent criticisms of the celebration of civil society as the "third path" to societal democratization point out, such analyses tend to lapse into abstract discussions of relations between the state and civil society, devoid of a specific historical or social context (Fine 1997; Tempest 1997; Blaney and Pasha 1993). This absence also contributes to an inadequate view of civil society as a uniform and homogeneous space without social inequalities and divisions.

Feminist criticism of civil society, countering liberal democratic theory and highlighting this problem of social inequalities, holds that the theoretical and practical exclusion or marginalization of women is constitutive of the development of civil society in the West (Fleming 1995; Pateman 1989). While challenging the presumed homogeneity and neutrality of civil society, this normative feminist criticism tends to downplay differences among women themselves, as well as the contested nature of civil society, because it focuses on the institutional origin of civil society and the principles guiding activities within it. Another strand of feminist approach to civil society attempts to modify this somewhat deterministic critique of androcentric civil society by stressing the multiplicity and heterogeneity of the public sphere (Landes 1995; Fraser 1992; Young 1987). While originating from the historical contexts of Western societies, this line of feminist analysis can serve as a conceptual tool to examine the impact of procedural democratization on women and, conversely, women's ability to shape this process in industrialized Asian societies. South Korea has witnessed the expansion of civil society since the 1980s and its qualitative transformation since the 1990s, especially after the inauguration of a civilian regime in 1993. By focusing on the growth of civil society and the emergence of autonomous women's movements in that context, this chapter intends to explore the following questions: 1) To what extent is the notion of civil society useful to our understanding of democratization in South Korea? 2)

In what ways does a focus on the women's movements in South Korea illuminate limits and possibilities of civil society that we would otherwise overlook?

The first section of this chapter will discuss the trajectory of civil society in post-military rule Korea after the establishment of procedural democracy in 1988. I argue that, while political conditions characterized by military authoritarian rule and national division suppressed the development of civil society in the midst of the emerging capitalist economy, those conditions also generated dissident movements and popular struggle contributing to political democratization. This has allowed not only for the expansion of civil society, but also for its qualitative transformation. The ongoing transformation of civil society is evidenced by the emergence and growth of "citizens' organizations" (*simindanch'e*) since the late 1980s. Crucial to the democratization of Korean society in the past decade or so, this new type of voluntary association is distinguished from old types of voluntary associations in terms of its autonomy from the state and its focus on social change.

The second section of this chapter will examine the androcentric tendency within Korean civil society in light of the aforementioned feminist criticism as articulated by Carole Pateman and Marie Fleming. Their critique enables us to assess the gendered evolution of civil society in Korea against the backdrop of political contexts shifting from military authoritarian rule in the 1970s and 1980s to procedural democracy in the 1990s. I argue that three features have contributed to this androcentric tendency: 1) the Confucian legacy that masculinized the public sphere outside the patriarchal household and mediated individual access to civil society, 2) the pervasiveness of violence in suppressed civil society generated by militant antagonism between civil society and the state, and 3) the reinvention of patriarchal tradition as a way to deal with postcolonial ambivalence toward rapid modernization. These historical and social conditions have discouraged women's participation in expanding civil society at the grassroots level.

The third section of this chapter will discuss the women's movements in the 1990s and 2000s, in order to illuminate both the contested nature of androcentric civil society and its fragility in contemporary Korea. The 1990s witnessed the revitalization of a broad spectrum of autonomous women's associations dealing with diverse issues, in tandem with other citizens' voluntary associations. Formed in 1987 as the umbrella of autonomous women's associations with feminist orientations, the Korean Women's Associations United (KWAU) has been the leading voice of the autonomous women's movements. It has developed collaborative and negotiatory relationships with the democratizing state, which together have promoted gender equality (Moon 2000). This recent development is particularly visible in the state's funding for projects run by various women's organizations and the emphasis of the KWAU on legislation, legal reform, and women's representation in elected offices. On the one hand, the women's movements led by the KWAU reflect multiplicity and heterogeneity within the androcentric civil society. On the other hand, lacking a broad grassroots base, the women's movements have relied heavily on a small number of devoted activists, most of whom were already participating in social movements under authoritarian rule. Although attempts have been made to broaden the base by the KWAU, women's participation in civil society in Korea has been curtailed by its androcentric tendency.

Mapping the trajectory of civil society in post-military rule South Korea

The restoration of procedural democracy allowed for the dramatic expansion of civil society in the Sixth Republic, particularly after the inauguration of Kim Young Sam's civilian administration (1993–97). This change was mirrored in the formation of numerous voluntary organizations aiming at social reform and transformation. In the late 1990s, there were approximately 700 social movement-oriented organizations in South Korea, roughly three-quarters of them created since 1987 (Cho 2000, 291). By 2005, the number of such organizations grew to over 3,000, and they are categorized as "civil society organizations" (siminsahoedanch'e), apart from other voluntary associations based on occupation, hometown, and school affiliations (Citizens' Newspaper 2005). This remarkable expansion of civil society was also manifested in the proliferation of labor unions and the explosion of the labor movement, particularly between 1987 and 1989 (see Chapter 4 in this volume). Their growth signified a departure from suppressed civil society, which had been dominated by "administered mass organizations" (AMOs), referring to "mass-based civilian organizations created by regimes to implement policies" (Kasza 1995, 7). Modeled after the modern conscript army, the AMOs were initially created by the political elites of Nazi Germany and Imperial Japan in the 1930s.[2] During the latter decades of colonial rule, Japan transplanted the AMOs to Korea as a mechanism to control the masses of colonized Koreans, organizing them on the basis of place of residence, gender, age, workplace, or industry. After liberation, the U.S. Army Military Government in Korea (1945–48) continued to exploit the various AMOs for the same purpose. Subsequent postcolonial regimes in Korea adopted this established practice to keep civil society in check.

The quantitative expansion of civil society has been accompanied by its qualitative transformation. There are three new noteworthy trends. First, the antagonistic and violent relationship between civil society and the state has been replaced by the emergence of collaboration, as well as checks and balances, between the two. This is not to obscure the fact that the state continued to deploy repressive measures to cope with intense, often wild-cat, strikes precipitated by the absence of any tradition of labor–management dialogue.[3] Yet, the legitimacy of the ruling regimes has led to a decline in militant anti-regime protests that were the core aspect of suppressed civil society in the pre-1988 period. This shift can be observed in the decline, on the one hand, of radical underground organizations advocating the revolutionary overthrow of the ruling regime and capitalist society, and, on the other hand, the rise of legal organizations pursuing the improvement in quality of life by means of institutional reform and continuous education of the public on various social issues. Social movement organizations of this new type have applied for government funds for their projects since 2000.[4] They have also collaborated with the state, especially since the inauguration of Kim Dae Jung's administration (1998–2002), the first government led by a former political dissident (Cho 2000, 284–6).[5]

However, Korean civil society in the 1990s and 2000s remains fragile in that the new type of social movement oriented organization tends to lack a strong grassroots base in its dues-paying membership. With a few exceptions, such organizations have only a few hundred members each – or even fewer – and a small number of activist individuals tend to have multiple memberships across different organizations. Exceptional organizations with larger membership include the Korean Federation for Environmental Movements with approximately 52,000 members, the People's Solidarity for Participatory Democracy with roughly 13,500 members (*Tomorrow Newspaper*, January 17, 2005), and the Citizens' Coalition for Economic Justice with roughly 35,000 members (*Chungang Daily*, November 25, 2003). The combined membership of all the social movement organizations in Korea has been estimated at 1.5 million, but fewer than half of these are active dues-paying members (Cho 2000, 294). This suggests that less than 2 percent of the entire population actually participate in the social movement organizations, although tens of thousands of others may be drawn into actions or campaigns spearheaded by these organizations. Active members of these organizations are predominantly educated members of the middle class and/or people who were previously involved in dissident activism and labor movements during the period of authoritarian rule (ibid., 256). This overall profile of membership suggests that, despite its dramatic growth and qualitative transformation, civil society in Korea remains confined to a relatively small segment of the public sphere.

The second characteristic of Korean civil society in the 1990s involves the diversity of issues and concerns addressed by new citizens' organizations. These organizations specialize in a broad spectrum of issues, ranging from the human rights of women, workers, rural farmers, and sexual minorities, to peace and unification, the environment, and anti-nuclearism. While these organizations each focus on specific issues, they often collaborate with one another by forming coalitions around such urgent social issues as national health insurance, a more equitable distribution of wealth, and family law reform. In contrast, heavily influenced by Marxism, pre-1988 organizations tended to focus on issues of labor exploitation and dictatorship (H. Yi 1997, ch. 6).

Finally, a few leading associations among the new type of social movement organization have adopted the market model for their routine operations. In other words, such organizations have begun to choose social movement issues and then rely on public relations to disseminate their positions and recruit dues-paying members, who provide financial support for organizations working on issues that matter to them. This mode of operation inevitably entails the professionalization of social movement organizations. For instance, the Citizens' Coalition for Economic Justice, founded in 1989, had over 70 permanent staff in its central office in the Seoul area and over 50 permanent staff in its provincial branches, working on specific committees (Cho 2000, 264). The People's Solidarity for

Participatory Democracy, which was founded in 1994, had over 60 regular staff in 2005.[6] This rationalized organizational structure differs significantly from that of dissident organizations in the pre-1988 period, which were characterized by members' direct participation in protests and other resistant activities based on ideological commitment, emotional ties, and individual sacrifice for a collective cause (ibid., 219).

In the context of escalating popular protests against the military regime, autonomous and "progressive" women's associations concerned with social change emerged. In 1983, when Chun Doo Whan's regime began to loosen up its repression of voluntary associations (KWAU 1990, 59), the Women's Equal Friends Society (*yŏsŏng p'yŏnguhoe*) was formed to establish a grassroots women's movement reaching beyond a handful of educated elite women. In the same year, the Women's Hotline (*yŏsŏngŭi chŏnhwa*) was formed to deal with the urgent problem of violence against women. In February 1987, 21 women's organizations with a feminist orientation came together under the Korean Women's Associations United (*yŏsŏng tanch'e yŏnhap*). While the number of the KWAU's member organizations has fluctuated somewhat over time, it has a total of 28 member organizations in 2005.[7] Their conscious distance from and oppositional stance toward the repressive state initially set them apart from other pre-existing or emerging women's organizations.

While the gap between these different types of women's organizations narrowed significantly throughout the 1990s, the KWAU initially occupied a position in direct opposition to that of women's AMOs – for instance, the New Village Women's Association (*saemaŭl punyŏhoe*), the Central Association of Housewives' Classes (*chŏn'guk chubukyosil chung'anghoe*), and the Federation of Housewives' Clubs (*chubu k'ŭrop yŏnhaphoe*).[8] In contrast to the KWAU, these organizations boasted mass membership, numbering approximately 250,000 to 2,000,000 members (Ministry of Political Affairs 1997: 240–5; KWDI 1991: 231–2). They often served as an instrument to implement state policies concerning population control and economic development and a way to propagate state ideologies concerning national security, anticommunism, and nationalism.

Numerous women's organizations occupied positions in between the autonomous KWAU and the women's AMOs. A majority of these intermediate organizations were occupational or religious associations. The two major organizations in these categories are the Korean Women's Associations Council (*yŏsŏng tanch'e hyŏbŭihoe*) and the Korean Young Women's Christian Association (YWCA). Founded in 1959, the KWAC is the oldest umbrella organization of professional and occupational associations. It started a family law reform movement in the mid-1970s and worked to eliminate discriminatory retirement practices against women and to promote consumer protection and women's political participation. Formed in 1922, the oldest and largest women's association, the YWCA has been involved in diverse issues, ranging from factory workers' rights and the reduction of foreign debts to women's unemployment (Citizens' Newspaper, June 8, 2005). Apparently apolitical and generally conservative under authoritarian regimes for decades, however, most of these middle organizations lacked a critical feminist consciousness or a concern for social change in their activities. This orientation can be observed in their activities and goals, which have been confined primarily to charity work, consumer protection, job training in feminized occupations, the promotion of friendship among members, and the offering of lectures and classes on domesticity for housewives and brides-to-be. While these activities can be considered expressions of women's concerns, and may serve their "practical gender interests," to use Maxine Molyneux's term (1985), they did not question socially prescribed feminine roles based on the normative identity of the middle-class housewife, or an authoritarian politics that excluded women as citizens. Neither did they come to join in anti-dictatorship movements.

The KWAU, in contrast, has played a central role in articulating the common goal of gender equality, as well as the specific needs and interests of such diverse groups of women as factory workers, clerical workers, urban housewives, rural women, and the urban poor (Yi 1991; Sin 1995). Its organizational structure has also differed from that of other existing women's organizations run by a few renowned "women leaders" with high visibility. While faced with the problem of small membership, the KWAU has tried to maintain a democratic structure without such hierarchical leadership (Yi 1998, 38; Yi 1996, ch. 8; Yi 1991). In a nutshell, the existence of the KWAU is emblematic of women's entry into growing civil society. The following discussion will address yet another way in which access to participation in civil society is limited by the historical and social conditions that have masculinized civil society in Korea.

Civil society in post-military rule in Korea: feminist criticism

The transformation of civil society in Korea from the public sphere, characterized by violent clashes between the state and anti-regime forces, into a sphere of emergent collaboration between the state and various social groups, does not mean that gendered social actors have equal access to it. To analyze the ways in which Korean civil society is androcentric against the backdrop of shifting political contexts, it is useful to draw upon feminist criticism of civil society in the West as articulated by Pateman and Fleming. Their criticism highlights the institutional origin of the coexistence of patriarchy and civil society.

Pateman, one of the earliest critics of androcentric civil society, focuses on the classical social-contract theories of the seventeenth and eighteenth centuries that envision civil society as a universal realm in which each individual acts as an equal citizen. Closely examining these theories, she asserts that "the social contract is a fraternal pact that constitutes civil society as a patriarchal or masculine order" (Pateman 1989, 33). In critiquing the way in which the social contract is constructed as a fraternal pact, she emphasizes the historical context in which social-contract theories emerged. She argues that they developed in the context of challenging "patriarchalism," which justified the political right to rule in terms of paternal authority over children. Rejecting this extension of the "natural" right to rule, based on the metaphor of the parent–child relation, to political rights, contract theories argue that individuals are equal as citizens.

At the same time, however, these theories do not question what makes paternal authority over children possible in the first place; that is, men's conjugal right to access to women's bodies. Consequently, what the social contract implies is the preservation of the husband's sexual rights over the wife's body and the expansion of this conjugal right to all men who are equal among themselves potentially as husbands. She argues that

> Civil individuals have a fraternal bond because, as men, they share a common interest in upholding the contract which legitimizes their masculine patriarchal right and allows them to gain material and psychological benefit from women's subjection.
>
> (ibid., 43)

Pateman further contends that the reproductive difference between women and men is constructed as fundamental to the creation of civil society. Women's reproductive capacity/burden, interpreted as their proximity to nature, passion, and the body, excludes them from civil society, which is supposed to be governed by reason and rational law. Women's sexual difference from men, as such seen as the very foundation of civil society, establishes that society as a profoundly masculine domain. Therefore, the only way for women to participate in it, Pateman maintains, is to join the fraternity by denying their own bodily difference. This is indeed the position of liberal feminism that has de-emphasized sexual differences in favor of gender equality, often misconstrued as sameness.[9] Yet, since the female body is considered as the unmistakable marker of the sexual difference, this denial is contradictory and precarious. Given that women continue to carry the visible and tangible embodiment of the sexual difference, their participation in civil society is at best marginal.

Marie Fleming develops a similar critique of Habermas's theory of the bourgeois public sphere based on its development in Western Europe in the late eighteenth and the nineteenth centuries. She approaches the gendered nature of this new sphere, starting from the principle of "the public use of reason". In explaining its connection to the masculinization of the public sphere, she focuses on Habermas's own recognition that the patriarchal conjugal family is a linchpin of the public sphere where all participants come together as equal citizens. Like Pateman, she explains the centrality of the conjugal family to the public sphere in conjunction with the making of the bourgeois identity vis-à-vis the old aristocrats. She argues,

> The idea of a third sphere [the intimate sphere of the family] makes it possible for him [Habermas] to argue that, while the bourgeois learned the art of rational-critical public debate from the urban nobility, the public sphere that they created – in literary works, but also in philosophy and law – became the expression of a sphere of subjectivity that was specifically bourgeois.
>
> (Fleming 1995, 122)

The exercise of reason, along with other principles of the public sphere such as impartiality and abstract equality among participants, becomes the hallmark of the bourgeois subjectivity which is distinguished from the affectation, partiality, and particularity associated with the aristocratic order in decline. At the same time, these attributes expunged from the public sphere are to be contained within the intimate sphere of family life, to which women are relegated as the other of the new bourgeois self. The bourgeois man's control over this private realm as the husband becomes the precondition for his participation in the public sphere. Hence, Habermas argues that "being the master of a household and of a family" cannot be overridden by "movable wealth and control over labor power" (ibid., 129). In other words, any man who is the head of his own household is to be admitted to the public sphere regardless of his property ownership. Yet this democratic openness precludes women, who are confined to the intimate sphere of family life.

The Confucian legacy and the masculinization of the public sphere

The patriarchal origin of civil society in the West is parallel to the Neo-Confucian construction of the public sphere outside patriarchal households (or a patrilineal kin group). Neo-Confucianism in Korea not only masculinized the public sphere through its gender ideology, but also established the family as the prototypical metaphor of social relations among individuals and groups. However, this masculinized public sphere did not mean that women in Korea were associated with the private sphere. Unlike the ideological and institutional construction of the family as the private sphere in Western societies, a household in Confucianized Korea was not organized around the notion of an island of romantic love between a (heterosexual) couple in the sea of rational calculation and pursuit of power that characterized activities in the public sphere (Coontz 1992, ch. 3). According to Neo-Confucianism, which the founders of the Chosŏn Dynasty (1392-1910) consciously chose as the state ideology, the spatial separation of sexes and the gender division of labor constituted the cornerstone of a new social order based on the principle of patrilineage. While relegating women to the domestic sphere of procreation and daily reproduction and production, this patrilineal order elevated men to heirs, with the symbolic authority to perform ancestor commemoration rituals and engage in politics outside the household (Deuchler 1992). Women's subordination as such within marriage and kinship was essential to the identity of the new society, as distinguished from the previous Koryŏ Dynasty (A.D. 918-1392). There is an intriguing parallel between Neo-Confucian (masculine) subjectivity, rooted in women's confinement within the domestic sphere, and bourgeois (masculine) subjectivity, rooted in the private/intimate sphere. Therefore, political activities outside the domestic sphere were and have continued to be generally considered masculine.[10] As I will discuss below, the ideological link between women and the domestic sphere has been firmly institutionalized by the gender division of labor within the family and without, and works as a barrier against women's participation in civil society.

Referring to the past, I do not mean to imply that Neo-Confucian tradition is merely reproduced in contemporary Korea. In the process of capitalist industrialization over the past decades, the modern gender division of labor between housewife and provider-husband has been superimposed on the Confucian gender division of labor. While the social context and the specific content of the gender division of labor has been transformed, there is an apparent continuity between Confucian and modern gender ideologies in women's relegation to the domestic sphere.

The experiences of diverse groups of Korean women actively involved in social movements in the 1980s illustrate the direct link between the expectation of women's family responsibilities and their lack of participation in civil society. Rural women's experience in an autonomous farmers' movement gives one clear picture of the negative link between women's domestic responsibility and their participation in expanding civil society. Women peasants had long been ignored by the state and by male-dominated agricultural organizations in rural areas. Toward the late 1970s, however, emerging farmers' organizations began to pay attention to women, as auxiliaries to their activist husbands. Taking advantage of this changing attitude, some single women also became actively involved in these organizations. These women, however, discontinued their activities after marriage due both to strong opposition from parents-in-law and to the constraints of pregnancy (Yun 1989, 192). By the late 1980s, when women peasants organized their own autonomous movement, some of those same former activists joined the movement, after the hiatus imposed by marriage and childbearing. Tellingly, widows played a far more active role in this emerging women farmers' movement than did their counterparts with husbands (Women's History Studies Association 1989, 22).[11]

At times, the negative effect of this conservative gender ideology on women's participation in civil society is not quite so straightforward. The dialectical interaction between the two can be seen in the example of women factory workers. During the 1970s, young single female factory workers kept civil society alive under Park Chung Hee's military regime by struggling against labor exploitation. By the end of the decade, many of them had left the labor movement upon getting married and becoming mothers (Women's History Studies Association 1989, 21). It is noteworthy that this disengagement took place despite the fact that many of them, after marriage, continued to work in informal sector jobs as part-time or temporary workers, since this type of job, albeit insecure, provided them with the flexibility in balancing domestic responsibilities and wage work needed for survival.[12] Some of these married women workers then returned to labor movements in the late 1980s explicitly in the role of wives of male workers. Sometimes, their support for their husbands contributed to the successful outcome of labor strikes by softening the image of the militant workers, thereby drawing public sympathy (ibid. 1989, 19–20, 37; Pak 1989, 136). The activism of these women, as wives, was made possible by the moral and/or practical support of their families, which released them from the psychological and actual burden accompanying the performance of housework and care work. At the same time, it is likely that they would not have received such support if they had been fighting for their own right to employment.

Violence in suppressed civil society and women's participation

The violent relationship between civil society and the state under the political conditions of military authoritarian rule and national division further accentuated the masculinization of the public sphere, and thereby discouraged women's access to it during the military rule. This process reflects the gender norms in many societies, including South Korea, that associate physical violence with masculinity, condoning and even encouraging men's use of it. This underlying social meaning of gender and violence is well reflected by the common phenomenon that women are excluded from, or marginal within, such institutions as the military and the police in most societies. This implies that gender ideology in South Korea, as in many other androcentric societies, perpetuates gender hierarchy in part by constructing the differences between women and men in relation to their access to, and use of, violence. In divided Korea, the institution of universal male conscription further normalized the link between masculinity and violence. The pervasiveness of violence in the public sphere discouraged participation in it by women far more than by men.

The experience of urban poor women involved in the struggle against the destruction of shanty towns by municipal authorities in the name of "urban redevelopment" in the 1980s poignantly illustrates the difficulty for women in participating in violent civil society. These urban poor women (wives, mothers, or daughters-in-law) belonged to a class generated by the explosive migration, since the 1960s, of rural populations to expanding cities in search of a livelihood. The urban poor suffered from the loss of communities and shelters as a result of urban redevelopment projects to build residential and commercial districts on the sites of demolished shanty towns (Cho and Cho 1992). In 1984, a spontaneous movement of the evacuated urban poor developed in the Mokdong area of the city of Seoul. By 1987, several groups had coalesced to form the Seoul City Association of the Evacuated Urban Poor to deal with the problem of forced dislocations. For the women in this association, this type of political action meant an additional burden to the multiple tasks of wage work, housework, and childcare. Moreover, reflecting the conservative gender ideology, the general public perceived their street protests, often involving physical confrontation with the police and real estate developers, as "crazy" and "embarrassing." Influenced by the hegemonic gender ideology, a majority of the active women themselves also thought that they had become rough and ill-tempered in the process of repeated struggle (Cho 1989, 180–1).

The dilemma of women activists involved in male-dominated progressive movements also offers a glimpse into women's often ambiguous relationships to civil society. In 1989, the KWAU, the major umbrella organization of autonomous women's associations, formed in 1987, joined the National Federation of Nationalistic and Democratic Movements (NFNDM), a coalition created to achieve democracy and reunification. This decision led to the withdrawal of three moderate organizations from the KWAU. Despite this conflict, the KWAU pursued collaboration with the NFNDM to end the legacy of military authoritarian rule. Then, however, it was criticized by male-dominated organizations within the NFNDM for adopting a "reformist approach" to social change, since the KWAU's focus on legal and gradual avenues to social change was perceived as insufficiently militant to challenge the status quo. While agreeing on the NFNDM's goal, the KWAU could not afford to alienate its female constituency by engaging in violent activities (Chung 1997, 27–8).

However, it is misleading to depict the tension between the KWAU and the NFNDM only in terms of dichotomous gender difference. Prior to the establishment of the KWAU, women activists were divided over the methods and focus of their social movement. While one section emphasized extra-legal political struggle resembling urban guerrilla warfare under military rule, another was more concerned with legal reforms. What is noteworthy here is that the latter was the one more concerned with the autonomous women's movement and could therefore not ignore the fact that the majority of women, whether housewives or employed, were perturbed by activities undertaken by the militant wing of the political struggle to overthrow the military regime (Chung 1997, 27).

The national division and military confrontation between the two Koreas have implications for women's participation in civil society: both contribute to its masculinization. This process stems from the presence of large defense budgets and the subsequent dependence of the state on families to provide social welfare including care for children, the infirm, the old, and the disabled. The militiary regimes have spent disproportionate amounts of the public budgets on militiary expenses.[13] Especially alarmed by the Nixon Doctrine, the Park regime escalated its military buildup throughout the 1970s to achieve "self-reliant defense." This concern also led the regime to launch, prematurely, a gigantic project to develop heavy and petrochemical industries in 1973. A year after this industrial shift, the regime embarked on *yulgok saŏp*, a long-term, systematic military buildup plan (Kim and Hong 1996, 297, 290). In 1987, the South Korean government used approximately one-third of its public budget on military spending (Kim 1992, 163). A dire consequence of the state's inability or unwillingness to expand social welfare was that families were forced to continue to perform their welfare function. In fact, the transitional regime under Roh Tae Woo (1988–92) reaffirmed this old practice by emphasizing that families would be primarily responsible for individual welfare, and that the state would provide support only when families failed to do so (Ministry of Health and Social Affairs 1989). This position had a negative implication for women because it has been primarily women, as mothers, wives, daughters-in-law or grandmothers, who have taken responsibility for a wide range of caring work for family members.

Reinventing patriarchal tradition and postcolonial ambivalence toward modernization

The androcentric nature of suppressed civil society under authoritarian regimes has been significantly modified, acquiring a new dimension in the process of procedural democratization in the 1990s. The qualitative transformation of civil society discussed above has particularly reduced its militant and confrontational nature. Yet, civil society of the 1990s exhibits a new aspect of androcentrism, which has developed in tandem with popular nostalgia for the past the nation has "lost" as a result of compressed industrialization. This postcolonial ambivalence toward modernization and westernization has been fertile soil for the politics of reinventing patriarchal tradition to cope with the anxiety stemming from compressed social change. Such traditionalism, equating Confucian patriarchal tradition with the core of national or cultural identity, serves to reaffirm the gender division of labor in the household, which circumscribes women's participation in civil society.

This problematic use of tradition needs to be understood in the historical context of colonization and neo-colonialism (Heng 1998). Korea's earlier experience of modernization took the form of violent and humiliating encounters with Western powers and then colonization by Japan, which emulated those powers. This experience of colonization by the only non-European power, which had successfully adopted Western technology and institutions, intensified the urgency for Koreans to pursue modernization and embrace the modernity that the West represented. And yet, this pursuit entails a complicated problem of collective identity crisis because embracing Western modernity inevitably involves becoming like the other and the presence of the powerful other challenges one's own identity. At the turn of the century, the Korean nationalist elite, like its counterparts elsewhere, attempted to resolve this tension by splitting the nation into material and spiritual dimensions (Chakrabarty 2000, chapter 6; Chatterjee 1993). They produced the ideology of tongdosŏgi (Eastern way, Western technology), which justified the adoption of instrumental aspects of Western modernity on the one hand and the preservation of Korean morality and culture on the other hand.

The colonial dilemma over modernization and national identity has become acute as Korea has rapidly industrialized over the past three decades. Nostalgia for "Korean tradition" has grown as its material life has increasingly resembled that of the United States, which has exercised military dominance and strong economic influence over postcolonial Korea. Moreover, the ever growing presence of American popular culture in the recent decade has escalated public concerns over Korea's "essential or unique culture" (koyuhan munwha). Reverberating the nationalist ideology of tongdosŏgi, Park's military regime took an initiative to "revive" traditional culture in the second half of the 1970s (S. Moon 1997, 39). In particular, this regime emphasized anti-democratic interpretations of such Confucian values as loyalty to the ruler (ch'ung) and filial piety (hyo) as the core of invaluable tradition (Kim and Hong 1991, 233). This official nationalist concern for Korean identity was followed by a parallel development in civil society.

Throughout the 1980s there was a growing interest in exploring and learning "Korean tradition" on college campuses, and by the 1990s, the postcolonial search for Korean tradition had taken a far more popular form. While not all such attempts reaffirmed patriarchal tradition, most of them did. (One notable exception is a series of travelogues written by an academic, based on his exploration of remote areas of the country, in a populist effort to identify ignored and hidden aspects of Korean cultural heritage.)[14]

To capture an interesting moment of convergence between state nationalism and popular nationalism in their pursuit of lost tradition, this section focuses on two popular cultural texts produced in the 1990s. Sŏp'yŏnje (1993), a film directed by Im Kwŏn-taek, was not only a box-office success but was also acknowledged as an "intangible cultural asset" (muhyŏng munwhaje) by the government (Choi 1998, 22). The film narrates the story of a poor itinerant family, including Yubong, a p'ansori (a traditional form of singing) master, Songwha, his adopted daughter, and Tongho, a boy put under his care. Yubong is determined to transmit this declining art form of p'ansori to his young apprentices. He demands painstaking discipline and total dedication to mastering this art form. Reaching his late teens, however, Tongho rebels against the harsh discipline and poverty and finally leaves the family. Alarmed by Tongho's rebellion, Yubong tries to keep Songwha by feeding her herbs that gradually take away her eyesight. While she finally masters the art of p'ansori, she spends the rest of her life on the margin of society, due to her blindness.

The captive daughter echoes the colonial legacy of the appropriation of women's bodies and their reduction to the site of the power struggle between male nationalist elites and colonial administrators. As Lata Mani (1998) analyzes, in her study of the colonial debate on sati in India, the widow's body in immolation serves as the site where British colonial power and Indian nationalists waged their contest over Indian tradition. The former condemned it as a brutal practice oppressing women, exploiting the issue to justify Britain's "civilizing mission," whereas the latter defended it as an element of India's cultural identity, stressing its voluntary and spiritual quality. The women actually or potentially affected by sati are entirely absent from this discourse; they exist merely as a field of discursive power. In parallel, Songwha's incapacitated body is caught between the official and the popular nationalist search for moorings of cultural identity. The woman Songwha represents is called upon to serve as a repository of Korean tradition, to alleviate the anxiety stemming from the tumultuous social change generated by compressed modernization.

The implication for women's participation in civil society of the conservative cultural practice is apparently negative. It reaffirms women's role as a symbol of culture or collective identity and continues to deprive them of their subjectivity as active citizens. The implicit message underscores women's sacrifice for the sake of the nation (or of whatever collectivity to which they belong). This image of selfless and sacrificing women has been institutionalized in women's relegation to domestic relationships as their primary and almost only roles. To be fair, the conservative cultural practice has been challenged by social change in general and by women's movements in particular. At the same time, however, this very change has led again to a reactionary sentiment, well illustrated by the recent success of a novel, ironically entitled Sŏnt'aek (choice), by a renowned male writer (M. Yi 1997). This novel is a fictional reconstruction of the life of the author's paternal female ancestor, Righteous Madam Chang (chŏngbuin Changssi), who lived in the Confucian Dynasty of the late sixteenth and the seventeenth centuries.[15] The author mentions in the epilogue that this novel is meant to offer "an image of the exemplary woman" from the past. Provocatively, the author conjures up Madam Chang's spirit to narrate her exemplary life for the instruction of the daughters, mothers, and wives of contemporary Korea. While she embodies Confucian womanhood as characterized by her selfless devotion to her in-laws' patrilineal household, her spirit argues repeatedly that she has chosen this path over the pursuit of her own literary and artistic success, in spite of her own talents, recognized by her own father and his friends since her childhood. Although circumscribed by the social environment of her time, the spirit insists, her life was a choice because there is no human choice free from external constraints.

Although this attempt to conjure the idealized Confucian woman of the mid-Chosŏn Dynasty into the eve of the third millennium might sound extremely anachronistic, it reflects a widespread backlash to the recent changes in women's consciousness and lives, characterized by their questioning of conventional gender roles and their growing entry into the public sphere as professionals, politicians, and social activists.[16] While a few feminists reviewed the novel critically, it was a top bestseller for several months after its publication in early 1997.[17]

The politics of reinventing patriarchal tradition and reducing women to its mere repository is not conducive to women's participation in civil society, since "tradition" dictates that women stay in their "natural" place within the household. To do otherwise would suggest that they are not authentic. Furthermore, the domestic responsibilities legitimized by conservative gender ideology preempt women's participation in civil society not only conceptually but also practically.

These constraints upon women's participation in civil society do not mean that there are no barriers to men's participation. The masculine role of providing for the family may not leave spare time for a man to engage in civil society either. For example, corporate culture in South Korea poses a serious obstacle even to middle-class men's participation in civil society, demanding, as it does, their total dedication to their companies even at the expense of time spent with their own families (Cho and Hong 1995). Yet these men's interests are usually represented by labor unions and other occupational associations. Moreover, this masculine role performed in the public sphere is still far more conducive to involvement in civil society than is the feminine role of wife and mother. This difference brings the relationship between families and civil society to the fore.

As Pateman and Fleming argue, the exclusion of the family from civil society is the very precondition for equal participation of (male) citizens in it. This ideological separation draws on the legacy of (Western) liberal political theory that establishes the boundary between public and private around the family. An exception to this theoretical tendency is Drude Dahlerup (1994), a Danish feminist, who attempts to redraw the boundary between private and public by including families in civil society. As Iris M. Young (1987) argues, such inclusion does not have to result in the total collapse of the realm of self-determination or privacy. Rather, it means that no one or no action should be pre-emptively forced into the realm of invisibility from the public.

The peasant movement in the late 1980s in South Korea sheds light on the ambiguous boundary between civil society and family. Since the beginning of the Uruguay Round of international trade in 1985, Korean farmers, like their counterparts in other countries, had fought against the powerful global economy that has encroached on local producers' survival in the name of "free trade." Farmers could not give up their protests because their livelihood was threatened by the massive influx of foreign agricultural produce. The Korean government, meanwhile, had little leverage to resist this global trend since its economy depends upon the export of manufactured goods to the international market. When the confrontation between the farmers and the government extended over several weeks, the demonstration sites were turned into outdoor domiciles where people ate and slept (Women's History Studies Association 1989, 22). The family members involved in these protests as advocates or actual participants blurred the conventional boundary between civil society and the family. In addition, the active involvement of women in these protests was made possible by their families' willingness to break away from the rigid gender division of labor during the time of family crisis. The persistent ideology and practices of the gender division of labor in the family cast a shadow over the androcentric but contested civil society, where the women's movement has managed to forge its space. But I also suggest that in the course of the struggle the androcentric definition of the family was challenged as women participated in the struggle and families accommodated to new social relations.

The women's movement in the 1990s and 2000s: contentious, heterogeneous and fragile civil society

The androcentric tendency in Korean civil society discussed above does not mean that the society is a seamless monolith that does not face ongoing contestation. Nor does women's marginality in civil society and their trouble with participating in it determine their perpetual marginalization, as the feminist conceptual critique of civil society might imply. The expansion of women's movements in contemporary Korea suggests that civil society is not a static entity but "the complex of relations of state, economy, individual, and associational life" characterized by "tensions, conundrums, and legitimations" (Blaney and Pasha 1993, 4).

The women's movements led by the KWAU in the 1990s became diverse and complex in the context of political democratization. The diversity of the women's movements is most noticeable in the presence of small-scale associations dealing with a wide range of issues, from sexual violence and harassment, domestic violence, work in urban and rural areas, prostitution, the environment, consumer issues and housework, children's education, childcare, and disability to peace and unification. While some organizations focus on a specific issue, others tackle a few different issues, often moving from one to another. For instance, the Women's Hot Line United (*yŏsŏngŭi chŏnhwa yŏnhap*) has devoted itself to the issues of domestic violence and sexual violence, offering counseling and support for abused women since 1983. Similarly, the Sexual Violence Counseling Center (*sŏngpongnyŏk sangdamso*) has supported victims of sexual violence since its establishment in 1991. The People's Friends Society (*minwuhoe*) has worked for a variety of issues, including food co-operatives, employment, maternity protection, childcare, the environment, and women's participation in local politics (KWHLU 1999; KWAU 1998).[18]

The diversification of issues within the women's movements led by the KWAU reflected the imperative to reach out to diverse groups of women in largely conservative local communities, hence the tendency to take on less controversial issues such as the environment, consumer issues and childcare, rather than those of sexual and domestic violence that speak directly to power relations between gendered individuals. Although the diversification of issues indicates the growth of the women's movements within the expanding civil society, the focus on less controversial issues tends to reproduce the feminine gender roles within the institution of (heterosexual) marriage and family. While none of these issues are either inherently or exclusively women's issues, the women's movement tended to frame them as an extension of women's concern, as mothers and wives, for the well-being of their families. By the same token, issues such as lesbian rights and disability, which affect a smaller number of women in the society, tend to be marginalized within the women's movements (Kim 1999; Yi 1999).

The growing complexity of the women's movement can be observed in its changing relationship to the state after the transition to procedural democracy. Reflecting the general trend in civil society of the 1990s, collaboration and negotiation began to replace the antagonism that existed previously between dissident women's associations and the state and the dominance that the state wielded over the AMOs and other in-between women's organizations. Founded as an oppositional group outside the state, the KWAU registered with the state as an incorporated body by 1995. Since then, the KWAU has begun to pay attention to local and national elections, so as to be able to influence legislative and policy-making processes. As a result, some KWAU activists have been elected to the National Assembly, and candidates sponsored by it have been elected to local assembly seats. Furthermore, after the inauguration of Kim Dae Jung's government in 1998, some KWAU representatives were appointed to government offices, mainly in the expanding women's policy apparatuses.[19] In parallel, the state's grip on women's AMOs and other in-between organizations has been significantly loosened, and many of these organizations themselves have begun to deal with issues of gender equality and women's empowerment in the context of political democratization, particularly with the rise of the state's policy to promote gender equality. Consequently, the sharp distinctions among autonomous women's organizations, women's AMOs, and in-between organizations have become somewhat ambiguous in ever-evolving civil society.

The convergence of different types of women's associations is also shown in their issues and activities. Prior to the transition to procedural democracy, autonomous women's associations were distinguished from other women's organizations not only in their struggle against workers' exploitation and military dictatorship, but also in their feminist concerns. In particular, there has been tension between the KWAU and the KWAC. While some members of the KWAC paid attention to issues of family law reform and the exploitation of women factory workers in the 1970s and 1980s, this umbrella organization had been used by or collaborated with the authoritarian regimes (Yi 1996, 254, 271).[20] These differences have been significantly reduced with the restoration of the civilian administration that has used the rhetoric of gender equality to forge its new identity apart from the previous regimes. Reflecting the new trend in civil society to adopt the market model, some autonomous women's organizations have tried to build their dues-paying membership bases by marketing issues appealing to diverse groups of women.

Yet, this convergence does not mean the collapse of differences among diverse women's associations. Rather, it points simply to increasing compatibility and coexistence among them. A positive consequence of this change is the growing practice of coalition formation among them. For instance, the Central Association of Housewives' Classes and the Federation of Housewives' Clubs collaborated with the KWAU to reform family law and equal employment law, and to legislate childcare law. Similarly, while there are still considerable differences between the two umbrella organizations in terms of ideology and organizational practices, the KWAU and the KWAC worked together for family law revision in the late 1980s and 1990s, for the establishment of a quota system to increase women's representation in politics and public employment in the mid-1990s, and for the elimination of the military service extra scores system in the late 1990s (Yi 1998, 34).

The new collaborative relationship between the state and the women's movements is visible in two ways. First, the state began to provide some financial support for women's associations by legislating the Women's Development Basic Law in 1995. Prior to this change, the state had financed the AMOs and semi-AMOs to exercise tight control over them. In contrast, the basic law requires the central and local governments to fund projects designed by women's associations that can promote gender equality and women's welfare (Kim 1998, 43, 53). Since the late 1990s, women's associations have received support for their programs and projects from the women's development fund after the institutional process of applications and reviews. Yet a close examination of the state's financial support for women's associations between 1995 and 1997 reveals its instability and unevenness. While the central government's funding of women's associations comes from established budgetary items and the women's development fund, the number of associations and projects, as well as the total amount of support fluctuated greatly (Kim 1998, 63, 82). The growth of the women's development fund has been very sluggish, and further aggravated by the aftermath of the 1997 Asian economic crisis (*Women's Newspaper*, September 22, 2000). On a positive note, the women's development fund, usually a few thousand U.S. dollars per project, has helped autonomous women's associations, which are usually indigent, to turn their ideas into useful products. For example, Seoul Women Workers' Association was able to publish a practical guidebook on sexual harassment in the workplace and distribute its copies among working women (*Kungmin Daily*, September 7, 2005). Overall, the emergence of the public fund available to women's associations to promote gender equality and women's welfare symbolizes the development of an interdependent relationship between the women's movements and the state.

Second, another dimension of the new collaborative relationship between the state and the women's movements since the 1990s is illustrated by the extensive involvement of the coalition of various women's associations in legislating and reforming laws fundamental to the promotion of gender equality and women's empowerment: the Infant Care Act (1991), the Sexual Violence Special Act (1993) and its reform (1997), and the Domestic Violence Prevention Act (1998). These legislative efforts constituted major activities of the women's movements throughout the 1990s. This dimension of the women's movements built upon their previous struggle to reform the Family Law, which was significantly revised in 1989 and the Equal Employment Act, which was repeatedly revised in the 1990s after its initial enactment in 1988. Since all of these laws challenged conventional ideas about social relations of gender and sexuality in Korean society, the women's movements had to confront varying degrees of conservative resistance to legislative attempts. The KWAU played the leading role in coping with such resistance by actively publicizing the issues through local and national mass media, drafting bills in collaboration with professionals, and lobbying politicians. It organized numerous formal and informal discussion meetings with experts and political parties, held public lectures, and used major elections to put pressure on the government and the legislature to pass these laws adequately reflecting women's interests. Although the laws that were passed fell short of the bills drafted by women's associations, this partial success is a remarkable achievement for the women's movement, especially given its short history and scarcity of human and material resources. Foremost, it made the women's movement nationally visible within androcentric civil society and established as a definite social force with which the state has to reckon.

Women's movements since 2000 have been further differentiated as new feminist associations spring up and remain outside the KWAU, which has served as a centripetal force among "progressive" women's associations.[21] These novel women's associations tend to be concerned with human rights of such social minorities as foreign women (workers) married to Korean men, lesbians, sex workers, women with disabilities and single women. The shifting attention away from the majority of Korean women who are heterosexual, married, and able-bodied is a logical outcome of the KWAU-led women's movement which succeeded in improving the lives of the majority of Korean women. This does not mean the end of the ongoing daily struggle against discrimination and violence in family life, workplace, and public sphere by many women who belong to the social majority.[22] Yet such change has begun to give rise to a perception among younger feminists that the KWAU-led women's movements have become the mainstream. Reflecting the changing sensibility, the novel women's associations redefine the center of their women's movement as sexual minorities, which encompasses not only lesbians, but also women who are relegated to the margins of society due to their differences from the majority of women. These new organizations have begun to articulate voices different from the mainstream women's movements on specific social and political issues. For example, Solidarity for Women's Liberation, founded in 2003, distances itself from the underlying assumption of mainstream women's associations that equates womanhood with maternity and motherhood within the boundary of a heterosexual family and intends to pursue solidarity with women who are social minorities.[23] The Sisters' Network, founded in 2004, announced critical stances toward the Ministry of Women and Family for a similar reason and has criticized the prostitution special law which has been implemented to "protect prostitutes as victims" and "punish employers and customers" since September 2004.[24]

Differentiated from the mainstream women's movements' focus on law and policy as the vehicle of social change, the innovative new women's associations emphasize their cultural approaches to women's empowerment. They utilize film, theatre, song, painting, photography, and other forms of cultural performance and festival to express their ideas and alter popular sensibilities. Although the mainstream women's movements also use these cultural resources to celebrate the institutionalized Women's Week (July 1 to 7 each year) and promote their objectives, a significant difference between the mainstream and the innovators lies in the latter's distance from the state and institutionalized politics. Some younger feminists are critical of older feminist activists who became parliamentary members and ministers of the national government. They tend to view the feminist entry into the center of political power as being conducive to an authoritarian attitude to ignore differences among women (*Women's Newspaper*, October 29, 2004). Those feminists who share this sensibility tend to view the legislation and implementation of the prostitution special law, actively supported by the KWAU, as an indication of such authoritarian attitudes that ignore views and experiences of sex workers themselves.

The development of the Korean women's movements in the 1990s and 2000s illustrates the contested nature of androcentric civil society and heterogeneity of women's "counterpublics" within the civil society (Fraser 1992). Two factors were crucial in allowing the women's movements to carve out their own space: 1) the transitional and relatively fluid nature of the democratizing state, and 2) the presence of a small number of dedicated activists who had previously been involved in anti-regime and labor-organizing democracy movements. The three regimes that ruled Korean society in the 1990s were transitional in different ways. Although Roh Tae Woo's regime represented transition from the military rule to procedural democracy, Mr. Roh was a general and the hand-picked successor to Mr. Chun. While Kim Young Sam's regime represented transition from military to civilian rule, Mr. Kim came from the conservative political establishment in the Yŏngnam region which had produced political leaders for decades. Kim

Dae Jung's regime, finally, represents transition to a civilian regime ruled by the opposition force, albeit allied with a conservative political party, for the first time in contemporary Korea, and with rulers, furthermore, from the Honam region which had been politically and socially marginalized. The consecutive presence of these transitional regimes generated the relative political fluidity that allowed women's movements to forge space throughout the 1990s.

Small groups of highly committed activists, especially in the KWAU and its member organizations, seized this political opportunity to revitalize the "progressive" women's movements. Their efforts symbolize both the promise and the fragility of civil society in Korea. On the one hand, as shown above, the women's coalition movements have been successful in pressing the state to establish the legal structure to promote gender equality and protect women against violence and discrimination in public and domestic spheres. On the other hand, the KWAU has been less successful in recruiting grassroots members to broaden its membership base. Most of its 28 member organizations have very limited memberships, ranging from only several dozen to a maximum of 300. This problem is particularly acute among member organizations in provincial areas, as opposed to the greater Seoul area. Exceptions include the People's Friends Society, the Women's Hot Line, and the National Parents Association for Genuine Education, which have a few thousand to over 10,000 members.[25]

The small numbers of grassroots members in the mainstream and new women's associations, overall, reveal the fragility of Korean civil society in the midst of its quantitative expansion and qualitative transformation. First, it generates chronic financial difficulties for these associations, which can undermine their viability in the future. This financial problem can create a vicious cycle of failure to reach out to various groups of women in local communities, resulting in the further scarcity of membership fees. A majority of women's associations, especially in provincial areas, do not have permanent staff and therefore rely upon dedicated volunteers for routine operations (Kim 1998, 39). For instance, the KWAU financed its activities in part with grants from the Evangelische Zentralstelle Entwicklungshilfe (Protestant Association for Co-operation in Development) in Germany, and in part with fundraising sales by member organizations. Yet the EZE discontinued its support after Korea became a member of the OECD in 1997. As a result, the KWAU has faced the challenge of how to secure grants from the Korean state while maintaining its autonomy (Yi 1998, 40). The financial difficulty has become acute in the aftermath of the 1997 Asian economic crisis and many of these women's organizations struggle to survive in the 2000s.

Second, the visibility of a small number of devoted activists and volunteers and scarcity of dues-paying members highlight the hybrid nature of Korean civil society, in which the notion and practices of liberal citizenship remain alien to the majority of Korean women, whose lives are embedded in domestic relations, often regardless of employment. This problem of women's citizenship is also observed in contemporary Japan. As Robin Leblanc shows in her study of Japanese middle-class housewives (1999), experiences of citizenship for those – predominantly women – who perform housework and care for others are curtailed by these socially invaluable but unrecognized responsibilities. The practice of joining a women's association as a dues-paying individual member requires a certain level of social awareness and economic security. Even if these conditions are available, domestic responsibilities and the hegemonic family metaphor that interprets interpersonal or intergroup relations as the extension of domestic relations do not encourage women to act as individuals in the public sphere. In South Korea, women in their thirties and forties who bear and rear children are largely invisible in the People's Solidarity for Participatory Democracy, one of the leading citizens' organizations. In contrast, this group of women is the mainstay of the People's Friends Society, one of the largest community-based women's organizations, which has attracted grassroots women around the issues of safe and organic food available at its food co-operatives, parenting, and children's sex education.[26]

Civil society and a new imagining of human relations

The concept of civil society is useful for understanding the rather dramatic process of political change in Korea during the past two decades, to the extent that Korean society has experienced the proliferation of social movement oriented associations (which refer to themselves as "civil society organizations"). Their visibility reflects the quantitative expansion of civil society; their changing relationships with the state mirror the qualitative transformation of civil society. Nevertheless, civil society has remained primarily androcentric, as a consequence of the Confucian legacy that masculinized the public sphere outside the patriarchal household, violence pervasive in the public sphere under authoritarian military rule, and the reinvention of patriarchal tradition to deal with postcolonial ambivalence toward rapid modernization in the post-military rule era. The focus on the women's movements and women's associations developing within Korean civil society illuminates both its promise and fragility. On the one hand, the vibrant and diverse women's movements of the 1990s and 2000s highlight contested and heterogeneous civil society in the context of transitional politics and procedural democratization. On the other hand, the visibility of a small number of dedicated activists and the scarcity of dues-paying regular members in many women's associations reveal the fragility of contested civil society.

In light of this fragility, it is useful to reflect on Nancy Fraser's notion of "subaltern counterpublics" which, she argues, women and other social minorities need to create to achieve the goals of social equality, cultural diversity and participatory democracy. According to Fraser (1992), subaltern counterpublics refers to autonomous space within civil society to counteract informal barriers, such as the style of communication and decorum, that prevent social minorities from participating in the public sphere, otherwise formally inclusive and open. The creation of subaltern counterpublics makes the public sphere multiple and heterogeneous, which can ameliorate the lasting effects of established structures of inequality by allowing subaltern groups to empower themselves. Yet Fraser does not address explicitly how women can break out of the cycle of established structures of inequality in the first place to create autonomous space of their own. Nor does she discuss how such space can be sustained once it is forged. The experience of the Korean women's movements since the 1990s and 2000s suggests that women's counterpublics in androcentric civil society are bound to further differentiation as a dialectical consequence of success of the mainstream women's movements. It also suggests that heterogeneity of counterpublics is an inevitable aspect of evolving civil society.

A small number of activist women who are either single or wives of activist men have carved out women's counterpublic space in expanding civil society since the mid-1980s by creating autonomous women's organizations in South Korea. I would argue that carving out counterpublic space requires women to be relatively free from domestic responsibilities and to develop a facet of their identities distinguished from familial relations and kinship. These conditions can be met only through the transformation of rigid gender division of labor in the family and a new imagining of human relations beyond the liberal notion of the atomized self and the Korean self enmeshed in domestic relations. As long as the domestic identities of women as mothers/wives/daughters-in-law mediate women's citizenship, women's access to civil society is practically and ideologically hampered, and the liberal notion of individual rights remains largely rhetorical to them. That is, quotidian practices of housework, childrearing and extended family obligation primarily performed by women overshadow their citizenship rights that formal law is supposed to guarantee.

However, the establishment of women's citizenship does not have to follow a liberal model of the self as an atomized individual disengaged from social relations. The liberal view of citizenship as a set of rights and obligations granted by the state tends to impoverish its meaning by overlooking the human agency involved in the ongoing struggle to turn formal rights into a substantive reality. Since such struggle is always collective, individual citizens are bearers of the relational self. The case of the Korean women's movements in the 1990s and 2000s suggests that activist women who carve out counterpublic space do not see themselves and other women as isolated individuals. As indicated by their involvement in creating and maintaining associations, activist women pursue the improvement of women's lives and their empowerment as diverse groups whose lives are deeply embedded in social relations. The major challenge for activist women would include not only broadening of the grassroots base of autonomous women's organizations to sustain women's counterpublics, but also accepting their heterogeneity.

Notes

1 An earlier version of this chapter was published in *The Journal of Asian Studies* vol. 61, no. 2 (May 2002), pp. 473–500.
2 Kasza summarizes the similarities between the AMOs and a conscription army in five points. First, both are instruments to implement public policy. Second, their membership includes entire categories of people – women, youth, factory workers, etc. Third, their membership is overtly or covertly coerced, and exists in the absence

of competing organizations. Fourth, their leaders are appointed by regimes. Fifth, their activities and goals are also determined by regimes (1995, 74).

3 One of the most conspicuous examples of such continuity was observed in the recent police responses to a series of labor disputes at Daewoo automobile company in the city of Pup'yŏng. On April 10, 2001 the police militantly suppressed a protest of laid-off auto workers (26 April, 2001 *Hangyŏre* 21).

4 It is important to distinguish this project-based funding from the money given to the AMOs for their routine operation. This old practice, which persists even today in various forms, often confuses the public and has generated the problem of public misconception that all citizens' associations are funded by the government for their routine operations, including the wages of activist staffs.

5 Major examples of the new type of citizens' organization include the Citizens' Coalition for Economic Justice (CCEJ) and the People's Solidarity for Participatory Democracy (PSPD). Founded in 1989, CCEJ has attempted to influence state policy by actively lobbying government officials, publicizing policy issues and providing policy alternatives for the state. However, it has lost its public credibility as a result of recurring scandals involving its acceptances of and requests for funds from the government and public corporations (5 January, 2001 *Dong-A Daily*; 4 January, 2001, *Mail Economy Newspaper*). Founded in 1994, the PSPD has focused on monitoring of the state and the economic conglomerates to protect middle-class citizens, workers, farmers, and the poor, rather than directly collaborating with the state on policy matters. To maintain its autonomy vis-à-vis the state, it has relied on membership dues so far without being embroiled in financial scandals.

6 This information is base on my field work in South Korea from August 2004 to May 2005.

7 See KWAU homepage: http://www.women21.or.kr/news/W_Intro/w-intro.asp.

8 Administered Mass Organizations of women have ample historical precedents in societies under fascist (and communist) regimes. For instance, Nazi Germany organized the German Girls League for female youth between the ages of ten and fourteen, Faith and Beauty for young women between fifteen and twenty-one, and German Women's Enterprise for adult women. Similarly, Imperial Japan organized women into the Great Japan Federated Women's Association, the National Defense Women's Association, and the Patriotic Women's Association during the 1930s (Kasza 1995, 33, 87–8).

9 This is not just a theoretical position, but in fact many professional women in corporate America and other highly competitive professional fields end up single or married but childless.

10 Elsewhere I examined this conservative nature of procedural democratization that underlies extremely low representation of women in political leadership positions. See S. Moon (2003).

11 Certainly, this type of conjugal constraint is not unique to South Korea. See Hirschmann (1995) for a discussion of a similar dynamic in the context of South Africa.

12 A similar economic practice is observed in Taiwan. Married women concentrated in informal sectors of the economy as part-time or temporary workers are a particularly important feature of the Taiwanese economy, dependent as it is upon export-oriented small-scale "satellite factories" (Hsiung 1996).

13 Thanks to rapid economic growth, the absolute and relative size of the defense budget in South Korea steadily increased. This trend continued even after the end of the Cold War. Defense spending grew from 55 billion won in 1988 to 87 billion in 1992 and 127 billion in 1996 (Kim 1996, 157). Only after the Asian economic crisis, did the government announce its plan to freeze the 1999 defense budget (13 August 1998, *Korea Times*).

14 The first volume of this travelogue was published in 1993 and the second in 1994. These books have remained bestsellers for several years, and over one million copies

had been sold by the end of the 1990s. In a parallel manner, the Japanese have also been interested in domestic travel as a means to discover the old or primitive self in the context of irreversible social change (See Ivy 1995, chapter 2).

15 *Chŏngbuin* was one of the official titles granted to wives of high civil officials of the Chosŏn Dynasty (1392-1910). These wives were expected to be exemplary women who embodied the ideal Confucian woman, practicing chastity, filial piety towards parents-in-law, and bringing up accomplished sons.

16 Mohan Rajeswari (1994) discusses a parallel case of conservative backlashes against the changing roles of women in India by examining the representation of women in popular melodramatic films. These movies tend to depict contemporary Indian women returning to "Indian tradition" one way or another.

17 The popularity of this novel was documented in the lists of best-selling books printed in daily newspapers, weekly magazines, and other publication references throughout 1997. In less than four months after its initial publication, the novel was in its 11th printing.

18 This information is also based on my aforementioned fieldwork conducted from August 2004 to May 2005.

19 Yi Mi-kyŏng, member of the National Assembly, used to be a co-representative of the KWAU. Han Myŏng-suk, also a former co-representative of the KWAU, became the first Minister of Gender Equality, established in 2001, and then served as the Minister of Environment. During Roh Moo Hyun's administration, she also served as the Prime Minister. Chi Ŭn-hŭi, a former representative of the KWAU, became the Minister of Gender Equality.

20 It is telling that *White Paper on Women* (1991) published by the Korea Women's Development Institute, a state-sponsored research center established to promote gender equality, mentions the problem of the antagonistic polarization between the women's associations represented by the KWAU and those represented by the KWAC, calling for tolerance for differences in ideology and activities (KWDI 1991, 244).

21 The list of these new women's associations includes Women Migrants Human Rights Center (2001), Women Against War (2001), Women's Solidarity for Similarity through Difference (2003), Solidarity for Women's Liberation (2003), Cultural Collective for Sexual Minorities (2004: a gathering to create cultural environment for sexual minorities), Sisters Network (2004), and Korean Lesbian Counseling Center (2005).

22 For instance, 17 years after the passage of the Equal Employment Law (1988), women's monthly wages on average are 63% of men's according to 2003 statistics (*Painaensyalnyus*, February 2, 2005). The wages gap between women and men employed in the 50 largest companies in South Korea in fact increased more than 50% during the past 5 years. In early 2005 men's monthly average income was 4,246,000 won whereas women's was 2,625,000 won (*Painaensyalnyus*, September 20, 2005). The problems of sexual violence and sexual harassment continue to threaten many women in the family, workplace, and public sphere (*Seoul Newspaper*, March 5, 2005; *Voice of People*, December 21, 2005).

23 See its website, www.feminist.or.kr/board/zboard.php?id=intro&page.

24 The implementation of the special law has generated a series of intense collective responses from prostitutes who redefine themselves as sex workers. For over 50 days, they gathered in front of the National Assembly building to protest against the law because it destroys their livelihood without viable alternatives. Their collective action evolved to make a claim about their right to organize a union to improve their working conditions. While some women's associations support their positions, the KWAU, which was instrumental in legislating this law has maintained that prostitution cannot be viewed as a form of labor or prostitutes a type of worker (*Citizens' Newspaper*, September 27, 2005; *Labor Today*, September 23, 2005).

25 The PFS, the largest among them, consists of community-based local branches that draw primarily housewives in 9 cities. The Women's Hot Line is now a national

organization with 25 local branches and has 2,728 supporting members in addition to its 1,744 regular members. It has trained over 1,500 domestic violence counselors through its training program since the 1980s. The NPAGE consist of 17 national branches and focuses on the problem of school education, appealing to all parents (KWAU 1998, Appendix 4).
26 This information is based on my aforementioned fieldwork.

References

Blaney, David L. and Mustapha Kamal Pasha. 1993. "Civil Society and Democracy in the Third World: Ambiguities and Historical Possibilities." *Studies in Comparative International Development* 28(1):3–24.

Chakrabarty, Dipesh. 2000. *Provincializing Europe: Postcolonial Thought and Historical Difference*. Princeton: Princeton University Press.

Chatterjee, Partha. 1993. "Communities and the Nation." In *The Nation and Its Fragments: Colonial and Postcolonial Histories*, edited by Partha Chatterjee. Princeton: Princeton University Press.

Cho, Mi-Hye. 1989. "Tosibinminyŏsŏngŭi silt'aewa ŭisik" (The living conditions and consciousness of urban poor women). In *Yŏsŏng 3*, edited by the Women's History Studies Association. Seoul: Ch'angjakkwabip'yŏng.

Cho, Pong-Jin and Sŏng-T'ae Hong. 1995. *Hoesagamyŏn chungnŭnda: kyŏngjejuŭi tamnonŭi pip'anŭl wihan pildŭstŏdi* (If you join a company, you are dead: a field study to criticize economistic discourse). Seoul: Hyŏnsilmunwhayŏngu.

Cho, Tae-Yŏp. 2000. *Han'gugŭi siminundong: chŏhangkwa ch'amyŏŭi donghak* (Korean citizens' movement: the dynamics of resistance and participation). Seoul: Nanam.

Cho, Un and Oakla Cho. 1992. *Dosibinminŭi samkwa gonggan* (The life and space of the urban poor). Seoul: Seoul National University Press.

Choi, Chungmoo. 1998. "Nationalism and Construction of Gender in Korea." In *Dangerous Women: Gender and Korean Nationalism*, edited by Chungmoo Choi and Elaine Kim. New York: Routledge.

Chung, Hyun-Back. 1997. "Together and Separately: 'The New Women's Movement' after the 1980s in South Korea." *Asian Women* 5:19–38.

Citizens' Newspaper, ed. 2005. *Han'guk mingandanch'e ch'ongram 2006*. Seoul: Citizens' Newspaper Co.

Cohen, Jean L. and Andrew Arato. 1992. *Civil Society and Political Theory*. Cambridge. MA: MIT Press.

Coontz, Stephanie. 1992. *The Way We Never Were: American Families and the Nostalgia Trap*. New York: Basic Books.

Dahlerup, Drude. 1994. "Learning to Live with the State." *Women's Studies International Forum* 17(2–3):117–27.

Deuchler, Martina. 1992. *The Confucian Transformation of Korea: A Study of Society and Ideology*. Cambridge, Mass.: Harvard University Press.

Fine, Robert. 1997. "Civil Society Theory, Enlightenment and Critique." *Democratization* 4(1):7–28.

Fleming, Marie. 1995. "Women and the 'Public Use of Reason.'" In *Feminists Read Habermas: Gendering the Subject of Discourse*, edited by Johanna Meehan. New York: Routledge.

Fraser, Nancy. 1992. "Rethinking the Public Sphere: A Contribution to the Critique of Actually Existing Democracy." In *Habermas and the Public Sphere*, edited by Craig Calhoun. Cambridge, MA: MIT Press.

Gold, Thomas. 1990. "The Resurgence of Civil Society in China." *Journal of Democracy* 1:18–31.

Hangyŏre 21. 2001. "'Kyeŏmch'iha' Pup'yŏng … silsŏnghan kyŏngcha'l!" (Pup'yŏng under "martial-law rule" … the mad police!). 26 April.

Heng, Geraldine. 1998. "'A Great Way to Fly:' Nationalism, the State, and the Varieties of Third-World Feminism." In *Feminist Genealogies, Colonial Legacies, Democratic Futures*, edited by M. Jacqui Alexander and Chandra Talpade Mohanty. New York: Routledge.

Hirschmann, David. 1995. "Gender Themes in Civil Society: Illustrations from South Africa." Working Paper 256, Women and International Development Program. East Lansing: Michigan State University.

Hsiung, Ping-Chun. 1996. *Living Rooms as Factories: Class, Gender and the Satellite Factory System in Taiwan.* Philadelphia: Temple University Press.

Ivy, Marilyn. 1995. *Discourses of the Vanishing: Modernity Phantasm Japan.* Chicago: University of Chicago Press.

Kasza, Gregory. 1995. *The Conscription Society: Administered Mass Organizations.* New Haven: Yale University Press.

Keane, John, ed. 1988. *Civil Society and the State: New European Perspectives.* London: Verso.

Kim Ch'ang-Su. 1996. *P'yŏnghwamandŭlgi, t'ongilmandŭlgi* (Making peace, making unification). Seoul: Taedong.

Kim Chin-Gyun and Sŏng-Tae Hong. 1996. *Kunsinkwa hyŏndaesahoe* (Mars and contemporary society). Seoul: Munhakkwahaksa.

Kim Chin-Gyun and Sŭng-Hŭi Hong. 1991. "Han'guksahoeŭi kyoyukkwa chibaeideologi" (Education and ruling ideologies in Korean society). In *Han'guksahoe'wa chibaeideologi* (Korean society and ruling ideologies), edited by the Korean Industrial Society Studies Association. Seoul: Noktu.

Kim Hong-Suk. 1998. *Yŏsŏngdanch'ee daehan chŏngbu chaejŏngjiwŏnŭi p'yŭngga mit taeane kwanhan yŏngu* (A study of governmental financial support for women's organizations: assessment and alternatives). Seoul: Korean Women's Development Institute.

Kim, Philo. 1992. *Two Koreas in Development: A Comparative Study of Principles and Strategies of Capitalist and Communist Third World Development.* New Brunswick, NJ: Transaction Publishers.

Kim Ŭn-Jŏng. 1999. "Chŏngsangsŏnge tojŏnhanŭn yŏsŏngdŭl" (Women challenging normality). In *Han'guk yŏsŏnginkwŏn undongsa* (A history of the Korean women's rights movement), edited by the Korean Women's Hot Line United. Seoul: Hanulacademi.

Koo, Hagen, ed. 1993. *State and Society in Contemporary Korea.* Ithaca: Cornell University Press.

Korea Times, The. 1998. "1999 Budget Guideline." Editorial, 13 August.

Korean Women's Associations United (KWAU), ed. 1990. *Minjuyŏsŏng 10* (Democratic women 10). Seoul: Minuhoe.

—— 1998. *Yŏllin hŭimang: Han'guk yŏsŏngdanch'eyŏnhap 10 nyŏnsa* (Open hope: a ten-year history of the KWAU). Seoul: Center for Korean Women's Studies, Dongdŏk Women's University.

Korean Women's Development Institute (KWDI). 1991. *Yŏsŏng paeksŏ* (White paper on women). Seoul: KWDI.

Korean Women's Hot Line United, ed. 1999. *Han'guk yŏsŏnginkwŏn undongsa* (A history of the Korean women's rights movement). Seoul: Han'ulacademi.

Landes, Joan B. 1995. "The Public and the Private Sphere: A Feminist Reconsideration." In *Feminists Read Habermas: Gendering the Subject of Discourse*, edited by Johanna Meehan. New York: Routledge.

Leblanc, Robin. 1999. *Bicycle Citizen: The Political World of the Japanese Housewife.* Berkeley and Los Angeles: University of California Press.

Mani, Lata. 1998. *Contentious Traditions: The Debate on Sati in Colonial India.* Berkeley and Los Angeles: University of California Press.

Ministry of Health and Social Affairs. 1989. *Punyŏpokchisaŏp chich'im* (Guidelines for women's welfare projects). Seoul: Ministry of Health and Social Affairs.

Ministry of Political Affairs. 1997. *Yŏsŏng paeksŏ* (White paper on women). Seoul: Ministry of Political Affairs.

Molyneux, Maxine. 1985. "Mobilization without Emancipation?: Women's Interests, the State and Revolution in Nicaragua." *Feminist Studies* 11(2):227–54.

Moon, Seungsook. 1997. "Begetting the Nation: The Androcentric Discourse of National History and Tradition in South Korea." In *Dangerous Women: Gender and Korean Nationalism*, edited by Chungmoo Choi and Elaine Kim. New York: Routledge.

—— 2000. "Overcome by Globalization: the Rise of a Women's Policy in South Korea." In *Korea's Globalization*, edited by Samuel S. Kim. Cambridge: Cambridge University Press.

—— 2003. "Redrafting Democratization through Women's Representation and Participation in the Republic of Korea." In Korea's Democratization, ed, Samuel S. Kim. Cambridge: Cambridge University Press.

Pak Sŏk-Pun. 1989. "Ch'abyŏrŭi sasŭrŭl ttulko chŏnjinhanŭn yŏsŏngnodongja undong" (The advancing women workers' movement that breaks the chains of discrimination). In *Yŏsŏng 3*, edited by the Women's History Studies Association. Seoul: Ch'angjakkwabip'yŏng.

Pateman, Carole. 1989. "The Fraternal Social Contract." In *The Disorder of Women: Democracy, Feminism and Political Theory*, edited by Carole Pateman. Stanford: Stanford University Press.

Rajeswari, Mohan. 1994. "The Crisis of Femininity and Modernity in the Third World." *Genders* 19:223-56.

Silliman, Sidney G., and Lela Garner Noble. 1998. *Organizing for Democracy: NGOs, Civil Society, and the Philippine State.* Honolulu: University of Hawaii Press.

Sin Yŏng-Suk. 1995. "Yŏsŏng undongŭi yŏksajŏk koch'al" (A historical study of the women's movement). In *Yŏsŏngkwa han'guksahoe* (Women and the Korean society), edited and revised by the Women in Korean Society Studies Association. Seoul: Sahoemunhwayŏnguso.

Tempest, Clive. 1997. "Myths from Eastern Europe and the Legend of the West." *Democratization* 4(1):132–44.

White, Gordon. 1996. *In Search of Civil Society: Market Reform and Social Change in Contemporary China.* Oxford: Clarendon Press.

Women's History Studies Association. 1989. "Minjok minju undongkwa yŏsŏng undong" (The national democracy movement and the women's movement). In *Yŏsŏng* (women) *3*, edited by the Women's History Studies Association. Seoul: Ch'angjakkwa bip'yŏng.

Yi Hae-Sol. 1999. "Han'guk lezbiŏn inkwŏnundongsa" (A history of the Korean lesbian rights movement). In *Han'guk yŏsŏnginkwŏn undongsa* (A history of Korean women's rights movement), edited by the Korean Women's Hot Line United. Seoul: Han'ulacademi.

Yi Hyo-Jae. 1996. *Han'gukŭi yŏsŏngundong: ŏjewa onŭl* (The women's movement in Korea: yesterday and today). Seoul: Chŏngusa.

Yi, Hyo-sŏn. 1997. *Hyŏndaehan'gugŭi siminundong* (The citizens' movement in contemporary Korea). Seoul: Chimmundang.

Yi Mi-Kyŏng. 1998. "Yŏsŏngundongkwa minjuhwaundong: yŏyŏn 10 nyŏnsa" (The women's movement and the democratization movement: a ten-year history of the KWAU). In *Yŏllin hŭimang: Han'guk yŏsŏngdanch'eyŏnhap 10 nyŏnsa* (Open hope: a ten-year history of the KWAU), edited by the KWAU. Seoul: Center for Korean Women's Studies, Dongdŏk Women's University.

Yi Mun-Yŏl. 1997. *Sŏnt'aek* (Choice). Seoul: Minŭmsa.

Yi Sŭng-Hŭi. 1991. "Han'guk hyŏndai yŏsŏngundongsa" (A history of the contemporary women's movement in South Korea). In *Yŏsŏnghakgangŭi* (Women's-studies lectures), edited by the Korean Women Studies Association. Seoul: Dongnyŏk.

Young, Iris M. 1987. "Impartiality and the Civic Public." In *Feminism as Critique*, edited by Seyla Benhabib and Drucilla Cornell. Minneapolis: University of Minnesota Press.

Yu, Hong-Jun. 1993. *Naŭi munhwayusan tapsagi I* (My exploration of Korean cultural heritage, vol. 1). Seoul: Ch'angjakkwabip'yŏng.

—— 1994. *Naŭi munhwayusan tapsagi II* (My exploration of Korean cultural heritage, vol. 2). Seoul: Ch'angjakkwabip'yŏng.

Yun, Yŏng-Sun. 1989. "'Nongmin moksumi ttonggŭminya?:' yŏsŏngnongminŭi samkwa t'ujaeng" ("Are peasants' lives pieces of shit?:" women peasants' life and struggle). In *Yŏsŏng* (women) *3*, edited by the Women's History Studies Association. Seoul: Ch'angjakkwa bip'yŏng.

7   Commemorating Kwangju

The 5.18 movement and civil society at the millennium[1]

Linda S. Lewis

Ah, ah – Oh Kwangju of May! Oh revolutionary Kwangju!
Oh city of youth who band firmly together, to fight.
In the struggle, flowers bloom; in the struggle, a new day comes.
Fight – fight – fight! Oh revolutionary Kwangju!
> From "The Song of Going to the Kwangju Battle,"
> a popular May protest song

Now, as an unhappy era has been brought to a close and history is victorious, 5.18 is approaching a second stage, changing to a spirit of universal humanity. Accordingly, the underlying tone of the commemoration events themselves must be stripped of the so-called anti-government struggle style of the past.
> Chŏng Su-man, Chairman, 5.18 Kwangju People's
> Uprising Bereaved Families' Association[2] (1997)

Each spring the May 18, 1980 Uprising[3] is remembered in Kwangju with parades, song fests, rallies, graveside memorial services and, all too often in the past, violent clashes with police. Oft-heard May "protest songs" like the one quoted above celebrate the revolutionary spirit of the city and its citizens, and the defiant tone of the anniversary events well into the 1990s typically reflected the oppositional political stance of the majority of the participants.

As the second quotation suggests, however, by the end of the decade even the leaders of the victims' groups in Kwangju had begun to disavow the "anti-government struggle style" characteristic of past commemorations. Indicative of this shift in public sentiment was the disappearance, in May 1998, of the familiar protest tunes; normally played and sung continuously all over town, by the eighteenth anniversary their militant, radical lyrics were deemed no longer appropriate to the occasion.[4] Along with depoliticization has come commodification, as well, as the Uprising has begun to be packaged as a tourist attraction. The twentieth anniversary saw the introduction of a cute cartoon 5.18 mascot, Nuxee, whose visage graces T-shirts, post cards, ballpoint pens and other souvenir items available for sale in the May 18 Cemetery gift shop, presumably designed to appeal to visiting groups of school children.

The transition to a civil society occurring in South Korea at the millennium is particularly problematic for 5.18 related groups in Kwangju. In a city whose very name evokes images of the evils of decades of authoritarian rule and the long popular struggle to end it, the success of the Korean democracy movement has in fact created an identity crisis within the 5.18 movement itself, a crisis that comes into focus each May in Kwangju during the 5.18 anniversary period. Where once the movement's constituent groups had opposition to the government and the fight to legitimate the Kwangju Uprising as a common goal and cause for mobilization, the challenge they face now in the post-*minjung* era is finding new aims and strategies, to sustain their own role(s) in civic affairs. Kwangju's leaders, intent on a fresh image for their city, must walk a fine line, capitalizing on a legacy of dissent without encouraging renewed anti-state activism and violent protest; new citizens' groups have emerged, to compete for a role in 5.18 commemoration politics; and the Uprising's direct victims, many still suffering after 20 years, face continued oppression and re-victimization at the close of the century. The focus of this chapter is the new aims and strategies (and their relative success) of 5.18 movement groups in "revolutionary Kwangju," after democratization.

May in Kwangju: an overview

During the Chun Doo Hwan era (1980–1987), the very act of commemorating 5.18 was a form of protest against the government; on May 18, 1981 (the first anniversary of the then so-called "Kwangju Incident," or *Kwangju Sat'ae*), Bereaved Family Association members attempting to hold graveside memorial rites for the dead were barred from Mangwŏldong cemetery,[5] and the Association's leader was detained under the National Security Law.[6] Stories are told of students going cross-country over the hills, to evade police and reach the burial ground, and of visitors to the cemetery being escorted away by the authorities when they tried to assemble.

In fact, it was not until the fifth anniversary, in 1985, that Kwangju citizens could freely visit Mangwŏldong; in the spring of that year, with the inaugural session of the 12th National Assembly, the once-taboo topic of Kwangju became for the first time a matter of public discourse.[7] Even so, throughout the 1980s demonstrators were arrested every May in downtown Kwangju (as well as in other parts of the nation) in connection with 5.18 memorial events, and the Kwangju Uprising was only legally commemorated for the first time in 1989, when, as part of the "Liquidation of the Fifth Republic" movement, the "resolution" of Kwangju was once again on the national agenda.

It was still well into the next decade before the 5.18 anniversary celebrations could begin to take on a less political tone. As a *Chosŏn Ilbo*[8] editorial noted on May 4, 1990, the atmosphere that year was quite different. While the government saw May as a critically important month because of 5.18 related activities planned by students and workers, Kwangju citizens (the newspaper suggested) might not be so inclined to join in anti-government protests, in part because that year compensation had been paid to the victims. While various memorial services and rallies were planned, most of the scheduled anniversary events were cultural and academic ones, which would be unlikely to give rise to social unrest and mass mobilization. And, although in 1995 the campaign to prosecute those responsible for the deaths in Kwangju added political tension (and national media attention) to the fifteenth anniversary celebrations (the official slogan, of "Let's examine the truth of the May massacre, by trying the butchers!" was quite concrete), local government officials (now elected) participated for the first time in the memorial services.

By 1997, however, the transformation of the 5.18 anniversary commemoration from a massive anti-government demonstration to an extended civic festival was almost complete. While time may not yet have healed all wounds, it had answered most claims. The trial of those responsible was over; the official slogan – "For humanity, peace; for our people, reunification" (*illyu ege p'yŏng hwarŭl, minjok ege t'ongiltŭl*) – made no new demands on the government. For the first time May 18 was celebrated as a national commemoration day (*kukka kinyŏmil*), and the memorial service held that day in the newly consecrated 26.1 billion won[9] 5.18 Cemetery was conducted by the Ministry of Home Affairs, not 5.18 movement groups, as in the past. And, while the 17th Anniversary Events Committee stated in the official program that "Our efforts to completely resolve the May problem will continue,"[10] such a vague declaration was very different in tone from the explicit oppositional political agendas put forth in past Mays.

The celebratory tone of the anniversary events by the late 1990s most obviously reflects the changing national political context, in which, with the achievement of a democratic civilian national government, 5.18 has been redefined, from mob riot to heroic struggle. The memory of the 1980 Kwangju Uprising has been written into the newly constructed national narrative of democratization, legitimized and sanctified, its victims extolled as patriot martyrs and Kwangju's citizens, as heroes. This point was dramatically underscored in 2000 by the attendance of President Kim Dae-jung, himself a 5.18 victim,[11] at the memorial services in Kwangju. Tight security at the 5.18 Cemetery that day resulted in competition for admission tickets and the exclusion of ordinary people from the event – an irony not lost on many of Kwangju's citizens.

This highlights the fact that from a local, rather than national, perspective, the "civic festival" atmosphere of May in Kwangju in the 1990s also represents the emergence in the city of new, competing claims to the direction and leadership of the 5.18 movement itself. As Koreans could more freely investigate and discuss the events of 1980 after the democratization of 1987, so too could differing points of view about their meaning and essential nature be expressed in Kwangju, as well. Kwangju intellectuals, professionals, civic leaders – middle-class citizens and members of the local elite who perhaps through guilt as well as caution remained passive through the 1980s – could begin to vie for a role in the 5.18 movement and a voice in its resolution.

In this respect, the situation in Kwangju reflects the nascent *minjung/simin* movement distinction appearing in the national political discourse. As Abelmann points out in examining farmer activism in the post-*minjung* 1990s,[12] there was in Korea by the mid-1990s a "widespread fatigue and even disgust" with the culture of dissent; "Many people distance themselves not only from the military authoritarianism of the recent past, but also from the righteousness and drama of dissent – from the totalizing projects of both the left and the right." In Kwangju, the symbolic center of oppositional politics throughout the 1980s, the noisy "drama of dissent" has been long-playing. And, while there is civic pride in Kwangju's identity as a "righteous town" (even city government publications by the late 1990s began to boast of an "historical tradition of spirited resistance against injustice")[13] there is also growing public weariness with the city's reputation as a site for the violence of anti-government demonstrations and their suppression.

It is in May in Kwangju when the uneasy coalition of 5.18-related groups[14] as well as government officials and other citizens' organizations concerned about the image and future of their city unite under the anniversary banner; as such, an analysis of the May commemoration offers insights into Kwangju civic sentiment at a given moment, as well as into the nature of oppositional politics and dissent in South Korea as a whole. The anniversary celebrations are a prism through which, over the years, diverse local and national agendas have been refracted. During May contested claims to the legacy of 5.18, differing goals and intentions, and significant splits within the 5.18 movement itself are revealed. As one observer noted (of the seventeenth anniversary), as the various groups concerned with the anniversary do not share a unified point of view, and as the memorialization period extends over a full month, the commemoration is an assortment of events put together "department store style" (*paekhwajŏmsik*).[15] Thus, while members of the anniversary committee could call, in 1997, for an end to the "antigovernment struggle style" of memorial events (and indeed, one of the governing principles for screening events in 1997 was that they be non-political and non-commercial in nature),[16] there was no guarantee that individual groups and organizations would forsake the oppositional political tone of the past.

In fact, the problem for the constituent elements of the 5.18 movement by the late 1990s was how to maintain their own momentum and relative position(s) of power and civic influence in a society in which democratization had been largely achieved. As long as the various 5.18 related groups, as well as most of Kwangju's citizens, shared as a common goal the legitimation of the events of May 1980 and the restoration of the city's honor and national image, the unity and purpose of the movement was assured; and naturally, the anniversary events were largely conducted in the anti-government *minjung* movement idiom characteristic of the 1980s. But, by the 1990s (as we have seen), both the national and local political terrain had changed. In Kwangju, the new emphasis was forward-looking. In the words of the Chairman of the 17th Anniversary Events Committee:

> It is not to remember the painful past, but to prepare for a new future … we have entered the 17th anniversary of the 5.18 Peoples' Uprising at a point in time at which we count on Kwangju's efforts for the 21st century. Starting with the 17th anniversary, we would like to prepare Kwangju's message for

the world, and for the future. Expect Kwangju's energy to be directed towards autonomy, democracy, and unification.[17]

These lofty but non-specific aspirations anticipate a "second phase" of the 5.18 movement in which Kwangju assumes a national, and international, leadership role as a model for the development of democracy, and the "5.18 spirit" (*5.18 chŏngsin*) serves as an inspiration to people world-wide. Yet the 5.18 movement itself seems to be, like much of post-1987 civil society in Korea, a movement "at a loss."[18] The year 1997 was marked by the ascendancy in Kwangju of new citizens' groups, whose purposes and tactics differ from those of the 5.18 victims' associations who have customarily assumed leadership of the 5.18 movement and claimed ownership of the uprising's legacy in the past. At the beginning of a new democratic era in Korea, Kwangju's 5.18-related constituent elements have had varying degrees of success in redirecting their energies, in overcoming the identity crisis that (apparent) victory has brought, and in some cases, in reimaging themselves as not anti-state, as we shall see.

Kwangju Citizens' Solidarity and the internationalization of the "Kwangju spirit"

Of the new citizens' groups that are in the ascendancy in Kwangju, the most active (and successful) of those connected to the memorialization of 5.18 is Kwangju Citizens' Solidarity – KCS (*Kwangju Simin Yŏndae Moim*). KCS was started in 1993 when a loose coalition of citizens' groups and concerned individuals joined together in opposition to plans for the construction of a large 5.18 monument.[19] The group functioned so well that members decided to continue working together and have a voice in 5.18-related civic affairs.[20] Composed of a relatively small core group of fewer than fifty like-minded individuals, almost all professionals (lawyers, doctors, college professors, and journalists), KCS is deeply concerned with overcoming the problem of the isolation of Kwangju and the surrounding Honam region. Its strategy is the promotion of the globalization of the "Kwangju spirit," through education about 5.18 and the forging of links with the international human rights community, particularly among Korea's Asian neighbors.

Accordingly, KCS's efforts during the annual anniversary celebrations have focused on academic conferences and symposia that bring foreigners to Kwangju, to share in the commemoration of 5.18 and to learn from its example. KCS literature envisions Kwangju as a "Mecca of Democracy" comparable to the Paris Commune and Auschwitz; Kwangju's "solemn struggle for democracy has moved the hearts of people across the world who have truly loved peace and freedom," and "People will remember Kwangju forever as a torch for freedom, peace, and equality which are universal virtues of mankind."[21] By capitalizing on Kwangju's legitimacy as the symbolic center of the now-successful Korean democracy movement and promoting the continuing vitality of the "Kwangju spirit," KCS seeks to transform what remains, from the perspective of other 5.18 groups, a local/regional tragedy and national "problem," into a civic asset, utilizing the events of May to advance a new image of the city. This vision of the legacy of 5.18 emphasizes Kwangju's on-going importance as a national and international role model, rather than as a site of remembered suffering and resistance.

Thus, in May 1995 KCS held an international symposium on "Inhumane Acts and Their Resolution," which included as panelists representatives from the Argentinian human rights group, Mothers for the May Plaza Victims. A more ambitious project in May 1996 brought together from Korea and over twenty other countries almost 100 college students and young adults active in human rights organizations for a six-day First International Youth Camp for Human Rights and Peace. As the project's Rationale explained:

> In May 1980 ordinary citizens and students of Kwangju rose up against the Military dictatorship demanding the creation of a democratic government and observance of human rights. ... Based on this Kwangju spirit, we've kept moving against all the obstacles of democracy in the last 16 years. It hasn't been easy. ... Over the past decade, South Korea has made dramatic strides in the arena of international business and technological advancement. However, the struggle for full democracy, human rights and social justice continues to lag behind this economic prosperity. We've observed that similar situations exist in other countries in Asia and around the world. For that reason, we invite people of good will, especially the youth and students who will carry the burden of this continuing struggle in the future to join us in Kwangju to share experiences and reflections on our common task of making a better society for all.[22]

Participants attended the major 5.18 anniversary events in Kwangju, as well as met together in sessions to share "concrete information on the exploitation and oppression of people in undemocratic societies."[23]

Finally, on the 18th anniversary in 1998, KCS organized a conference jointly with the Asian Human Rights Commission (Hong Kong) at which Asian human rights activists gathered in Kwangju to declare the newly drafted Asian Human Rights Charter.[24] In proclaiming the importance of Kwangju as a venue for the declaration of this charter, KCS stated that

> The Kwangju massacre stands symbolic on the failure of almost all the Asian countries to develop meaningful democracy during the 20th century. However, the determination of those who faced the massacre and gave their lives and the determination of the people of the Kwangju city to defend the honor of those who died and to keep the flame of solidarity alive and further the continuous influence of the Kwangju Massacre in the political life of south Korea as a whole is symbolic of the aspirations of the people to part from repression and militarism and to seek an altered world where human life is respected. ... The spirit of the Asian Human Rights Charter too is the same for all the people of Asia. In this sense having the declaration of the Asian Human Rights Charter in Kwangju has a very comprehensive meaning.[25]

By linking the "determination" of those who actually participated in the Kwangju Uprising (and, even, died in 1980) with the "determination" of the ordinary citizens of Kwangju who have worked since then to redeem the national reputation of their city, KCS asserts the right of everyone, and not just those who were direct victims of the uprising, to lay claim to the legacy of 5.18, and to the moral legitimacy its heritage now bestows. All Kwangju citizens are its rightful heirs – and perhaps all Koreans, too, as the hegemonic view of the successful democracy movement of 1987 is that it was made possible through the widespread popular support of the middle classes. This broader, more symbolic, interpretation of the meaning of the "Kwangju spirit" empowers all Kwangju citizens, and, at the same time, dilutes the privileged status of the direct victims' groups and weakens their *a priori* claims to civic leadership roles.

In fact, KCS members consciously seek to distance themselves from the direct victims' groups,[26] who they consider first of all to be too "emotional" in their representations of the Kwangju Uprising. KCS members express the idea that the overly hysterical and impassioned tone of victims' testimony is counterproductive; their rhetoric makes outsiders uncomfortable, and they come across as too biased to be effective spokespeople for Kwangju.

In contrast, KCS actively promotes accounts which appear more disinterested and nonpartisan, particularly the testimony of non-Koreans. In 1997, the KCS anniversary project was the publication of the personal recollections of foreign correspondents who had covered the Kwangju Uprising. At a press conference in Kwangju on May 17 celebrating the publication of *Kwangju in the Eyes of the World* (attended by most of those who had contributed essays to the volume), the chairman of the *Mudŭng Ilbo*[27] in his remarks said that the book, which appeared in both Korean and English versions, excluded Kwangju residents not only to make the events of May 1980 more accessible to the outside world, but also to make the volume more objective. As the Preface to the book itself asserts,

> In the search for truth, objectivity is always deemed the prerequisite. History, like science, demands an unimpassioned observer to chronicle its events. It hopes that, from his unbiased vantage point, this onlooker will be able to balance the scales, absorb the circumstances, intentions, motivations, and consequences, and come out with a story that tells the whole tale. Thus the modern world has chosen the foreign correspondent as its historian – hoping that his eyes, unmoved by patriotism or ideologic concerns, will not be blinded; praying that his story, unfettered by censorship or national security concerns, will be related in its entirety.[28]

The foreign reporter is " … the voice that shall be believed"[29]; implicitly, the voices of the victims themselves are inherently "unobjective" and thus less believable, inevitably tainted by personal and ideological concerns.

In addition, KCS also opposes the contentious attitude of the direct victims' groups. One member in 1996 cited, as an example of the continuing oppositional priorities of other Kwangju groups, the efforts of a prominent 5.18 activist to put on trial not only the leaders of the Kwangju Massacre, but also the soldiers who had done the actual killing[30] – a campaign KCS members did not support.[31] This is not to suggest that KCS members in the mid-1990s felt that the Kwangju Uprising was "over"; rather, the remaining issues they were concerned with involved government responsibility and accountability in a symbolic, rather than a concrete sense. That is, admissions of guilt and contrition, and educating the nation about the facts of 5.18, were more important than punishing individual paratroopers, or even giving more money to the victims.

In a scholarly presentation at a KCS-sponsored symposium in 1995, the lawyer Pak Wŏn-sun[32] argued that the government was trying to solve the problem of Kwangju solely through "compensation"– that is, offering comfort money to the victims – rather than "reparations," which would involve the acknowledgment that the government had acted illegally, and thus needed to do much more than give monetary restitution to direct victims. Citing a 1994 survey in Kwangju showing that 53 percent of ordinary citizens and 63 percent of civic leaders thought that "finding out the truth" (*chinsang kyumyŏng*) was the most important unresolved issue about 5.18,[33] Pak pointed out that, in light of international standards for reparations, this demand for government honesty was not unreasonable;[34] instead, the policy of the Kim Young Sam government treated the "Kwangju problem" (*Kwangju munje*) as a regional event that could be settled quickly, through money.[35] And indeed, by the mid-1990s, the victims had been awarded compensation in a series of government acts,[36] and 100 *p'yong*[37] of the former army base, *Sangmudae*, was given to the people of Kwangju as collective restitution;[38] and, in 1997 the expensive new 5.18 national cemetery was completed.[39]

As a result, in the eyes of most Kwangju citizens, the 5.18 victims' associations had, by the late 1990s, already benefited sufficiently from the government's largesse, and public sympathy for them had run its course. Any further claims or demands are seen as selfish and greedy, and concrete proposals that address these groups' specific needs are thought of as narrowly self-serving. As one KCS member explained, what separates the various 5.18 associations is self-interest:

> When the groups were struggling for compensation, others could sympathize with them. But now, most Kwangju people are fed up with the 5.18 groups. Even more, people outside Kwangju are fed up with them. ... To lead the 5.18 movement, they should have a high level of morality, but these groups have lost their legitimacy ... through the compensation and cemetery, they [in this case, the bereaved families' association] have money and [a] good position – but they just fight among themselves, for relative power within the organization. Some people are good, but others are not.[40]

In contrast, KCS envisions its projects as serving the public, rather than the private, interest.

KCS has been able to mobilize resources beyond the Korean peninsula; these projects have required money, English-language ability, global connections and the sophistication to conceive of them in the first place. There are KCS members who have traveled overseas, lived in the United States, and/or have significant networks and ties (through occupation, family or educational experiences) that extend well beyond Honam. The group has proven skillful at raising funds for their projects; they have a website; they have formed an English-study circle. KCS has internationalized its efforts in ways significantly beyond the means of other 5.18-related groups in Kwangju.

Yet, it could be argued that theirs is still a transnational project with a remarkably local agenda: a bigger role in city affairs, a larger voice in the future direction of Kwangju's development, the boosting of civic pride, and, ultimately, the rehabilitation and enhancement of Kwangju's (and the Honam region's) image within the nation. While bringing interested groups to Kwangju does educate foreigners about 5.18 and spread the "Kwangju spirit," the impetus for these projects is clearly also the impact they have had on KCS prestige and power within the local community itself.

5.18 direct victims' associations: the injured and the bereaved at the margins

The competitive resources of the direct victims' groups, in contrast, seem limited almost exclusively to moral authority. In general, the large number of groups in the loosely defined 5.18 movement are organized on the basis of degree and kind of participation in the Kwangju Uprising itself, and the competing agendas and fragmentation within the movement since, to a large extent, have their origins there, as well. During the 1980s leadership came from within the coalition of "directly affected" or "direct victims" (*p'ihaeja*) groups – that is, the respective associations composed of the three major kinds of victims: bereaved family members, the injured, and those arrested for their role in the uprising.[41] It is these groups (and their members) that have historically had the most legitimacy, the most power, and the strongest claims to the memory of May 18; but it is also these groups who, with the shift in the 1990s away from the politics of dissent and class confrontation, and the waning of the *minjung* movement, have lost the most. In the absence of new agendas and strategies, the direct victims' groups face renewed disenfranchisement and marginalization in civic affairs.

Ironically, it is the Bereaved Families Association (*5.18 Kwangju Minjung Hangjaeng Yujokhoe*) that seems to have suffered the biggest eclipse in status and power. Although it is not the largest of the direct victims' groups, it has been the most influential, perhaps because of its claims to, and long struggle over, the victims' gravesites. In Korean culture, particular importance is attached to the proper performance of funeral and mourning rituals, including death-day observances.[42] On May 29, 1980, just after the Uprising, the military took victims' corpses to a small corner of the public cemetery in garbage trucks, and dumped them. The same day, 126 bodies were buried on a hillside, and relatives managed to hold a joint memorial service; two days later, they formed the "5.18 Kwangju Heroic Uprising Bereaved Families Association"– the first 5.18 group to be organized. Since then, members' activities have included continuous demonstrations and testimony about 5.18, and, as chief mourners for the heroic dead, these families have customarily played a central role in the anniversary events.

As has already been mentioned, on the first anniversary, on May 18, 1981, BFA members trying to hold graveside memorial rites were barred from Mangwŏldong cemetery, and their leader was detained by police; it was not until the fifth anniversary, in 1985, in fact, that citizens could freely visit the cemetery. The image of grieving relatives being kept from the graves of their lost loved ones, deprived of the right to properly mourn their own massacred children, siblings, spouses, or parents was potent, and the decade of persecution and harassment the 5.18 bereaved suffered at the hands of the government throughout the 1980s only solidified their moral claims. By 1995, when the anniversary could be freely remembered, crowds of up to 10,000[43] gathered on May 18 at the Mangwŏldong cemetery for the BFA's annual graveside memorial rites (*hŭisaengja ch'umosik*). The major television networks set up desks amid the grave mounds for their newscasters, and camera crews seeking a panoramic view of the huge spectacle perched atop a towering crane. The Mayor of Kwangju, allowed to appear for the first time at these rites, was one of three chief mourners. And, at the conclusion of the ceremony the large number of invited guests seated on the dais (a group of civic leaders that included local politicians, university administrators, and religious figures) followed the relatives of the dead, in paying homage at the offering-laden altar.

By 1997, however, the event had changed significantly. With the opening of the new cemetery, the BFA's community *chesa*[44] was displaced from the actual death anniversary, to May 17; in its place, the government held its own "5.18 Democratization Movement Memorial Service" (*5.18 Minjuhwa Undong Kinyŏmsik*) on May 18. Although the relatives of the dead sat in places of honor, it clearly was not their event. The next year, in 1998, the families' traditional rite, again held on May 17, was attended by only a few hundred people, while the government's service, complete with military band and a speech by the Prime Minister, drew as many as 10,000;[45] by 2000, the President's appearance assured the primacy of the civil ceremony.

This shift from the central spot on the commemorative events calendar is symbolic of the group's displacement from power. With no further agenda beyond what has already been achieved, it is difficult to imagine how the BFA can maintain its privileged place in civic affairs. Ironically, their very success, in the monumental scale of the new cemetery and its tacit recognition of the 5.18 dead as national heroes, precludes any further demands, and the concomitant co-optation by the government of a major role in the memorialization process forecloses any immediately apparent opportunities for (even symbolic) leadership. While the groups' 1997 official anniversary message concludes with the statement that "There are still many tasks that remain, in order for the 5.18 Peoples' Uprising to become the foundation for this country's democracy, and an important experience that leads towards world peace and the expansion of human rights," it outlines no concrete goals or plan of action for the coming year.

Other direct victims' groups, most notably the injured, still have unmet needs, which they are struggling to successfully articulate in a less-than receptive environment.[46] After all, of the 3,416 "official victims" (*injong toen p'ihaeja*),[47] the majority (over 95 percent) are survivors of one kind or another,[48] who continue to suffer from the events of May 1980. Research has shown that over 91.7 percent of 5.18 victims evince post-traumatic stress disorders. Among the victims, 42 percent suffer from physical ailments, 19 percent from mental problems, and 31 percent from both; in addition, their degree of life change events (7.1 times), anxiety (3.2 times), and depression (2.7 times) is higher than non-victims in Kwangju.[49] They are also, in general, less educated and poorer than average. About 70 percent of those who died were working class (factory workers, service sector laborers, petty traders, farmers) or unemployed, and evidence suggests the same is true for 5.18 survivors, as well.[50] Furthermore, throughout the 1980s, the direct victims tended to remain poor, with many actually suffering downward mobility.[51] In fact, the observation that these people have "for the past 17 years and even now ... been confronting death"[52] is not empty rhetoric: since 1980 an additional 120 victims have died,[53] survivors are at higher risk for drug addiction (from pain killers), alcoholism, and suicide,[54] and family members of the 5.18 dead and missing are more likely to suffer associated deaths, often from what Koreans call *hwappyŏng*.[55]

The Association of 5.18 Injured (*5.18 Minjung Hangjaeng Pusangja Hoe*) was the second victims' group founded, on July 13, 1982;[56] its numbers have steadily dwindled over the years (as members have either recovered or died)[57] to "about 300"[58] in the mid-1990s. The Association's primary goal is medical treatment (*ch'iryo*): getting adequate care, paying for it, and living with the effects of chronic illness and disability. Although most have health insurance, in the majority of cases it does not cover all medical expenses;[59] those who are disabled also have difficulty finding work.[60] Many of the victims suffer from chronic pain from bullet "splinters," or fragments, left in their bodies, for which the only relief is increasingly larger doses of drugs.[61] Another common problem is lead poisoning (from bullets); this has had an impact on victims' general health, although for many years they were not even aware of this themselves.[62] Needless to say, caring for the victims is also stressful for their families, who may in turn need financial and psychological support.[63] Several of the critically ill would benefit from treatment in U.S. trauma centers; the Association of the Injured did manage to send three victims to Los Angeles in 1996,[64] but the group has had great difficulty in raising even the relatively small amount needed to send several more of the seriously injured overseas for medical attention.

To address these problems, in 1996 the Association for the Injured began, as its part of the uprising anniversary events, to hold an annual scholarly meeting (*haksul daehoe*), the purpose of which was to educate the public about issues related to the injured, and as a forum for presenting the group's agenda. At the first one, on May 25, 1996, the results of research on the victims' health after fifteen years was discussed. The second, in 1997, was devoted to the presentation of a concrete proposal for a comprehensive treatment/public welfare center for

5.18 victims (*ch'iryo mich chaehwal pokji sent'ŏ*);[65] the third, in 1998, focused on the feasibility of seeking compensation for psychological damages (*chŏngsinjŏk paesang*). By labeling these events as "scholarly," presenting factual information and sound arguments in a scientific context, and soliciting the help of locally or regionally recognized (non-victim) academics, the group hopes to depoliticize their agenda and win broader public support. These represent new tactics, consciously adopted in an effort to share in the new-found national "legitimacy" of the Kwangju Uprising, and to compete for the public money that is as a result available since the late 1990s in Kwangju for 5.18 related projects.

Unfortunately, the fact that these meetings have been attended by a relatively small number of people (fewer than 200) who are mostly victims themselves, and the organizers have had difficulty in finding academics and medical professionals willing to participate, is indicative of the general antipathy in Kwangju towards the injured. Despite the compelling argument that, if the 5.18 spirit means respect for human dignity, then taking care of the victims should be a civic priority, most citizens prefer that 5.18 be "over." Ironically, the trials of former presidents Roh and Chun in 1995 (which the 5.18 victims' groups actively sought, and then attended) helped provide just such a public sense of closure.

The Association of the Injured would perhaps have more success if it could align itself more closely with other national and/or international social movements; repositioning the injured as people with disabilities, rather than victims of government violence, for example, is an intriguing idea. But how could they accomplish this? Obviously, the class composition of the 5.18 related groups reproduces the original socio-economic divisions existing in Kwangju in 1980, at the time of the uprising. As the dead were by and large poorer and less educated than average, so, too, are their surviving relatives and comrades, who, in the changing political context of the late 1990s, lack the skills and resources to avoid revictimization, through public neglect of their very real physical, social, and psychological problems.

National social movements: students and labor in the post-Minjung era

In addition to these local groups, there are also other national social movements that have historically claimed 5.18 as part of their own *minjung* struggle narrative and thus, have in the past played an active role in the uprising anniversary. Two of these, the student movement and the democratic labor movement, have remained a presence in Kwangju in May throughout the late 1990s, although (as we shall see) their public reception has been quite different.

As late as 1996, college students were highly visible participants in the uprising anniversary festivities. That year, hundreds of students marched in the "eve parade" (on May 17), and held rallies night after night on the blocked off main thoroughfare, *Kŭmnamno*, singing 5.18 songs, chanting anti-government slogans, dancing to *samulnori* bands, and setting small bonfires in the street. In the words of one American college student observing the scene, it was a sort of "political Mardi Gras"– lively and festive, but with a militant edge. In 1997, however, there was no "eve parade" on May 17, and the students were kept to the margins, pushed out of the official program. Their role that year was as disrupters rather than as participants, battling riot police late into the night, every night for a week, in the streets around the Provincial Office Building. Even during the daily graveside memorial events, riot police generally kept student groups contained in the old cemetery area, which has in the years since become the de facto anti-government/anti-American protest site and the staging ground for forays into the new cemetery; in one incident on May 18, 1997 a group of about 200 militant students charged the main altar and attempted to tear down the memorial wreaths sent by government officials. However, the students were repulsed by a dozen bereaved family members who, quickly mobilizing from the various gravesites where they had been holding private family rites, confronted the students, and, angrily berating them, tried to chase them away from the central plaza.

Thus, by the late 1990s, activist students were no longer welcome, even on the sacred terrain in Kwangju where not so long before, on anniversaries past, they had joined with Kwangju citizens in fighting the riot police. This anti-student stance was a conscious policy on the part of the anniversary events organizing committee. Earlier, in April 1997, a local university student had died in a demonstration; his body was still in the hospital, and the students wanted to hold a public funeral for him concurrent with the anniversary events. Sentiment in Kwangju, however, was turning against this kind of student activism.[66] With the image of Kwangju improving in the eyes of the nation, civic leaders feared the co-optation of the 5.18 commemoration program by radical students, and opposed the continued association of Kwangju with violent anti-government protests. Even the media were unanimous in condemning the students' plans, and students were denied an official part in the proceedings. So, although students (not just from Kwangju, but from all over the country) made their presence known – marching about the city, holding noisy rallies, trying almost daily to get to the center of town, and disrupting organized memorial events[67] – public opinion was not sympathetic, and they were unable to muster support for their cause.

If activist students had not attempted to promote their own national anti-government agenda during May in Kwangju, or had not been so intransigent in the face of popular disenchantment with their tactics, perhaps they could have continued to have an important role in the commemoration events. Student unwillingness to comply with the "new," less confrontational, unprovocative, peaceful – essentially depoliticized – tone of the anniversary events espoused by Kwangju's civic leaders in the late 1990s caused their displacement to the margins.

Obviously, this mirrors the situation on the larger national scene, where the student movement was, by the late 1990s, becoming more radical, and less influential. Particularly in the wake of the Yonsei University incident of August, 1996 and the government's subsequent successful efforts to stigmatize *Hanch'ongnyŏn*[68] as anti-state, the student movement was, by May 1997, more isolated; even Kwangju's tolerant and long-suffering citizenry could finally also say "enough."[69]

In contrast to the students, another waning national social movement with a claim to the symbolic capital of the Kwangju uprising, the labor movement, has been more successful in maintaining its stake in the anniversary commemoration, and using the May events to advance its own political agenda in post-*minjung* Korea. In 1997, the same May the students were banished, democratic labor (*minju noch'ong*) successfully inaugurated a new union, the National Democratic Taxi Labor Union (*Chŏn'guk Minju T'aeksi Nodong Chohap Yŏnmaeng*) in Kwangju. In an event[70] that brought together national and local democratic labor leaders, Anniversary Events Committee members, 5.18 survivors, and taxi drivers from around the country, both the role of taxi drivers (and by extension, all laborers) in the Kwangju Uprising was remembered and extolled, and the establishment of the new union was celebrated.

May 20 is customarily set aside in Kwangju as "Democratic Drivers' Day" (*Minju Kisa ŭi Nal*), in recognition of the decisive role played by drivers at this point in the Uprising. On that day in 1980, taxi and bus drivers, angered at the actions of martial law troops,[71] gathered at *Mudŭng* Stadium and decided to drive straight into the lines of soldiers massed around the provincial office building. A long line of several hundred vehicles – the "taxi troops"– paraded through town and advanced on the soldiers; many drivers were killed or injured,[72] but their heroic actions rallied their fellow citizens, who then battled on through the night.[73]

In 1997 the commemorative event included a re-enactment of the vehicle demonstration. Following a sound truck carrying Kwangju dignitaries and labor leaders, a parade of about 1,000 drivers[74] – on foot, in a line of almost 100 taxis, four abreast, or riding in the buses in which they had come from other parts of the country – proceeded downtown to the provincial office building where, in a brief ceremony, labor protest songs were sung, and a statement was read honoring Kwangju's "democratic drivers" and proclaiming the goals of the new labor union. Tying the two events together, the union's "struggle resolution" (*t'ujaeng kyŏlŭi mun*) declared (among other things) that "Following the examples of the struggle of our senior comrades, the Kwangju taxi drivers, and the Taegu taxi laborers' demonstration, numerous vehicle demonstrations, and a general strike, we resolve that we will strive without surrender for the realization of taxi laborers' rights and interests, and human existence." In addition, "we will take the lead in campaigning for the independence of laborers and the development of this country's democracy, as we inherit the fighting spirit of our senior taxi driver comrades who fought, risking their lives, against the guns and swords of the martial law troops."[75]

Thus, the labor movement activists who participated in the event managed to use the 5.18 anniversary as a forum at which they could put forth their own concrete political program (the speeches and proclamations also outlined more specific goals and union demands), successfully evoking the moral power and legitimacy of laborers' role in the Kwangju Uprising, in support of a larger, contemporary national democratic labor agenda. And, far from being pushed to the margins by Kwangju civic leaders, labor-movement-sponsored events were part of the official anniversary program.

The reason for this, it would appear, is that the activities of labor were peaceful and low key. Although in previous years representatives from labor groups carried provocative banners and chanted militant slogans, in 1997 they avoided such displays, and consciously distanced themselves from the more radical students.[76] In addition, labor unions brought in participants from outside the Honam area. In 1997, 5.18 leaders were publicly lamenting the fact that, although the proclamation of 5.18 as a national commemoration day theoretically made the anniversary a national, rather than regional, event, in reality it remained a local celebration. How to overcome this problem is a cause for civic concern,[77] and that year, the Democratic Drivers' Day event provided a notable exception. One participant from outside the region confessed that normally he would not want to be anywhere near Kwangju on May 18, but since the Kwangju Uprising was indeed an important historic event in the creation of his union, he had overcome his misgivings to attend. During the 1980s, *minjung* movement solidarity apparently overrode regional prejudices; in the post-*minjung* 1990s, Kwangju appears to face renewed national indifference.

Kwangju in May: into the twenty-first century?

It would be ironic if the price of the restoration of Kwangju's honor, the result of state appropriation of 5.18 and the consequent national recognition and memorialization of May, is the erasure from public memory of the long struggle to realize that very goal – particularly, memory of the suffering of 5.18 victims. In the government's discourse on the national democratization movement and Kwangju's place in it, citizens are asked to celebrate the achievement of democratization, without also remembering the *minjung* activism of the 1980s that brought the long process to fruition. In Kwangju, the legacy of that activism does linger, if only symbolically, in the imagery conjured by the very naming of the event itself: those in Kwangju continue to use the "5.18 Kwangju People's Uprising" (*5.18 Kwangju Minjung Hangjaeng*), while the government in the 1990s has re-inscribed it the "5.18 Kwangju Democratization Movement" (*5.18 Kwangju Minjuhwa Undong*). In May, street arches, banners, and signs in Kwangju commemorating the anniversary carry both designations, depending on whether they have been erected by the government, or by 5.18 movement and Kwangju civic organizations, students, labor unions, or other activist groups. Yet the trend, even in Kwangju, is away from the activism and oppositional political style of the past.

There are, as Sunhyuk Kim suggests, several dangers in this transition to a civil society in Korea. One is that South Korean civil society "should learn to tolerate and promote greater diversity and pluralism"; as new interest groups arise, "Labeling some issues as trivial and instead imposing 'greater' goals is merely the mirror image of the authoritarian past."[78] In the case of the 5.18 groups

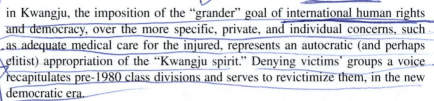

in Kwangju, the imposition of the "grander" goal of international human rights and democracy, over the more specific, private, and individual concerns, such as adequate medical care for the injured, represents an autocratic (and perhaps elitist) appropriation of the "Kwangju spirit." Denying victims' groups a voice recapitulates pre-1980 class divisions and serves to revictimize them, in the new democratic era.

Furthermore, "functional groups in a civil society" should not be "ashamed and guilty of projecting and pursuing their own sectoral interests",[79] and charged with being simply "petty" interest groups. That the Association of the Injured would, for example, propose the building of a comprehensive treatment facility is a perfectly reasonable goal, one that deserves better than dismissal as "selfish" and "greedy" by their fellow citizens.

Unfortunately, as has been suggested, the direct victims' groups in Kwangju in general lack the resources and skills to successfully compete on behalf of their own interests. Outside the inclusive umbrella of the now moribund *minjung* movement, they must struggle to be heard. While participation in the *minjung* movement may have been a mixed blessing for many different groups during the 1980s,[80] without it, people like the 5.18 victims have much less power. Obviously, they must find new tactics and allies, and ways to reposition themselves in the changed political environment of the late 1990s, if they are to make the transition from being part of a resisting civil society, struggling against authoritarianism, to playing a role in a new generation of social movements in Korea.

Notes

1 This chapter is based on ethnographic research carried out in Kwangju between 1995 and 2000, primarily in May of each year.
2 As quoted in the *Chŏnnam Ilbo*, 5.19.1997, p. 20.
3 The "Kwangju Uprising" (or "5.18") was a popular revolt against the South Korean government that took place in the southwestern city of Kwangju and lasted for ten days in May, 1980. What began as a peaceful demonstration against the imposition of military rule turned into a bloody citizens' uprising when the people of Kwangju, outraged by the brutality of government troops sent in to suppress the demonstration, pushed the soldiers to the edge of town and proclaimed a "free Kwangju." The government eventually retook the city with tanks and tear gas, but not without great cost in human lives and government credibility. Memories of the Kwangju Uprising were a rallying cry for opposition forces throughout the regime of military strongman Chun Doo Hwan (1980–1987), and the event had much symbolic importance in the Korean democracy movement of the 1980s. See Linda S. Lewis, *Laying Claim to the Memory of May: A Look Back at the 1980 Kwangju Uprising* (forthcoming, Honolulu: University of Hawaii Press) for a detailed account of the event itself. Also see Donald N. Clark, ed., *The Kwangju Uprising: Shadows Over the Regime in South Korea* (Boulder, Colorado: Westview Press, 1988) for an analysis of the event's meaning and significance and Jae-eui Lee, *Kwangju Diary: Beyond Death, Beyond the Darkness of the Age* (Los Angeles: UCLA Asian Pacific Monograph Series, 1999) for a Kwangju-centered description of the uprising.
4 The notable exception seemed to be at the display sponsored by the Association of the Detained (*5.18 Minjung Hangjaeng Kusokja Hoe*) where loudspeakers continued to blast out the familiar melodies. When questioned about why only their group, and

not the others, was playing the 5.18 protest songs, members replied that, as they had actually done the fighting in 1980, for them these songs still had special meaning, and thus they (in contrast to others) were unwilling to go along with the popular consensus and give up on their music.

5   Referring to the municipal cemetery outside of Kwangju where many of the 5.18 victims were originally buried.

6   See 5.18 Kwangju People's Uprising Bereaved Families' Association (or BFA),[*5.18 Kwangju Minjung Hangjaeng Yujokhoe*], *Record of the Kwangju Peoples' Uprising* [*Kwangju Minjung Hangjaeng Pimangnok*] (Kwangju: Namp'ung, 1989), p. 357.

7   In a speech on May 18, 1985 Democratic Justice Party chairman and future President Roh Tae Woo said of 5.18: "It was not only regrettable that social confusion followed the October 26 incident [the assassination of President Park Chung Hee], but also it was a national tragedy that in the vortex of that confusion, as many as 191 human lives were lost." This was the first public mention of its kind by a government and ruling party leader (*Tonga Ilbo* editorial, 5.20.85).

8   A major national daily newspaper.

9   About $32.6 million.

10   5.18 People's Uprising 17th Anniversary Events Committee (or AC) [*5.18 Minjung Hangjaeng 17 Chunyŏn Haengsa Wiwŏnhoe*], *5.18 Peoples' Uprising 17th Anniversary Collected Materials* [*5.18 Minjung Hangjaeng 17 Chunyŏn Charyojip*], pamphlet published by the AC, Kwangju, 1997, back cover.

11   Kim Dae-jung, a native of the area, was convicted and sentenced to death for his alleged role in "masterminding" the Kwangju Uprising; the sentence was later commuted, and he was allowed to go into exile in the United States.

12   Nancy Abelmann, "Reorganizing and Recapturing Dissent in 1990s South Korea," in Richard Fox and Orin Starn, eds., *Between Resistance and Revolution* (New Jersey: Rutgers University Press, 1997), pp. 250–251.

13   See Kwangju City Government pamphlet, *Information about the Glorious Achievements of 5.18* [*5.18 Yujŏkji Annae*], p. 2.

14   The Kwangju telephone directory in 1996 listed at least thirteen 5.18 related groups. Over the years various coalition groups have come and gone, as have some associations (occasionally nationwide) for specific campaigns, e.g. the "Prosecute the Murderers" movement of the late 1980s.

15   Lawyer Kim Dae-bong, as quoted in the *Chŏnnam Ilbo*, 5.19.1997, p. 20.

16   See the Introduction to the 5.18 People's Uprising 17th Anniversary Events [*5.18 Minjung Hangjaeng Che 17 Kinyŏmhaengsa Sogae*] a pamphlet prepared by the 5.18 People's Uprising 17th Anniversary Events Committee [*5.18 Minjung Hangjaeng Che 17 Kinyŏm Haengsa Wiwŏnhoe*], p. 2.

17   From the chairman's introductory remarks in the *5.18 Peoples' Uprising Information Pamphlet* [*5.18 Minjung Hangjaeng 17 Chunyŏn Charyojip*], published by the 17th AC, p. 1.

18   Sunhyuk Kim, "Civil Society in South Korea: From Grand Democracy Movements to Petty Interest Groups?" *Journal of Northeast Asian Studies* (Summer, 1996), p. 94.

19   The group is not against the building of monuments, per se; it simply sought a voice in the decision-making process. In fact, in 1994 members were active in the campaign to build a stone tower at the Mangwŏldong cemetery and in the movement to preserve the *Sangmudae* prison and courtroom as historical sites.

20   Thirteen citizens' groups came together to formally found the original organization in 1994; less than a year later it was re-established as an independent organization with individual members. It remains, by design, a rather small group, of under 50 participants. See "Introduction, Kwangju Citizens' Solidarity," Kwangju Citizens' Solidarity, http://www.ik.co.kr/kcs/ (1996).

21   See Kwangju Citizens' Solidarity, "Kwangju: Mecca of Democracy," pamphlet published in 1995, p.2.

22 See Kwangju Citizens' Solidarity, "Proceedings of the First International Youth Camp for Human Rights and Peace" (Kwangju: 1996), pp. 16–17.

23 Ibid., p. 17.

24 Over 200 NGOs directly participated in the drafting process of the Charter, which began in 1994. The final drafting meeting took place in Hong Kong in 1996, and its public declaration in 1998 coincided with the 50th anniversary of the Universal Declaration on Human Rights. See "Program: Declaring the Asian Human Rights Charter," Kwangju Citizens' Solidarity, http://www.ik.co.kr/kcs (1998).

25 Ibid.

26 Very few of the Solidarity members are themselves 5.18 "direct victims." The ones I personally know of who are were college students or professors at the time, and are in the category of people who were detained and/or arrested in connection with the event (rather than the injured, members of bereaved families, etc.).

27 A local newspaper which, along with the Journalists Association of Korea, co-sponsored the event.

28 Kwangju Citizens' Solidarity, *Kwangju in the Eyes of the World* (Kwangju: P'ulpit Publishing Co., 1997), p. x.

29 Ibid.

30 Personal communication, KCS executive committee member.

31 And which did not succeed.

32 "Kwangju Continues: The Kwangju Uprising From the Perspective of Compensation" [*Kwangjunŭn Kyesoktoego Issda: Paesangŭi Ch'ŭngmyŏnesŏPon Kwangju Hangjaeng*], presented at an international symposium entitled "Inhumane Acts and Their Resolution" [*Paninnyun Haengwiwa Ch'ŏngsang*], Kwangju, May 17, 1995, *Proceedings* p. 33.

33 Ibid., p. 18.

34 Ibid., p. 17.

35 Ibid., p. 15.

36 According to Pak Wŏn-sun (pp. 30–33), there have been several chances for victim compensation. In June 1980, W 4,200,000 was given from private donations as death compensation (including for funeral expenses). A government compensation law was enacted in August 1990 and W 142 billion 700 million was distributed to 2,227 people. In a second compensation plan, the Kim Young Sam government later gave out W 37 billion 900 million to 1,831 people. These plans have been somewhat controversial, with many claims being denied and some victims refusing, on principle, to accept the money.

37 A Korean unit of area, of about 6 square feet.

38 *Sangmudae* was in 1980 a large army base on the edge of Kwangju. The area has now been turned into a mammoth apartment complex, but the buildings where prisoners were detained and secret military court trials were held in the aftermath of 5.18 have been preserved, and a May 18 Memorial Park and Theme Park is planned for the site. In addition, a Memorial Hall and Memorial Square will be built downtown on the site of the Provincial Office Building, when in the future those buildings are torn down. See Kwangju City Government pamphlet, *Information About the Glorious Achievements of 5.18* [*5.18 Yujŏkji Annae*], p. 16.

39 See Ibid., pp. 13–15; also Kwangju City Government pamphlet, *5.18 Sacred Place Pilgrimage* [*5.18 Sŏngji Sunnye*], p. 4; also *Korea Times*, 5.17.97, p. 3.

40 Personal interview, 5.22.97.

41 During the 5th Republic these basic groups themselves splintered as categories became more complicated and refined – in part due to the government's differential treatment, in terms of compensation, of different classes of victims. For example, among families of those who are missing, some petitions for 5.18 official victim's status have been granted by the government, and some have not, thus creating two groups with different claims, interests, and goals vis-à-vis the government, and within

the 5.18 movement itself. There have also been splits due to ideological and tactical differences.

42 See Roger Janelli and Dawnhee Yim Janelli, *Ancestor Worship and Korean Society* (Stanford: Stanford University Press, 1982) for the definitive discussion of these practices.

43 As reported in the *Kwangju Ilbo*, 5.18.1995, p. 1.

44 Confucian-based ancestor memorial rites.

45 As reported in the *Chŏnnam Ilbo*, 5.18.1998, p. 1.

46 See Juna Byun and Linda S. Lewis, eds., *The Kwangju Uprising After 20 Years: The Unhealed Wounds of the Victims* (Seoul: Dahae Publishers, 2000) for extensive analyses of the situation of the 5.18 victims at the turn of the century.

47 1994 Kwangju City Government statistics, which reckon 154 victims, 47 official missing, 2,710 injured, and 505 questioned, detained, or convicted. Other groups calculate the number as higher; for example, there are 107 "unofficial" missing, and the Association for the Injured claimed 4,326 in 1990 (as quoted in Juna Byun, "5.18 Democratization Movement Victims' Current Obstacles and Countermeasures" [*5.18 Minjuhwa Undong P'ihaejadŭlŭi Changaehyŏn Kwa Daech'aek*], a lecture presented at the 2nd Annual 5.18 Injured Associations' Scholarly Meeting, Kwangju, May 24, 1997). In addition, 120 victims died between 1980 and 1997 (as quoted in a report on "Those Who Died After 5.18" [*5.18 Minjung Hangjaeng Sangihu Samangja*] presented by Kim Sŏng-su at the same event).

48 This number does not include victims' families, who are also recognized as being at increased risk. The rate of death may also be increasing; in one eight month period in 1994–1995, nine of the injured died (as cited by Juna Byun), and in 1998 two famous victims finally succumbed (personal communication, Juna Byun).

49 Juna Byun, "Fifteen Year-Aftermath Syndrome of Victims from the Kwangju Civil Uprising of May 18, 1980, South Korea," unpublished paper, 1996. See also Juna Byun, "The 15 Year Aftermath Trauma" in Byun and Lewis.

50 Catholic Church, Kwangju Diocese Justice and Peace Committee [*Ch'ŏnjukyo kwangju Daekyogu Chŏngŭi P'yŏnghwoa Wiwŏnhoe*], *A Study of Kwangju Citizens' Social Consciousness, Through Popular Feelings About the Kwangju Uprising* [*Kwangju Simin Sahoe ŭisik Chosa*], (Kwangju: Pitkoŭl Publishing, 1988), p. 53.

51 Ibid., p. 52. In Byun's 1995 sample, 32.35 percent were jobless in 1980, but the percentage had risen to 64.71 percent in 1995. While these figures do not control for many variables, it is clear that the socio-economic status of the victims (and their families) has, in general, deteriorated since the Uprising.

52 Juna Byun, 1997, p. 8.

53 As of May 1997, as cited by the Chairman of the Association of Bereaved Families of Those Who Died After 5.18 (*5.18 Sangihu Samangja Yujokhoe*) at the 2nd Annual Injured Association Scholarly Meeting.

54 See Jae-eŭi Lee, "Kwangju's Democratic Citizens Bemoan Successful Coup D'etat" [*Sŏnggonghan K'udet'ae Sinŏm Hanŭn Kwangju Minju Simin*], in *Modern Praxis* (14, 1995), pp. 82–107 for examples of these problems.

55 Causation as explained by the survivors' families (personal communication, Juna Byun). *Hwappyŏng* is a Korean culture-bound syndrome in which death is attributed to excessive *hwa*, or pent-up anger, frustration, and resentment.

56 Kwangju City May 18 History Compilation Committee [*Kwangju 5.18 Saryo P'yŏnch'an Wiwŏnhoe*], *The 5.18 Kwangju Peoples' Uprising [5.18 Kwangju Minjung Hangjaeng*] (Kwangju: Tosŏ Publishing, 1997), p. 143.

57 One member, now bedridden, reminisced about how at first the victims, mostly young and unemployed, used to help each other, even pushing each others' wheelchairs around.

58 Personal communication, Association of the Injured Chairman.

59 Pak Yŏng-sun, "1997 Survey of 200 5.18 Peoples' Uprising Injured Victims" [*1997 Nyŏndo 5.18 Minjung Hangjaeng P'isaengja 200 Myŏng Silt'ae Pogosŏ*], unpublished paper presented at the 3rd Annual Association of the Injured Scholarly Meeting, Kwangju, May 16, 1998. See also Byun, "Introduction," in Byun and Lewis, p. 32–33.

60 See Sangkyu Kim, "The Government's Responsibility and Role in the Victims' Rehabilitation," in Byun and Lewis for a discussion of treatment of the disabled in Korea.

61 One of those hoping for treatment in the U.S., whose spinal cord was severed, says the bullet splinters are like scattered sand, impossible to remove, but causing pain as his blood circulates. The pain is still 50 percent as much as when he was first hit, and his biggest wish "is to have my kid go to college. And then, before I die, if my pain could be gone for even one day, I would have nothing else to wish for. Because my body hurts so much, I can't help but think about that time [1980]. Whether I am active or not ... the broken nerves, spine, my lower body will not recover. I don't expect that. But to the extent that the pain stops – for a day, or a week – it seems impossible, until I die" (personal communication, Yongdae Kim, 1996).

62 Personal communication, Association of the Injured Chairman.

63 Many victims have in fact been abandoned by their families. As one paraplegic put it, "For my wife, it must be like being in a grave. It is a mystery to me, why the center of her heart has not exploded by now" (personal communication, Yong-dae Kim, 1996). See Jae-eŭi Lee, *Modern Praxis*, p. 84 for accounts of wives who have received awards for their devotion to bedridden husbands.

64 Two of them were children in 1980. One, Sang-chul Park was shot in the back, and after ten operations still suffered from partial paralysis and an open wound in his back that would not heal. See K. Connie Kang, *Los Angeles Times*, February 5, 1996 (B1).

65 See Juna Byun, "Conclusion," in Byun and Lewis for a description of the proposed center.

66 Previous to this, the radical student governing association, *Hanch'ongnyŏn*, had planned to hold their inaugural meeting in Kwangju. Local newspapers heard about the plan and reported it; public opinion was sufficiently aroused that *Hanch'ongnyŏn* was forced to change the proposed venue (personal communication, Jae-eŭi Lee).

67 As many as 5,000 radical students held street demonstrations on May 23. See for example Hŭng Ki Kim and Kil Yong Ku, *Kwangnam Ilbo*, 5.24.97, p. 23.

68 The National Federation of Student Councils. Initiated in 1993, in 1996 it was an umbrella organization representing student councils of some 180 universities and colleges in Korea, and was characterized by increasingly violent tactics and a radical platform. *Hanch'ongnyŏn* was responsible for nine days of violent demonstrations at Yonsei University, during which a building was seized.

69 Even students in Kwangju apparently felt the same way. A survey taken at Chŏnnam University in the aftermath of the Yonsei University incident found that 63.9 percent of the students and 50 percent of the faculty found *Hanch'ongnyŏn*'s cause acceptable, but its methods wrong. *The Korea Times*, September 7, 1996, p. 1.

70 Officially called the "5.18 Democratic Drivers' Day Memorial Service and Rally for Laborers' Determination to Keep the Spirit Alive" (*5.18 Minjugisa ŭi Nal mit Chŏngsin'gyesŏng ŭl wihan Nodongja Kyŏlŭi Taehoe*). "Keep the Spirit Alive" rallies are a common feature of the May events.

71 It is said that taxi drivers, in particular, because of their mobility, were especially aware of what was going on in the first days of the Uprising. There are many tales of taxi drivers who acted heroically – for example, in taking the wounded to hospitals – and who witnessed acts of brutality when soldiers stopped them and pulled out injured passengers. See Tim Warnberg, "The Kwangju Uprising: An Inside View," in *Korean Studies* 11 (1988) pp. 38–42; also Arnold Peterson, *The 5.18 Kwangju Incident* (Seoul: P'ulpit, 1990), pp. 193, 199.

72 Fully 8.5 percent (or 14) of 5.18 victims are classified as "drivers" (*unjŏnja*) – BFA, 1989, p. 325; also p. 199 for an account of one such death. In addition, many of the injured were riding in trucks and buses when they were shot. See for example the testimony of Pak Yŏng-sun, who was hurt while taking part in a "vehicle demonstration" (*ch'aryang siwi*) – Korean Modern Historical Materials Research Institute [*Hanguk Hyŏndaesa Saryo Yŏnguso*], *The Complete Collection of the Historical Record of the Kwangju May Peoples' Uprising* [*Kwangju Owŏl injung Hangjaeng Saryon Chŏnjip*] (Seoul: P'ulpit, 1990), pp. 689–691.

73 See Jae-eui Lee, *Kwangju Diary: Beyond Death, Beyond the Darkness of the Age* (Los Angeles: UCLA Asian Pacific Monograph Series, 1999), pp. 64–66 for a vivid account of this crucial event. There is also a very famous picture from this day, of a man standing atop a bus, waving a Korean flag. See Chong Kŏn Hwang and Nyŏng Man Kim, *Kwangju, That Day* [*Kwangju, KŭNal*] (Seoul: Sajinyesulsa, 1994), pp. 38–39.

74 As reported in the *Mudŭng Ilbo*, 5.21.1997, p. 1.

75 From a statement, "National Democratic Taxi Labor Union Struggle Resolution" (*Chŏn'guk Minju T'aeksi Nodongchohapyŏngmaeng T'ujaeng Kyŏlŭi Mun*) read at the provincial office building, Kwangju, 5.20.1997.

76 Reportedly, taxi drivers from out of town rode in buses in the parade, rather than walking, as planned, so that students could not infiltrate their ranks, and cause a disturbance when they reached the provincial office building (personal communication, union official from Taegu).

77 See panel discussion among 5.18 civic leaders, *Chŏnnam Ilbo*, May 19, 1997, p. 20.

78 1996, p. 95.

79 Ibid.

80 See for example James Thomas' study of the squatters' movement, in which he says of the *minjung* movement that "although this movement was the only national political force that acted on behalf of and provided consistent support to disadvantaged and disempowered groups, it never focused exclusively on the interests of those groups." "Contested from Within and Without: Squatters, the State, the Minjung Movement and the Limits of Resistance in a Seoul Shanty Town Targeted For Urban Renewal," unpublished doctoral dissertation, University of Rochester, 1993, p. 235.

8 Protestant Christianity and the state

Religious organizations as civil society

Donald N. Clark

Introduction

Christian communities in South Korea are outstanding examples of civil society, as the term is generally understood.[1] They have always drawn their inspiration and power from impulses that are essentially non-political, at least in the sense of being strongly resistant to state domination. Their membership patterns cut across the political spectrum and are not defined by political labels. They provide arenas for tolerance, negotiation of differences, and internal training of new leaders. In *The Clash of Civilizations and the Remaking of the World Order* (see Chapter 1, p. 13), Samuel Huntington has much to say about the power of religion to shape the processes of modernization and revitalization, for example, in the Islamic world. Islam, however, is the traditional creed in the Middle East. Christianity started out as an ideology that was foreign to Korea, and there is much to ponder in the way it has been accepted, absorbed, and even transformed by the Korean people. This is especially so when one compares Korea with Japan and China, where Christianity also has a dramatic history but has never accounted for more than a small percentage of the religious population. The fact that approximately 25 percent of South Koreans identify themselves as Christians raises questions about the nature of Korean society, the process by which Christianity was introduced to Korea, the interaction between Christian propagation and events and trends in modern Korean history, and the link between Christian ideology and political authority.

Christianity as a model of civil society at work

In many ways Korea's Christian communities act as models of civil society. They comprise a remarkable number and variety of associational "cells" in the form of church congregations that cohere because of particular denominational, historical, regional, and class and income factors. These "cells" meet, recruit and induct new members, train leaders, follow rituals, share beliefs, and strive toward common organizational goals cooperatively and without much interference from the outside. Taken as a whole, Korea's Christian churches include representatives of all social strata and all walks of life, all ages, and, as individuals, all shades of the political spectrum. Their right to meet and practice their religion is guaranteed by the state and protected by the legal structure within certain well-recognized (and mostly agreed-upon) limits. Korean churches engage in self-education and the dissemination of information.[2] And they are autonomous and "democratic" in their structures inasmuch as their members accept the rules voluntarily and the leadership responds to the membership even in the most authoritarian of churches – for the very reason that members are free to "vote with their feet" and join other churches (and do so) in a competitive "membership market."

Protestants and Catholics in Korea

This chapter focuses mainly on Korea's Protestant churches, though the Catholic experience is also essential at points. Indeed, in the human rights struggles of the 1970s and 1980s, the Catholic establishment took the lead in confrontations with the state, notably in the March First Declaration in 1976 opposing the dictatorship of President Park Chung-hee under his *Yushin* "Revitalizing Reforms," and in the democracy movement of 1987, when Cardinal Stephen Kim Suhwan allowed the grounds of the Cathedral of the Immaculate Conception of St. Mary in Myŏng-dong to be used as a sanctuary for dissidents and demonstrators.

The distinction between Catholics and Protestants, however, mirrors Korean history and attitudes. In terms of their theology, church organization, and experience, Korean Catholics and Protestants do not normally see themselves as belonging to the same tradition or even the same religion. Though both streams were built up by missionaries from abroad, the Catholics remained much longer under missionary authority and continue to practice under the umbrella of one central church authority, while the Protestants reflect the multiple denominations represented by the many missionary organizations that have operated in Korea since 1884, and to these have added sub-denominations of their own, reflecting splits in leadership and fine differences in theology. The cacophony of Korean Protestantism contrasts with the discipline of Korean Catholicism, a reminder that not too long ago, before ecumenism took hold, the two sides regarded each other as "separated brethren" at best and heretics at worst. While there has rarely been anything in Korea like the violence of Catholic–Protestant struggles in Europe and Latin America, Koreans identify the term "Christianity" (*kidokkyo*) with Protestantism (which is, strictly speaking, "reformism," or *kaeshin'kyo*), and refer to Catholicism as something very different, called *Ch'ŏnjukyo* (the religion of the Lord of Heaven).

The Protestant–Catholic distinction reflects the history of Christianity throughout Asia, since Catholicism reached China and Japan much earlier, in the sixteenth century, while Protestant missionaries did not arrive until the early 1800s. Catholicism reached Korea in the late eighteenth century, 100 years before Protestantism. During that first century Korea's Catholics had to meet underground and were often caught and killed by the state for practicing dangerous heterodoxies. They associated with fringe members of the ruling class (the educated specialist *chung'in* class) and disaffected intellectuals. But when Korea's first Protestant community was founded in Hwanghae Province in the 1860s by Korean peddlers returning from trips to Manchuria where they met Scottish missionaries, they believed they were beginning a new religion. For example, the terminologies were different. The Protestants called God *Hanŭnim*, using an old Korean word for the Creator, while the Catholics used the term for "Lord of Heaven" learned from Chinese Catholics, which was *Tianzi* (*Ch'ŏnju* in Korean). Protestants also had a different class base. The first ones were peddlers, and when Western missionaries arrived in the mid-1880s they made it a point to present the Gospel to commoners and members of the lower classes. Protestantism was therefore doubly disdained by Korea's ruling *yangban* who rejected it both on ideological and class grounds.

Today, Protestant Christianity (*Kidokkyo*) continues to be regarded as a different religion from Catholicism (*Ch'ŏnjukyo*). The Protestant experience has diverged sharply from the Catholic through most of the twentieth century, and the two, while tolerating each other, have not mingled. One is therefore obliged to tell the story of Korean Christianity in two parts, the Protestant and the Catholic. Here we focus on Protestant history and institutions because they are by far the larger of the two streams of Christianity and, until the recent dramatic increase in Catholic membership, by far the more visible.

Phases of Protestant civil society experience in Korea

Christianity has been a part of Korean history for more than two centuries, beginning with the introduction of Catholic ideas by Korean traders and envoys returning from China in 1784. Reformed Christianity (i.e., Protestantism) began to spread only after the arrival of the first Western missionaries in 1884–1885. The twelve decades of Protestant history since then can be divided into five or six phases of growth during which Korean Protestantism defined and redefined itself and was subjected to severe tests, eventually maturing into a strong and vital force in civil society.

In their formative period (1884–1910), Korea's first Protestants and Protestant missionaries had to deal with the legacy of Christianity as an outlawed religion, suppressed, if no longer by the central government under the royal court,[3] by local officials and members of the *yangban* class whose distaste for Christianity was manifested through the posing of bureaucratic obstacles to its spread.[4] At the same time, Christianity acquired converts from among the "disaffected classes," the sort who would otherwise have joined the Tonghaks (in the southwest) or who were less disposed against foreign ideas (as in the northern P'yŏng'an and Hamgyŏng provinces which were closer to China, more used to foreign contact, and turned out to be the most fertile area of Christian propagation). Certain intellectuals were also drawn to Christianity, notably those who were part of the enlightenment stream, with Independence Club leaders So Chaep'il and Yun Ch'iho as frequently mentioned examples but including many others as well. The convergence of the enlightenment movement and Protestant Christianity was symbolized in the numerous Christian schools that became famous in Korea as centers of modern education and the independence movement, as well as religious institutions.[5] The prestige of Christianity was much enhanced by the reputation of these schools as they directly addressed the political and social crises that confronted Korea as it was succumbing to Japanese colonial domination. Korean Christians also founded civic and patriotic organizations that stood for Korean self-strengthening during this period.

The early part of the Japanese occupation (1910–1920) took Korean Protestantism into a different phase of civil society development by forcing it to confront the new colonial regime. One such confrontation was the so-called "Conspiracy Case" (in Korean, *paego'in sakŏn*, or "105 Incident") of 1911–1913, in which Korean Christians and certain foreign missionaries were accused of plotting to assassinate Terauchi Masatake, the Japanese Governor-General. By that time, the Japanese had identified Protestant Christianity as an element in the new colony that posed potential control problems, and the trumped-up charges in the Conspiracy Case were an attempt to purge the church community of any inclination to resist the new regime. The accusation that Protestant leaders had conspired to kill a second Japanese ruler in the same way that the Catholic An Chunggŭn (1879–1910) had killed Itō Hirobumi in 1909, did not stand up well in court, though the Japanese judges dutifully convicted the most prominent defendants and sentenced them to prison.[6]

A second test of the Protestant community's independence from government control was the colonial government's 1915 order that religion be excluded from the curricula of schools issuing government-recognized diplomas, an order that undermined the *raison d'être* of Christian schools.[7] And a third case, best known of all, was the conspicuous participation of Protestants and Christian church and school communities in the independence uprising of 1919–1920. All three of these episodes represented cases of Korean Christians negotiating the terms of their religious and organizational autonomy from the Meiji system that at least nominally provided for religious freedom under its constitution.

Following the 1919 independence movement, Korean Protestant pastors liked to compare their congregations to the Israelites of the Book of Exodus who suffered cruelties under foreign rule while awaiting deliverance. Protestant ideology under Japanese rule devised a modus vivendi with the state by spinning out a pious ideology of separation from the world, a stress on spiritualism, and a focus on the individual's relationship with an all-powerful and saving God. Human efforts were not to be the agents of Korea's liberation; rather God would find his own way to free the Koreans in his own good time. Meanwhile, though they might engage in Gandhi-style self-strengthening by "buying Korean" and participating as little as possible in the exploitative colonial economic system, they could find ways to coexist with the occupying Japanese while God was preparing for his intervention.[8]

In the middle years of the colonial period, Protestants like Yi Sangjae were prominent as leaders of civil society organizations such as the YMCA. Christian educators like Yun Ch'iho operated schools and sought to bolster Korean consciousness through education, and Christian writers contributed to magazines that spread an enlightened vision of Korean freedom. Christians were part of the united front of nationalists and socialists known as the Sin'ganhoe ("New Trunk Society," or "New Korea Society"), that lasted for two years from 1920 to 1929. Christian thinkers like Kim Kyosin struggled with "Western" aspects of Christianity in an attempt to adapt the religion to the Korean scene, publishing a journal named *Chosŏn Sŏngsŏ* ("The Bible in Korea") and arguing for a Korean version of the Japanese Mukyōkai ("No Church") movement. Chosŏn Christian College (Yŏnhi College) served as a center for Protestant intellectuals as they pursued their "cultural nationalist" activities of language and history studies in an attempt to protect Korean culture from obliteration by Japanese colonial policies.

However, the last years of the Japanese period nevertheless forced Korea's Christians to make harsh choices when the colonial regime created a state-controlled church, or *Kyodan*, as in wartime Japan.[9] The prelude to this development was the well-known imposition of Shintō worship on the Koreans as part of Japan's *Naisen ittai* policy of integrating Korea fully into the Japanese empire. The Japanese meant to strengthen the Koreans' own self-identification as subjects of the Emperor and members of Japan's spiritual framework (its *kokutai*, or national "body") by making them go to Japanese-built Shintō shrines in Korea and performing respectful bows and other obeisances to indicate respect for Japan's national heroes. The spirits of those to be honored included, first and foremost the emperor, but also the war dead who had sacrificed their lives in the effort to extend Japan's colonial control over Korea decades earlier.[10]

The Japanese generally presented Shintō ceremonies as "patriotic" and not "religious," emphasizing the distinction between "state Shintō" and "religious Shintō."[11] However, their form and the nature of the spiritual "presence" in the shrines offended the Korean Christian conscience.[12] If the ceremonies were in fact "worship," they violated the commandments in Exodus 20: 2–4 that forbade worship of any other god than the God of the Bible. No doubt there were many Christians who used the Ten Commandments as an excuse to avoid showing respect to the Japanese spirits (a refusal that meant imprisonment for many after 1938). But there were also sincere Christians who refused shrine worship purely out of religious conviction. In either case, those who refused were cast as disloyal subjects and subject to punishment as members of the Korean resistance.

Those who accepted the Japanese proposition that the shrine rituals were civil and not religious ceremonies, were cast by other Koreans as collaborators, betraying their Korean-ness, or "apostates" betraying their faith. Much enmity was generated among Christians because of individual decisions in this crisis. The bitterness lingered for decades after Liberation from Japan in 1945, plaguing all Christian denominations and confusing relations between church and state under Syngman Rhee and his successors. In South Korea immediately after the division of the peninsula at the 38th parallel, the main Presbyterian and Methodist denominations were torn apart by accusations of collaboration. Yun Ch'iho and Bishop Chŏng Ch'unsu are examples of leading Methodists who were criticized for having made broadcasts supporting the Japanese war effort and, in Chŏng's case, for having used church funds to make contributions to the Japanese military. Yun's death during the controversy is widely believed to have been a suicide, while Chŏng renounced the Methodist Church and became a Catholic. He disappeared and is presumed eventually to have gone to live in the north.

The Christian confrontation with the state in North Korea, 1945–1948

A different kind of confrontation between Christians and the state occurred above the 38th parallel in North Korea between 1945 and 1950. In this situation, the Protestant community started out in an autonomous position as one of the few organized structures surviving the Japanese surrender. Its acknowledged leader was Cho Mansik, a P'yŏngyang-based Presbyterian elder famous for his leading role in the Sin'ganhoe and as organizer of the "Korea Products Promotion Society" (*Chosŏn mulsan changnyohoe*). In August 1945, Cho Mansik became head of the South P'yŏng'an Province Committee for the Preparation of Korean Independence (CPKI; *Chosŏnkŏn'guk chunbi wiwŏnhoe*) and thus emerged as a main contender for leadership in the northern zone. The Soviets accepted Cho when they first arrived and made him Chief Executive of the Five Province Administrative Bureau (*Odo haengjŏngguk*), the interim government they created to consolidate the various northern branches of the CPKI and the local "people's committees" (*inmin wiwŏnhoe*). In October, however, the Soviets brought Kim Il-sung from the Khabarovsk area where he had been serving in an ethnic Korean brigade of the Soviet Red Army. Cho Mansik actually introduced Kim to the populace on at least two occasions, including a public rally in front of City Hall, only to find himself being pushed aside soon thereafter.

As an alternative to Communist power in North Korea, Cho Mansik founded his own Korea Democratic Party (*Chosŏn Minjudang*) in November 1945, drawing membership not only from P'yŏngyang but also from the Sinŭiju area, where the Presbyterian pastors Han Kyŏngjik and Yun Hayŏng had formed their own Christian Social Democratic Party (*Kidokkyo sahoe minjudang*) in September. This group had tried for broader appeal by dropping the "Christian" part of its name, but nevertheless had lost its leaders and much of its membership in the current of refugees fleeing to South Korea. Cho Mansik's Korea Democratic Party enjoyed remarkable early success by bringing together these and many other remnants and factions of anti-Communist north Koreans, winning an estimated half million members within three months, across all five northern provinces.[13]

The growth of this home-grown alternative to the left-wing leadership that was emerging with the help of the Soviet occupation soon led to violent conflict. In November, leftist workers attacked a meeting of the Korea Democratic Party in Yŏnamp'o, and a week later Christian students in Sinŭiju organized an anti-Communist demonstration that led to a violent clash at the city's Communist Party headquarters in which a number of demonstrators were shot and killed. In December, Christians rallied against the Moscow Agreement ending the trusteeship arrangement for the occupation of Korea, an arrangement officially supported by the Soviet Union and Korea's Communists. Cho Mansik's support for this protest, which flew in the face of the official Soviet position, led to his final removal from his nominal position at the head of the Five Province Administrative Bureau in January. Soon thereafter Cho was also taken out as head of the Korea Democratic Party, being replaced by the Communist Ch'oe Yonggŏn.[14] Cho's removal was a serious blow to North Korea's Christians and other non-Communists.

Violence between Christians and Communists again erupted on March 1, 1946, the first-ever commemoration of the 1919 Korean Independence Movement, when the Soviet-backed regime organized a patriotic celebration that was boycotted by Christians in favor of their own observance elsewhere in the city of P'yŏngyang. Certain Christians aggravated the situation by proclaiming that they, and not the Marxists, had been the driving force behind the 1919 uprising, bringing on condemnation from the regime for sowing disunity and putting sectarianism ahead of patriotism.

Later that same month, the Soviet occupation authorities executed a land reform that effectively stripped large landowners of their holdings, organizing absentee holdings in particular (i.e., land rented to sharecroppers) for redistribution to landless peasants. Many Christians were among those who lost part or all of their property in the process. Moreover, all property that had belonged to the Korean church, including church buildings, schools, hospitals, and income-producing lands owned by school foundations (*chaedan*), was reclassified as state property whether it had been owned by Korean Christian groups or foreign missionary societies. The land reform in effect reclassified citizens as collaborators with, or resisters against, the Japanese colonial regime and thus as supporters or enemies of the "revolution." There were public meetings where citizens pointed out other citizens as former collaborators. Many intellectuals, businessmen, and others who were seen as rich or as members of pre-Liberation elites were open to being marked for discrimination and, in some cases, expropriation and punishment.

In November 1946, the northern regime organized an election for members of the region's people's committees, the first step in the creation of a national assembly. Candidates in the election were supposed to represent a broad spectrum of national opinion and included some Christians, but the process was opposed by the region's Christians as a whole because it was clearly meant to legitimize Communist political control. When Christian leaders announced a boycott on grounds that the election was scheduled for a Sunday and thus violated their strict tenet of Sunday observance, the regime took it as a kind of last straw. The government denounced the boycott as an attack on order and an effort to destabilize the system in order to promote the fortunes of the American-backed rightists and collaborators in South Korea. Christians who took this stance were to be regarded as opponents of the "revolutionary state" and its policies, and therefore as enemies of the people.

Having marginalized the existing churches in this manner, the regime created a state-recognized church resembling the non-denominational "kyodan" model employed by the Japanese when they created their state-controlled church during the war. This was the "Christian League" (the *Kidokkyodo yŏnmaeng*), officially empowered to hold the property and supervise and limit the work of the North Korean Christian church. The League was headed by Kang Yang'uk, an ordained Presbyterian minister with family ties to Kim Il-sung.[15]

As thousands of North Korean Christians bitterly pulled up stakes and migrated southward to escape persecution, they carried with them a whole range of grievances against the Soviet-backed leftist regime. Fleeing often with only what they could carry with them, they saw themselves as victims of a foreign-backed Korean faction that had robbed them of their property, livelihoods, political and religious freedom, and their very futures, a government that had turned the dream of Liberation into a nightmare. Naturally, anti-Communism became the basis of their political, social, and religious orientation as they struggled to reconstruct their lives in the south. Younger refugees organized themselves into anti-Communist youth organizations that soon distinguished themselves as volunteer elements in the American-backed South Korean effort to hunt down and eliminate suspected Communists in workers' unions and peasant associations in the region's cities and villages. The most notorious of these organizations, the Northwest Youth (*Sŏbuk ch'ŏngnyŏnhoe*), served the southern regime as paramilitary elements alongside police and army units. In the southwestern province of South Cholla during the late 1940s they came to be hated for their indiscriminate violence against anyone suspected of being a Communist or Communist sympathizer. They were notorious for their participation in the army massacre of civilians on Cheju Island during the islanders' revolt against the Seoul regime in April, 1948.

Christianity and the state in South Korea

Protestant Christianity and the South Korean state have maintained a tense relationship virtually from the moment of Liberation in 1945. Two contradictory features bear special mention here. The first is the basic tendency of South Korea's Christian community to oppose Communism, in particular North Korean Communism, and thus to support the South Korean government's posture of military opposition to North Korea. The second, contradictory tendency is the church's resistance to political pressure and domination by the state, and its determination to set its own moral and social agenda as an institution of civil society. Most observers would agree that the former tendency has been stronger than the latter.

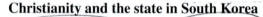

When the Americans occupied South Korea in 1945 and instituted what has been called their "interpreters' government," they sought to employ Koreans who could speak English and who knew something about American political and cultural ideals. They found many Korean Christians who had studied English in mission schools and could remember pre-war lessons in Western history and democratic ideals. The collaboration between the American Military Government and Koreans with Western orientation was immediately obvious to the general public, who saw affiliation with the Americans and knowledge of America including Christianity as an advantage in the new, postwar political system. When the exiled Korean nationalist leader Syngman Rhee ended his decades in the United States and was returned to Korea aboard General Douglas MacArthur's own airplane, it seemed clear that this American-educated Methodist was the embodiment of the future envisioned for South Korea. Notwithstanding the fact that the Americans who had to deal with Rhee found him dictatorial and undemocratic in many ways, Koreans took his leadership as an opportunity to test what it meant to live under a democratic government with a Christian (i.e., Protestant) leader.

As the emerging "American candidate" prior to 1948 and as President of the Republic of Korea from 1948 to 1960, Syngman Rhee played his American connection for all it was worth on the stage of Korean politics. American power after World War II seemed awesome to Koreans and the material and even spiritual qualities of American life seemed enviable. Without deprecating the authentic spiritual appeal of Christianity during that era or diminishing the importance of faith and belief for individuals, Christianity had an undeniable appeal as an ideology opposed to Communism and the religious system, as Koreans saw it, of the richest, most powerful people on earth. This perception enhanced the position of Christianity in the South Korean ideological spectrum and contributed much to its rapid growth.

Historical circumstances – primarily the lack of a viable non-Communist "Korean" alternative in the South in the early months of the Cold War – thus afforded Korean Christians a great social advantage. Rhee cultivated the "Christian government" aspect of his presidency by regularly attending the Chŏng-dong First Methodist Church, by receiving Korean and foreign Christian leaders, and by gestures such as putting chaplains in the military, American-style. Even while Rhee's Liberal Party sank deeper into corruption, railroaded legislation through the National Assembly, and used political violence against opponents, South Korea's Protestants largely supported him personally until the very end, when he was overthrown by massive protests following a rigged election in 1960.

Though "Christian prestige" was hurt by Rhee's disgrace and perhaps also by the fecklessness of Rhee's successor, Prime Minister Chang Myŏn, a Catholic Christian, Korea's Protestants continued to support the anti-Communist state. After the military coup of 1961 they continued to buy the state's anti-Communist rhetoric to such an extent that they accepted repressive security laws and kept silent as center-left elements in society were suppressed, censored, purged, and even executed. The symbiosis of church and state was clear in the participation by leading Protestant clergy in presidential "prayer breakfasts" invoking divine guidance (and favor) for General-turned-President Park Chung-hee and the country's ruling military apparatus. The symbiosis was nurtured in especially egregious ways by right-wing Christian leaders from the United States who frequently turned up in Seoul to praise the South Korean regime as a fearless defender in the worldwide crusade against godless communism.[16]

However, it was during the years of military rule that a significant part of Korea's Christian community, both Protestant and Catholic, began to oppose the undemocratic tactics of the Park regime. They criticized the design that the government was creating for economic development, based as it was on a low-wage, export-driven development model that provided little for the human rights

of workers and privileged the emerging business class. They were offended by the cynicism of the military junta that had promised a return to civilian rule but "retired" from the army and resumed ruling as civilians after government-dominated elections in 1963. The political opposition, consisting of a lineage of conservative politicians (some of them Catholics) who had opposed Syngman Rhee, supported the brief prime ministership of Chang Myŏn in 1960–1961, and criticized the "civilianization" of the military junta, gave rise to the impression of an opposition stance among Catholics in general. The emergence of the Catholic politician Kim Dae Jung and his run for the presidency against Park Chung-hee in 1971 further identified Catholicism with the opposition. The Catholic poet Kim Chiha became famous for his satirical attacks on the Park government and its cronies in the military and big business. Catholic clergymen like Bishop Daniel Chi Haksun and Cardinal Stephen Kim Suhwan helped protect demonstrators from the police and began to use their positions in society to speak openly against the government's use of secret police methods to silence critics.

Certain Protestants likewise demanded an end to the government's betrayal of democracy. Their stand was in the finest tradition of civil society, articulating and insisting on limits for state power and using non-governmental organizations and fora to uphold civil rights. While most of Korea's Christians maintained their attitude of support for the anti-Communist state in South Korea and remained preoccupied with theological issues and controversies that dated back to the Korean War and the colonial period, a more progressive wing of the Protestant Church focused on the contemporary Korean scene. At the center of this group was a liberal sub-denomination of Presbyterians known as *Kijang* (short for *Kidokkyo changnohoe*, "Christian Presbyterians," as opposed to the more conservative mainstream "Jesus Presbyterians"). The Kijang Presbyterians, led by the Reverend Kim Chejun and headquartered at the Han'guk Theological Seminary in Suwŏn, had a long liberal tradition of social activism going back to its regional origins in northeastern Korea and the ethnic Korean area of southeastern Manchuria called Kando (*Jiandao*), a cockpit of leftist opposition to Japanese colonial rule and the homeland of an important strain of Korean Communism. While the Kijang Presbyterians from that tradition had actually struggled to win converts from Communism and present the territory with alternatives to Communism as an ideology of liberation, in the South Korean context of the 1970s their message of social justice and criticism of the military regime was reinterpreted by many fellow Christians as woolly thinking and leftist fellow-traveling. Articulate Kijang spokesmen such as the brothers Mun Ikhwan and Mun Tonghwan, both of the Han'guk Seminary faculty, were viewed as politically unreliable and actually spent time in prison for violating some of the Seoul regime's national security laws, confined, in essence, for giving aid and comfort to the enemy. The Mun brothers and other Christian activists sacrificed much under the military regime but they also identified Christianity with the cause of social justice and kept alive the church's civil society function as an institution that was fighting to remain free from state dictation.

The confrontation between church and state became particularly acute in the 1970s, after Park Chung-hee declared a state of national emergency and began ruling by decree under what is known as the Yushin ("Revitalizing Reforms") constitution, a system that gave him dictatorial powers. The South Korean Central Intelligence Agency (KCIA) harassed church leaders and intimidated worshippers in congregations led by certain targeted pastors. Individuals like Pastor Pak Hyŏnggyu of the Che'il Presbyterian Church in Seoul were singled out for abuse because of their role in human rights demonstrations and public criticisms of the Park regime. The rationale for such harassment was always national security, the argument being that agitators like Reverend Pak were fomenting anti-state activity. It was useful for the regime to make examples of prominent dissidents, arresting them, holding them under house detention, and sometimes trying and sentencing them on charges of sedition and treason. A particularly painful case of this took place in the so-called People's Revolutionary Party (PRP) case of 1974, when the KCIA rounded up a group of workers and charged them as North Korean agents. The same workers had been charged ten years earlier in a case that had been bungled by government prosecutors, and it seemed that the government was looking for a second chance to make examples of the detainees. The government was noticeably rough and unconcerned with the civil rights of the alleged agents under Korean law, and church monitors began to object to the procedures, to demand better proof of the alleged conspiracy, and to organize support groups for the detainees' families. These monitors in turn were subjected to KCIA intimidation. In this atmosphere of Korean McCarthyism, the Catholic poet Kim Chiha, whose satirical works and pungent social commentary had been an embarrassment to the Park regime for several years, was silenced and imprisoned for his opinions which were alleged to have given aid and comfort to the enemy.

A particular target of the Park regime in the PRP case was an interdenominational advocacy unit of the Protestant National Christian Council named the Urban Industrial Mission (UIM) aimed at protecting workers from abuse in the workplace. UIM had a staff of Christians who went into factories and encouraged workers to band together to demand basic improvements including safer conditions, better pay, and humane treatment. At the time, any action that encouraged workers to organize was seen as a threat to the government's low-wage economic development strategy, and UIM was particularly troublesome because of its effectiveness and its international connections. Active in the leadership of UIM, for example, were American missionaries trained in community development and labor issues. They made themselves conspicuous in the PRP protests, standing with family members outside the gate of Seoul's infamous West Gate Prison in vigils calling attention to the legal irregularities of the PRP case. In the denouement of the PRP case the government prevailed and executed eight of the alleged PRP conspirators, and deported the two American missionaries most closely associated with labor advocacy.[17]

The rise of Catholic advocacy in human rights episodes like the PRP case followed the Vatican II call to witness for the poor and oppressed of the world.

In Korea, two further developments heightened the concern of the Catholic Church for local issues: the transfer of church leadership from foreign to local control in 1962 and the KCIA kidnapping and near-murder of Kim Dae Jung in 1973, in retribution for his vocal opposition to Park Chung-hee's "revitalizing reforms." Christian activism in Korea thereafter became a decidedly ecumenical affair, a rare convergence of Catholic and Protestant work. Though the bulk of Protestant membership remained pietistic and spiritually oriented, inclined to tolerate the government in the name of national security, strong minorities in both Christian traditions made human rights a special cause during the 1970s and 1980s. Leading members of the Protestant National Christian Council joined Catholic priests in issuing "declarations of conscience." A Catholic–Protestant coalition of clergymen, politicians, and intellectuals threw down the gauntlet at an illegal assembly in the Myŏng-dong Catholic Cathedral on March 1, 1976, with a manifesto on human rights recalling the spirit of the 1919 independence uprising against Japan and denouncing the Park regime for tarnishing that vision with political dictatorship and economic oppression. Its signers included Kim Dae-Jung, former President Yun Posŏn, former Foreign Minister Chŏng Ilhyŏng, National Council of Churches Secretary-General Kim Kwansŏk, Christian human rights activist Yi Ujŏng, and the great Quaker leader Ham Sŏkhŏn. Some of the signers were jailed for a considerable time and all of them, including former President Yun, were harassed continually for years thereafter by the KCIA. Their words, however, inspired the entire South Korean democracy movement well into the 1980s. The rise of General Chun Doo-hwan in the aftermath of Park Chung-hee's assassination in 1979 and the bloody suppression of the democracy movement in the Kwangju massacre of May 1980 created an atmosphere of real terror in South Korea that silenced much of the opposition that had roiled the 1970s. Christian publications were shut down, Christian broadcasting outlets were subjected to censorship and lost their reputation for independent news reporting, clergymen were ordered from their pulpits, and services were subjected to surveillance in a manner reminiscent of the worst years of Japanese thought control. Korea had changed, however, and even Chun Doo-hwan could not control the demand for democratic participation.

During these dark years, the dilemmas of Christianity were especially apparent in the divergence between two forms of Protestantism: the Pentecostal type that was displayed in the First Full Gospel Church on Yŭido Island in Seoul, and the Minjung Theology promoted by Christian intellectuals as they continued to identify with the working people in ways that flirted with the Marxist analyses so long forbidden in South Korea.

In the church on Yŭido, which had an active membership of more than half a million people in the 1980s, Pastor Cho Yŏnggi offered an attractive package of success theology that emphasized Christian happiness and God's rewards for the faithful, including material benefits. Every Sunday, in seven services that filled the stadium-sized sanctuary that seated 20,000 people per service, Cho preached his combination of New Testament salvation, political conservatism, and middle-class striving, summoning a vast evangelical constituency to go forth and conquer doubt and evil. Anti-Communism was an important component of his message, with the North Korean Communist regime representing the ultimate in evil to be conquered, in God's own time, by the faithful Christians of South Korea. In this Manichean context the Chun Doo-hwan regime in South Korea, for all its shortcomings, corruption, and murderous history, could be seen standing firmly on the side of righteousness.[18]

Minjung Theology, by contrast, sought roots in the Korean *minjung*, or "masses" and the Korean history of tribulation expressed in the emotion of *han*.[19] Among its proponents were three signers of the March 1, 1976 manifesto in Myŏng-dong Cathedral: Mun Tonghwan and An Pyŏngmu of the Kijang Presbyterians' Han'guk Seminary, and theology professor Sŏ Namdong of Yonsei University. In the 1970s and 1980s they responded to government oppression with a claim that the masses, or *minjung*, should be the subjects (not objects) of history and that Christians should be the instruments of God's own will to see justice done in the world. This was a call to activism and involvement in changing the political system that greatly offended the South Korean state and invited trouble for its prophets and catcalls from the sidelines of conventional, conservative Protestantism. Though its target was the "masses," in fact it appealed most to intellectuals and university students who saw in its theology a call for Koreans to rise up and demand national reunification, the expulsion of foreign forces from Korean soil, and a reclaiming of their honorable tradition. These messages were not entirely theological, and explanations of Minjung Theology were always somewhat cerebral even while they purported to speak to the common people. Yet despite its inconsistencies, Minjung Theology was an authentic expression of the hurt and anger that are undeniable parts of modern Korean experience. It was also a potent criticism of the pietistic Christianity that avoids tangling with the brutal realities of Korean life in the twentieth century and simply awaits a better world in the next life.

In the midst of this, Korean Protestantism grew and developed many non-political expressions that richly articulated its place in civil society. One underlying phenomenon was the rate and scale of growth in all Korea's Christian churches during the 1970s and 1980s. This growth was the result of the variety of messages being put out by the various Christian denominations and leaders, so that there was truly something for everyone. At Easter sunrise services on the great plaza on Yŭido Island hundreds of thousands of Christians massed each year to celebrate the Resurrection and to hear affirmations of hope for their future. Even larger crowds attended crusades addressed by internationally famous evangelists such as Billy Graham, and even Pope John Paul II himself, to congratulate Korea's Christians for their steadfastness and their historic importance as an example for the entire Christian world. A heady pride attached to belonging to a movement of such size and vitality, and the membership rolls swelled beyond all expectations. The word "explosion" (Korean *p'okbal*) was often used to describe the growth. By the early 1990s, the number of Christians in South Korea was thought to exceed eleven million, or a quarter of the population, with Protestants accounting for more than eight million.[20]

Along with this "explosive" growth came a proliferation of secondary organizations and institutions to give expression to every kind of interest and impulse in the church. Education and literacy have always been an important field of activity for Protestant churches in Korea, aimed, basically, at giving access to the Bible. Schools at all levels, therefore, have always been basic building blocks for Christianity, and their alumni associations are civil society institutions of the first order, institutionalizing loyalties and obligations that are far beyond the control of the state. As we have seen, the Japanese colonial regime had its problems with church-related schools and encountered considerable difficulty in controlling them. Since Liberation, the Ministry of Education has licensed schools and set requirements for teacher preparation, but the nature of private schools, whether secular or religious, has remained under the control of independent boards and associations. The government of Chun Doo-hwan in the 1980s was unable to control campuses and schools even when riot police and the motorcycle-helmeted *paekkoldan* ("white skull corps") freely ranged the grounds.

Related to educational institutions are the publishing houses, newspapers, and broadcasting organizations that comprise the Christian media. These range from producers of Christian literature such as the venerable Christian Literature Society (*Kidokkyo sŏhoe*) to the publishers of evangelical tracts that sometimes litter the streets of Seoul. These producers have associations of their own – for example, the Korean Christian Publishers Association, or *Han'guk kidokkyo ch'ulp'an hyŏbuihoe* – which help them govern themselves and protect themselves from pressure from the state. Christian booksellers and educators have national associations.[21] So do Christian women (Korea Church Women United: the *Han'guk kyohoe yŏsŏng yŏnhaphoe* and the YWCA). There are associations of Christian veterans, policemen, taxi drivers, and actors. Students have the Intervarsity Christian Fellowship (*Han'guk kidok haksaenghoe*), the Ecumenical Youth Council (*Han'guk kidok ch'ŏngnyŏnhoe*), the Christian Church Youth Association (*Han'guk kidokkyohoe ch'ŏngnyŏn hyŏbŭihoe*), and the best-known youth organization, the Korea Student Christian Federation (*Han'guk kidok haksaenghoe ch'ongyŏnmaeng*). The national umbrella organization that constitutes a loose federation of all these and many others is the National Council of Churches in Korea (*Han'guk kidokkyohoe hyŏbŭihoe*) with its headquarters in the "Christian Building" near East Gate, made famous as the site of many actions, decisions, and organizing meetings in the human rights campaign and resistance to military rule in the 1970s and 1980s. During that time, though much of the Protestant community reverted to its political and social conservatism and supported the basic anti-Communism of the state, the government never quite succeeded in imposing its control over this constellation of civil society organizations.

Aggregate growth in the number of Christians has also brought with it a proliferation of sects and denominations. Before World War II, Korea had only a few varieties of Protestantism, mainly Presbyterian, Methodist, Anglican, Baptist, and the Salvation Army. Since Liberation, however, and especially since the involvement of large numbers of overseas religious groups in the reconstruction of

Korea after 1953, many more denominations have taken root, planted by foreign missionaries but nurtured and now led by Korean pastors and laypeople. These include the Assemblies of God, Jehovah's Witnesses, and the Mormons. There are also some Korean "new religions" that draw on Protestant traditions but are actually cults. These include the famous Unification Church of Mun Sŏnmyŏng and the Olive Tree Church of the former Presbyterian elder Pak Taesŏn.[22] The division and subdivision of Korea's Protestant churches is a serious drain on the social potential of the overall movement. Most observers acknowledge this problem and the large church federations such as the National Christian Council represent attempts to reunite the factions on common ground.

Nevertheless, the official number of Protestant "denominations" was 96 in the mid-1990s, 59 of them Presbyterian, while the Catholics continued to have only one, at least officially.[23] Foreign missionaries who came to Korea representing varieties of Presbyterians, or Methodists, or Baptists in other countries often get the blame for setting factional precedents. However, this is only one reason. The Presbyterian Church in particular started splitting as soon as the missionaries began relinquishing control in the 1930s. In the beginning the issues concerned theological convictions and differences over Shintō worship. But the Church continued to divide and divide again in the 1950s and 1960s. This was in marked contrast to the ecclesiastical and organizational discipline made possible by the unified structure of the Korean Catholic Church under a single Archbishop (later Cardinal) appointed by the Vatican.[24]

An analysis of the 59 Presbyterian sub-denominations shows that although most Korean Presbyterians still belong to the five biggest groups, the tiny splinters that round out the list each consist of one or two churches that are associated with individual pastors who broke away from their parent denominations together with loyal followers to found their own groups. Establishing a new sub-denomination, however small, elevates the pastor to the status of "theologian," often enables him to found a "seminary" that employs "professors" and spawns graduates as "disciples" who go out and found "daughter churches" that recruit new members and raise new funds to help the denomination to grow.

The Presbyterian Church traditionally is supposed to have strong organizational discipline and a corporate structure designed to maintain standards of theology and conduct. In Korea, however, the real tradition has always been congregational, with the pastor personally at the center of things. In the material world of contemporary Korea there are many incentives to have one's own congregational church and defy denominational discipline. One purely financial incentive is the sheer value of the land on which an urban church sits. Another is the fact that a congregational church can keep the contributions of its members without having to forward any to the central organization. No matter how mainline denominational leaders decry the splintering trend as prideful and selfish, the list of splinter churches is evidence of their powerlessness to reverse the trend.

Ironically, then, it is middle-class prosperity and democracy that now poses the biggest threats to the future of South Korea's Protestant community. Many churches have grown rich and are even suspected of corruption, their budgets secret or lacking in transparency, their leaders exerting personal power far beyond their humble calling of service. Some of the biggest churches actually resemble empires, with business enterprises and newspapers and influence in areas outside the bounds of religion. This lack of accountability is a serious problem and sets the stage for scandals of the sort that already have done much damage to the integrity of the church.

Conclusion

The election of Kim Dae-jung as President in December 1997 marks a striking departure from the troubled 1970s and 1980s not only in politics but in the whole national agenda. The economic crisis and the urgent need to widen communication with North Korea have forced even the most conservative elements in South Korean society to open their minds to new possibilities. Christian organizations, both Protestant and Catholic, have been strongly on the side of reconciliation and the search for better answers. Even during the presidency of the Presbyterian elder Kim Young-Sam (1993–1998), years when hard-liners in South Korea contrived to choke off contacts with the north and even appeared willing to let masses of people starve in order to hasten "victory" over Communism, the Christian community raised prodigious amounts of money to buy food and medical supplies for the North Koreans. While some Christians persist in dreaming of a scenario where North Korea one day will lie open to a "Christian occupation" and talk excitedly about "reclaiming" North Korea for Christ, other, cooler heads advocate conciliation and respect for their suffering brethren to the north. Korean Protestants of the ecumenical sort hope that President Kim Dae-Jung continues to maintain that tone with his Sunshine Policy.

In the 1990s, with so many of the economic, social, and political goals of earlier struggles realized or within their grasp (notwithstanding the recession of 1997–1999), Koreans in general are enjoying unheard-of prosperity. In this climate the rate of church growth has slackened and in some churches membership has actually fallen. One obvious explanation is that it is human nature to rely less on religion when the temporal world is in satisfactory shape. But perhaps the truth lies in a corollary: that the Korean church has always thrived in adversity and has actually needed it in order to grow. The Christians of Korea have always embraced a theology of suffering and deliverance, comparing their nation to the Israel of the Old Testament. The Catholics recall their history of martyrdom in the nineteenth century and use it as a call to faith and unity. Korean Protestants likewise compare their pre-war history under the Japanese in North Korea, and under military rule in South Korea, to the experience of the Israelites under the tyranny of Egyptian pharaohs and Babylonian kings. If Korean Protestantism has proven itself in times of opposition to the state, an even greater test may come as it struggles to maintain its vitality in a time of unprecedented wealth and freedom.

Notes

1 For a succinct and useful definition of civil society, see Larry Diamond, "Rethinking Civil Society: Toward Democratic Consolidation," *Journal of Democracy* vol. 5, no. 3 (July 1994).

2 Institutional examples of this include the Christian Literature Society, the Korean Bible Society, Christian bookstores and religious book outlets in major secular bookstores such as Kyobo, Christian mass media such as CBS, the Christian Broadcasting System (*Kidokkyo pangsong*), Christian newspapers, and magazines and journals for Christian women, youth, farmers, etc.

3 Horace Allen, a Presbyterian missionary in Korea in the guise of physician to the American Legation in Seoul, administered Western-style medical aid to the gravely wounded Prince Min Yong'ik during the *kapsin* coup of December 1884 and thus won the gratitude of King Kojong who granted him his wish to begin a clinic. The clinic, known as the *Kwanghyewŏn*, was begun in 1885 as the first Protestant mission institution in Korea. Eventually it developed into Severance Hospital and Severance Union Medical College, named for its chief donor, Cleveland philanthropist Louis H. Severance. In 1957 Severance merged with Chosun Christian University (Yŏnhŭi University, founded in 1915 as Yŏnhŭi College) to become Yonsei University. Accordingly, Yonsei claims to be the oldest university in Korea (apart from the Confucian Academy or Sŏnggyun'gwan), dating its beginnings from the *Kwanghyewŏn* clinic in 1885.

4 The literature on early Protestant missions in Korea includes many examples of this conflict with local officials and members of the *yangban* class. See Fred Harvey Harrington, *God, Mammon, and the Japanese* (Madison: University of Wisconsin Press, 1944); Lillias H. Underwood, *Fifteen Years Among the Topknots* (Boston: American Tract Society, 1904); Everett N. Hunt, Jr., *Protestant Pioneers in Korea* (Maryknoll, N.Y.: Orbis Books, 1980); Daniel M. Davies, *The Life and Thought of Henry Gerhard Appenzeller* (Lewiston, Maine: The Edwin Mellen Press, 1988); and Martha Huntley, *To Start a Work: The Foundations of Protestant Mission in Korea (1884–1919)* (Seoul: Presbyterian Church of Korea, 1987).

5 These include Paejae, Ewha, Sungsil, Yŏnhi, Kyesŏng, Myŏngdong, and the YMCA, to name only a few.

6 For the Conspiracy Case see *The Korean Conspiracy Trial: Full Report of the Proceedings in Appeal, by the Special Correspondent of the 'Japan Chronicle'* (Kobe: The Japan Chronicle, 1913); Yun Kyŏngno, *Paego'in sakŏn gwa Shinminhoe yŏn'gu* (Studies on the "105 Incident" and the New People's Association) (Seoul: Ilchisa, 1990), and F. A. McKenzie, *Korea's Fight for Freedom*, reprint edition (Seoul: Yonsei University Press, 1969), pp. 218–238.

7 When this order was first announced it was met by spirited opposition from Korean Christians and the various missionary organizations. After considerable discussion the government offered a compromise consisting of a ten-year grace period for the phasing out of religious teaching. At least one mission (the Northern Presbyterians) made plans to end its school program altogether during this grace period rather than operate wholly "secular" schools with scarce mission funds. However, before ten years had passed the Korean Independence Movement led to the institution of the milder "cultural policy" in the colony, and under Governor-General Saitō Makoto the regulation was amended to permit the teaching of religion in government-recognized schools. This prolonged the life of the missionary-sponsored school network until the late 1930s.

8 See Kenneth M. Wells, "The Rationale of Korean Nationalism Under Japanese Colonial Rule, 1922–1932: The Case of Cho Mansik's Korean Products Promotion Society," in *Modern Asian Studies*, 19: 4 (1985), pp. 823–859.

9   The forced consolidation of Christian church denominations into a single state-recognized *Kyodan* ran parallel to the consolidation of other Japanese centers of influence; for example, political parties that were combined into the *Taisei yokusankai* (or "Imperial Rule Assistance Association) and Japan's various news organizations into a single state-controlled information outlet, the Dōmei news agency.

10 The headquarters shrine of Shintō in Korea was the Chōsen Jingū on the shoulder of Namsan above South Gate in Seoul. This shrine contained *mitamashiro* regalia associated with the imperial cult, including one of the Emperor's swords. Before they could build the shrine on the site, the Japanese had to remove the main shrine of Korean shamanism, known as the *Kuksadang*, to Inwang-san where it remains to this day. The years since Liberation have seen a number of ironic uses of the Chōsen Jingū site, including use of the former shrine buildings as a temporary home for the Presbyterian Theological Seminary immediately after its forced relocation from North Korea, as the location of a large statue of Syngman Rhee that was pulled down after 1960 and more recently a statue and hall in memory of An Chunggǔn, the assassin of Korea's first Japanese ruler Itō Hirobumi. The site now features another patriotic statue of the independence leader Kim Ku, and a tall building that was built originally as a children's center in memory of Yuk Yǒngsu (Mme. Park Chung-hee) and later became an annex of the National Central Library. Among other shrines constructed in Seoul was a memorial shrine to Itō Hirobumi in what is now Changch'ung-dong on the present site of the banquet hall of the Shilla Hotel.

11 The significance of this distinction is developed fully by Helen Hardacre in her book *Shintō and the State, 1868–1988* (Princeton: Princeton University Press, 1989).

12 It should be noted that in Japan, this issue was worked out much earlier, in the 1890s, when the Japanese Christian Uchimura Kanzǒ found a way to bow before state deities while holding "mental reservations." Thereafter, the Japanese Christian Church generally saw no conflict between imperial symbolism and the Ten Commandments. Korean Christians rejected the advice of Japanese Christians to take a similar stance.

13 In addition to the Pyongyang and Sinǔiju-based Christian parties there were several other smaller groups including the Christian Liberal Party (*Kidokkyo chayudang*) led by Kim Hwasik, which was eclipsed by Cho Mansik's group but reemerged in 1947 briefly as the Liberal Party (*Chayudang*) before being put out of business.

14 Cho Mansik spent the late 1940s in prison, and although there was once a short-lived plan to trade him to South Korea for imprisoned leftists there, the plan was never implemented. He is presumed to have perished in the early part of the Korean War.

15 Kang Yang'uk was a cousin of Kang Pan-sǒk, Kim Il-sung's mother. The Kang family were Christians – as is well known, Kang Pan-sǒk herself was a Presbyterian deaconess – and Kang Yang'uk was a graduate of the Presbyterian Theological Seminary in Pyongyang and an ordained Presbyterian pastor. He remained head of the Christian League in North Korea until his death in 1983, rising in the meantime to the rank of vice-premier of the Democratic People's Republic of Korea. For an account of Christian influences in Kim Il-sung's childhood via members of the Kang family, see Yong-ho Ch'oe, "Christian Background in the Early Life of Kim Il-sŏng," *Asian Survey*, 26:10 (October 1986), pp. 1,082–1,091.

16 Over the years, these included the National Association of Evangelicals under Dr. Carl McIntire, which brought to Korea an aggressive anti-Communism that was picked up by one wing of the majority Presbyterian denomination and combined with an interesting mix of existing regional and historical grievances from within Korea to create a breakaway denomination that still comprises nearly half of all Korean Presbyterians, the Taehan Yesukyo Changnohoe (Haptong). See *Kidokkyo taeyǒn'gam, 1993* (The 1993 Christian Yearbook of Korea) (Seoul: Kidokkyomunsa, 1994), p. 268. Other infusions of American right-wing religious politics came with youth organizations like Campus Crusade for Christ, and Christians-in-Action, whose

missionaries in Korea went under the unfortunate acronym CIA during the 1970s and 1980s.

17 Documents circulated by missionaries in Seoul and declarations by the Catholic Priests for the Realization of Justice and the Support Committee of the Families of the Arrested, in the author's possession. For the People's Revolutionary Party case see U.S. 93rd Congress, 2nd Session, House of Representatives, "Human Rights in South Korea: Implications for U.S. Policy," Hearings Before the Subcommittees on Asian and Pacific Affairs and on International Organizations and Movements of the Committee on Foreign Affairs, July 30, August 5, and December 20, 1974, *passim*. The two deported Americans were Methodist missionary George Ogle, of UIM, and Father James Sinnott, who had been organizing fishermen and factory workers on islands in the Yellow Sea of Korea's west coast. For Kim Chiha's part in the case see Sugwon Kang, "The Politics and Poetry of Kim Chiha," *Bulletin of Concerned Asian Scholars*, 9: 2 (April–June, 1977), pp. 3–7.

18 For the First Full Gospel Church on Yŭido, see Donald N. Clark, "History and Religion in Modern Korea: The Case of Protestant Christianity," in *Religion and Society in Contemporary Korea*, eds. Lewis R. Lancaster and Richard K. Payne (Berkeley: Institute of East Asian Studies, 1997), pp. 203–206. For a tongue-in-cheek description of an evangelical service in South Korea that captures another side of the same phenomenon, see Kwang-ok Kim, "Ritual Forms and Religious Experiences: Protestant Christians in Contemporary Political Context," in the same volume, pp. 230–236.

19 "Han" is an elusive term but is often translated as "bitter resentment," something that smolders after generations of oppression by unjust systems and masters. See Suh Nam-dong (SŏNamdong), "Towards a Theology of *Han*," in *Minjung Theology: People as the Subjects of History*, ed. Commission on Theological Concerns of the Christian Conference of Asia (Maryknoll, New York: Orbis Books, 1981), pp. 16–17.

20 Of these, the largest number belong to one of the 59 registered Presbyterian "denominations" followed by Methodists (five varieties), Baptists, and assorted evangelicals including Pentecostal sects that include the famous "megachurch" on Yŭido Island that today claims to be the biggest church in the world with a membership of 725,000 and a pastoral staff of 700.

21 The booksellers have the *Han'guk kidokkyo sŏjŏm hyŏbŭihoe* while the Christian educators' associations include the *Taehan kidokkyo kyoyuk hyŏphoe*, the *Han'guk kyoyuk hyŏphoe*, the Federation of Christian Schools in Korea (*Han'guk kidokkyo hakkyo yŏnmaeng*) and the Association if Christian Schools in Korea (*Han'guk kidokkyo hakkyo yŏnhaphoe*).

22 Basic tenets of both these sects are set forth in a special volume on Korean new religions in the series *Transactions of the Korea Branch of the Royal Asiatic Society*, 43 (1967).

23 For an English translation of the complete listing of the various denominations and sub-denominations of Korean Christianity that appeared in the Korean Christian Yearbook (*Kidokkyo taeyŏn'gam*) for 1994 see Clark, "History and Religion in Modern Korea," in Lancaster and Payne (eds.), pp. 196–202.

24 Although French, German, Irish, and American Catholic missionaries established missions in different parts of Korea that might easily have turned into regional denominations under Protestant systems of governance, the authority of the Pope in Rome and the structure of the worldwide church that continues to be maintained today under Cardinal Stephen Kim Suhwan created a unity in the Catholic church that would be impossible for the more independent Protestants.

9 Beyond the DMZ

The possibility of civil society in North Korea

Charles K. Armstrong

Dominance and hegemony

> Above all else, totalitarian discourse effaces the opposition between the state and civil society; it seeks to make the presence of the state manifest throughout the social space, that is, to convey, through a series of representatives, the principle of power which informs the diversity of activities and incorporates them in the model of a common allegiance.
>
> Claude Lefort[1]

Since the disintegration of communist regimes in Eastern Europe at the end of the 1980s and beginning of the 1990s, many outside observers have been waiting for the North Korean regime to follow its erstwhile allies into the dustbin of history. But unlike Eastern Europe and the Soviet Union, or for that matter the South Korean military government, North Korea did not succumb to the "Third Wave" of democratization. Almost two decades after the fall of the Berlin Wall, despite a famine that killed hundreds of thousands of North Koreans in the mid-1990s, the Democratic People's Republic of Korea (DPRK) is still with us, its political system essentially unchanged. Some would argue that this is the result of the unusually effective coercive apparatus of the North Korean state, which, even after 15 years of economic involution, retains a powerful hold on its people. As a corollary to this argument, a view held by certain scholars, conservative South Koreans and American congressmen among others, North Korea's odious and fundamentally illegitimate regime is "propped up" by international economic aid; take away this artificial support, and the long-oppressed North Korean people would rise up against their government and the regime would quickly collapse. Usually, in this scenario, absorption into the ROK in the South soon follows.[2]

There are several problems with this argument. First, North Korea is not like the weak and Soviet-supported states of Eastern Europe and Mongolia; there are counter-examples that may be more valid – notably Vietnam, Cuba, and above all China, Marxist-Leninist but independent and highly nationalistic regimes which continue to survive, and in the case of China, to manifest great strength. Second, even if the regime did collapse, the possibility should not be dismissed that an even more oppressive and militarized leadership would take its place, resistant to unification with the South. Third, and most important, a scenario of collapse along the lines of Romania or East Germany assumes that there is widespread if subliminal resistance to the regime that could be rapidly organized to engineer its overthrow. In short, those who promote regime change in North Korea and look with equanimity at collapse assume that there is a civil society in North Korea (or at least a potential one), held in check only by the coercion of the ruling party-state, and that this civil society can play a central role in resisting and replacing that regime, analogous to the situation of Eastern Europe in the 1980s. Without such a pre-existing civil society, the collapse of the current North Korean regime may not lead to anything remotely resembling peaceful and democratic unification. Post-collapse possibilities include a North Korea colonized by the South (perhaps with the collusion of China), a devastating war on the Korean peninsula that could draw in other surrounding countries and the United States, and other consequences yet unforeseen.

In this chapter, I will argue that we may indeed be seeing the emergence of civil society in North Korea, as a result of social and economic changes in the last decade, but that it will be some time before it can play any autonomous role to influence the political system. To understand the weakness of civil society in North Korea, it is crucial to understand the historical evolution of the DPRK, and therefore this chapter focuses on how North Korea came to be the kind of state that it is, one which has drastically reduced the autonomous space for civil society more by absorbing its energies than by merely suppressing it. This is largely a product of events in the first 15 years of North Korea's existence as a regime, from liberation from Japanese colonial rule in 1945 until the end of the 1950s. I conclude with some provisional comments on the emergence of civil society in the North today, and why the marked deterioration in the standard of living since the 1980s has generated no active dissent, much less open revolt. North Korea, for all its profound problems, may continue to exist and evolve for some time into the future.

All states operate through a combination of coercion and compliance; or as Machiavelli expressed it, in the personalized manner appropriate for both sixteenth-century Italy and dynastic North Korea, the Prince must strike a balance between fear and love.[3] The North Korean state, like its Stalinist and Japanese militarist predecessors, was no stranger to the instruments of coercion and fear. But on the whole, North Korea's post-colonial nationalism, war mobilization, isolation and education have produced a population that, at least until recently, appears to have been generally loyal to the regime. This is one clear point of difference between North Korea and the late socialist societies of Eastern Europe and the Soviet Union, as well as contemporary proto-capitalist China. Whereas in daily life under erstwhile "actually existing socialism," inner belief in the official ideology was less important than "following the external rituals and practices in which this ideology acquired material existence,"[4] in North Korea belief *does* matter. Indeed, ideology becomes even more important as economic conditions deteriorate and the state relies increasingly on non-material incentives to rally the population.[5] In this sense, unlike in colonial conditions wherein the imperial state practiced "dominance without hegemony," to use Ranaji Guha's phrase,[6] the DPRK until the present has exerted both dominance *and* hegemony, the latter being the creation of values and meanings to which the mass of the population subscribes.[7] The Japanese colonial state was unable to do this, nor were successive authoritarian regimes in South Korea.

For almost the entire existence of the DPRK, North Korea has been a society based on mass mobilization, emphasizing national self-reliance or *juche*, North Korea's leading ideological concept since the late 1950s. For a brief period in the 1960s and 1970s, there was a shift in emphasis from war mobilization to material improvement in daily life.[8] In the years since, daily life has become much grimmer for most North Koreans. Everyday life was reduced to a struggle for survival in the famine years of the 1990s, even for much of the elite, and although conditions improved with the introduction of foreign aid, much of the population remains near the edge of subsistence. According to the testimony of defectors, some North Koreans would prefer to go to war rather than continue to suffer as they do.[9] There are now some signs of "fissures within the conscious mythmaking" of North Korean ideology, even in officially-sanctioned literature.[10] At the level of the general economy, the state has given official recognition to private markets and, in 2002, initiated a series of wage and price reforms that marked a major departure from earlier economic practices. The public distribution system for delivering basic foodstuffs has collapsed in much of the country, and with that collapse, socialist consumption has given way to the gradual, piecemeal emergence of private consumerism. Since the economic crisis began to emerge in the early 1990s, long before the famine, there had been signs of liberalization and the growth of local markets in the North Korean economy, what one American observer calls "reform by stealth."[11] There is, of course, great danger in this shift, as the regime is well aware. Market-oriented economic reforms encourage self-interest and consumerism, weakening the dependence of the people on the state, and therefore the state's control over the people, precisely what the DPRK leadership points to (with good reason) as the source of the downfall of communism in Europe and the rise of revisionism in China. The dominance of the North Korean regime is not yet seriously in question. Its hegemony, however, may already be weakening at the level of everyday life. If so, there is as yet little sign of an independent or even quasi-independent civil society emerging. For the moment, North Korea remains a society of national mobilization, in which civil society is pervaded and dominated by the state.

North Korea's socialist nationalism emerged out of a crisis of post-colonial society. Something similar could be argued for other Marxist-Leninist states in the Third World, which combined a Soviet-Stalinist "model" with the imperatives of post-colonial nation-building: Vietnam, China, Cuba, Angola, and Mozambique, among others; and, following a different model of development, right-wing authoritarian regimes such as Park Chung Hee's South Korea. In North Korea multiple crises converged to create one of the most totalizing, if not totalitarian, regimes of the twentieth century: Japanese colonial militarism and the Korean nationalist reaction; Soviet occupation and the implementation of Stalinist techniques of governance; a highly compressed, state-directed transformation from a predominantly agrarian economy to a predominantly industrial one; and war with South Korea and the United States that began in 1950 and continues to this day. Unlike all other Marxist-Leninist states, with the possible exceptions of Enver Hoxha's Albania and Pol Pot's short-lived Democratic Kampuchea, the DPRK never moved beyond the stage of a mobilization economy to that of a more consumer-oriented economy. Attempts to orient the country in a more "reformist" direction and replace Kim Il Sung with a collective leadership in the late 1950s, in the wake of de-Stalinization in the Soviet Union, were firmly crushed.[12] Until the economic breakdown of the mid-1990s, after which the contours of a "mixed" public–private economy began slowly to emerge, the DPRK maintained an extraordinary degree of control over its citizens' movements and activities, and relied primarily on non-material incentives and disincentives to mobilize North Koreans for collective action.

The socialization of citizens into collective subjectivities, defined by the state and oriented toward the state's goals, involves the redirection of individual preferences away from private (especially material) interests and toward public projects. Ultimately the totalitarian state's intent is to absorb the entire social body into a single subjectivity, with "one heart, united" (*ilsim dangyŏl* in North Korean terminology). That is, the goal of the mobilizing state is the creation of a collective subjectivity embodied in the (North) Korean nation and represented by its leader. Between the formation of the DPRK in the late 1940s and the emergence of juche as North Korea's guiding ideological principle in the late 1950s, North Korea developed this subjectivity at the intersection of individuals, collective identities and the state; it remains to be seen whether this can be maintained in the face of globalization, economic reform and increasingly visible material inequality.

The construction of the social

North Korea's revolutionary project, begun in the late 1940s, involved sweeping social reforms (including above all land redistribution) as well as the construction of new social categories and group identities. The latter entailed both horizontal and vertical divisions: the categorization and organization of individuals into groups according to gender, age and occupation (farmers, workers, youth, women, and white-collar workers or intellectuals), on the horizontal plane; and delineation according to class background on the vertical plane. In terms of social organization, the Japanese colonial wartime regime, which was the DPRK's immediate predecessor, and the Stalinist state which was its proximate model, proved to be quite isomorphic. That is, both regimes mobilized society through "administered mass organizations" (AMOs), a technique adopted by the South Korean state as well, especially under Park Chung Hee (see Chapter 6 in this volume). As Robert Scalapino and Chong-Sik Lee pointed out in reference to the Korean Workers' Party of the DPRK, "no modern party, communist or otherwise, had ever placed so much emphasis on the politics of mass mobilization."[13]

While North Korean AMOs were organized on the horizontal plane – focusing especially on workers, farmers, young people and women – the post-war North Korean regime also attempted to clarify the vertical division of society by carefully recording the social stratum (*sŏngbun*) of each individual. Then, the state attempted to reverse the previous hierarchy and to put those of "good *sŏngbun*" on top. That is, the result of the North Korean revolution, as became clear after the Korean War, was not the elimination of social hierarchy as such, but a radical change in the *content* of hierarchy. The hereditary three-tiered structure of "core class", "wavering class", and "hostile class" became explicit in North Korea from the 1960s onward, and was based on the actions of oneself or one's ancestors during the colonial period and the Korean War. Such stratification seems almost the reverse of socialist equality, but in a way it resonated with Korean tradition: Chosŏn Korea also had a three-tiered social order, consisting of yangban (aristocrat), commoner, and outcaste.[14] The content of hierarchy was vastly different between Chosŏn Korea and the DPRK, but both proved to be remarkably long-lasting and stable.

The Korean War deepened the North Korean state's reliance on social mobilization. Only metaphorically a war economy when the DPRK was founded in 1948, with the outbreak of war in June 1950 North Korea became a genuine wartime state, and in the face of American hostility and the absence of a peace treaty, has remained one ever since. In the post-war period, the migration of thousands of North Korean citizens to the South was detrimental economically but beneficial politically to the North Korean regime, effectively eliminating much potential dissent. Post-war purges and the strengthening of social surveillance, justified by the ever-present fear of South Korean agents, furthered the penetration of state into society and the denial of any legitimate forms of criticism against the government. The war also created a new class of suspicious persons, those whose relatives had fled to South Korea and the U.S.; they and their descendants lay permanently outside the "core" class of reliable regime supporters. By the 1960s, the DPRK had largely solidified the vertical division of North Korean society that had begun two decades earlier.

Mobilization and militarization

The political economy of North Korea, from its beginnings until very recently, has been based on mass mobilization and collectivism – that is to say, the sublimation of individual consumer desires into large-scale collective projects. For more than 20 years, a program of heavy industry, limited consumer goods, withdrawal from the capitalist world-economy and planned production seemed to work well, giving North Korea an impressive rate of economic growth far beyond that of the South.[15] By the 1970s, however, such a development path was showing limited returns, and by the 1990s the North Korean economy was in a seemingly intractable state of crisis. Like the erstwhile centralized economies of Eastern Europe, North Korea showed great gains in the early stages of industrialization, but was unable to compete with a capitalism that had developed beyond the stage of mass-production to one that has variously been described as "post-Fordist", "post-modern", or "disorganized."[16] In particular, such economies have failed markedly to satisfy popular demand for consumer goods, in sharp contrast to what their populations perceive is the case for their advanced capitalist neighbors. Fifteen years before the collapse of the Soviet Union, the East German scholar Rudolf Bahro predicted that "the apparatus in Moscow will find itself sitting on a volcano of unsatisfied material needs ... [t]he propaganda machine is completely powerless against the mere appearance of the 'affluent society'."[17] It is precisely the appearance of the affluent society, especially in South Korea, that the DPRK has tried to shield its citizens against.

The first part of society to be mobilized for increased productivity was the peasantry. Immediately after the 1946 land reform, Kim exhorted peasants to increase their productivity and transform North Korea "from a region of food shortage to a region of abundance."[18] Implicit in Kim's call for greater agricultural productivity was the problem of food production. Agricultural output was severely hampered by North Korea's separation from the grain-producing areas in the South, a shortage of fertilizer, lack of farm tools, and the confiscation and slaughter of oxen by the Soviet occupation forces in the fall of 1945.[19] The first 18 months after liberation was characterized by a serious food shortage, as both internal documents and intelligence reports repeatedly stress. A local People's Court document attests that right after liberation, production was in a "state of anarchy" and food was in short supply.[20] Shortly after attaining power, the Provisional People's Committee enforced strict food rationing, including the prohibition of meat and rice in restaurants.[21] Throughout the pre-Korean War years and beyond, food was rationed according to type of work, with particular favoritism toward the military.[22] North Korea, like other socialist systems, has always been a "shortage economy," if more literally than most.[23]

Although North Korea was still a predominantly agricultural society in the late 1940s, even at that stage its leaders were committed to heavy industry as the centerpiece of the country's economy, much as South Korea's president Park Chung Hee was in the early 1970s. The Japanese industrialization of northern Korea in the 1930s and early 1940s had helped to put North Korea in a unique position among Asian socialist states to follow a Stalinist model of development.[24] The North Korean people were exhorted to construct a democratic, "enlightened industry" essential for "developing the state economy and improving the people's material and cultural level."[25] In August 1946, the North Korean Provisional People's Committee (a precursor to the DPRK) passed a law on the nationalization of major industries, the last in its series of major social reforms. Overwhelming Japanese control of colonial industry made the transition to state ownership relatively easy: with the Japanese gone, there were few private owners from whom to expropriate.[26]

The first of two one-year plans for "National Economic Rehabilitation and Development" was adopted in February 1947. Kim Il Sung announced that only under a single state plan "can the economy be restored and developed really fast and the people's standard of living raised." The plan called for a 92 percent growth in industrial production over the previous year, concentrating on construction, steel, coal, chemicals, power, and transportation, especially railroads.[27] As U.S. intelligence reports noted, North Korea's state economic planning followed the Soviet model, but also had its precursor in the state capitalism of the Japanese Government-General.[28] The main architects of the 1947 plan were Kim Kwan-jin, a lecturer at Keijo Imperial University who came North in September 1945 and became advisor to the Planning Department, and Yi Mun-han, who had studied economics in Japan and headed the Department of Industry.[29] Several hundred Japanese technical experts were retained as advisors in state-run industries.[30] Here as in other aspects of social mobilization, the Japanese predecessor and Soviet model reinforced one another.

As in the early years of the Soviet Union and the People's Republic of China, economic development was pursued with the tactics and terminology of war, including "campaigns", "mobilization", and "assault movements." Socialist states, particularly North Korea, have had a great deal of difficulty abandoning this method of promoting production and moving into a "post-mobilization" stage of development.[31] Born out of war, such societies approached the economy as if they were conducting warfare.[32] In North Korea this approach to the economy has been reinforced by the fact that the regime has seen itself to be literally at war, or at least on a war footing, against South Korea and the United States for more than 50 years.

The Korean War caused utter devastation throughout the peninsula, but especially in the North, which lost nearly half its industrial output, one-quarter of its agricultural output, and millions of its citizens through death and migration.[33] The post-war reconstruction effort was carried out with much the same militaristic methods as the war itself, and the pre-war economic program before that. Indeed, the line between the army and the civilian reconstruction workforce was often a blurry one: Korean People's Army (KPA) draftees were sometimes retained in factory work rather than sent into the army, and active KPA troops were utilized in civilian reconstruction projects.[34] Local peasants were involved in clearing rubble from factories and repairing streets. Hundreds of office workers labored after hours to repair the main thoroughfare of Stalin Street in Pyongyang (renamed Victory Street in 1956).[35] The Democratic Youth League (DYL), which had played a central role in political organization before the war, mobilized children and young people to rebuild schools and cultural facilities.[36]

The reconstruction effort rehabilitated North Korea's industrial sector in a remarkably short time, but the effect on the standard of living of ordinary North Koreans was mixed. In December 1953, the DPRK government cancelled all pre-Korean War debts owed by the peasantry, a decree that was understandably well-received by the hard-pressed Korean farmers.[37] But the Party leadership debated fiercely about the priorities to be given to overall industrialization versus focusing on the increasing production of consumer goods and improving the livelihood of the masses. At the Sixth Plenum of the KWP Central Committee, for example, some representatives advocated eliminating the ration system and increasing wages, while others wished to increase quantities of rations instead. Ultimately the Central Committee decided to keep the rationing system in place but to reduce the price of certain consumer items and increase wages. In April, the regime increased workers' wages by an average of 25 percent, although there were still complaints of excessively high prices.[38]

As it did before the war, the post-war DPRK leadership put first priority on rebuilding heavy industry. Kim Il Sung's report to Soviet ambassador Suzdalev at the end of July 1953 emphasized the need for rapidly rebuilding North Korea's heavy industrial base, particularly machine-tools.[39] In the first two years of post-war reconstruction some 80 percent of industrial investment, or nearly 40 percent of total investment, went into heavy industry, a proportion quite similar to China at the time or East European countries a few years earlier.[40] North Korea's emphasis on heavy industry was partly due to the existence of a pre-war industrial infrastructure built in the latter part of the Japanese colonial period. Although much of this infrastructure had been heavily damaged or destroyed in the Korean War, re-building was a simpler task than building from scratch – the plans and technical knowledge already existed, and experts from more advanced fraternal countries were there to help. But, as Kim had indicated earlier, the North Korean leadership was keen on redirecting industry from the distortions of colonial development. For example, Kim pointed out, the Japanese had built major factories on the coasts, convenient for shipping to Japan but far from the sources of raw materials and poorly suited for Korea's domestic needs. Therefore existing plants should not merely be reconstructed, but new factories and the infrastructure serving them should be built to better serve the needs of North Korea.[41] The new economic plans laid out a careful sequence of rehabilitation and development leading toward industrial self-sufficiency, beginning with sources of power and raw materials (especially electricity generation and mining), and moving on to the production of basic industrial goods such as iron, steel, machine tools, ships, automobile parts, and chemicals, including chemical fertilizer.[42]

The Soviet Union supplied much of the technical advice and material assistance, but the North Koreans' ambitions did not always follow Soviet guidelines. Until the war, the Soviet Union had seen North Korea largely as a source of primary goods, which would be exported in exchange for manufactured goods from the European parts of the socialist bloc. After the war, however, North Korean planners wanted to focus on manufactured goods, including goods for export outside the Soviet bloc, something the Soviet advisors did not think practical. The 1954–56 plan paid a great deal of attention to textile production, an area that had overwhelmingly been concentrated in the South before division, in order to make the DPRK more self-sufficient in clothing and textiles, another policy which the Soviets advised against.[43] The thrust of the post-war rehabilitation plan was toward autarky rather than incorporation into a Soviet-centered international division of labor. The establishment of a "socialist division of labor" was not something that had been of much interest to Stalin, who preferred to extract what the USSR needed from occupied territories after World War II and otherwise let the "satellite" countries fend for themselves. Khrushchev attempted much more forcefully to rationalize economic relations among socialist states, an attempt North Korea resisted to the

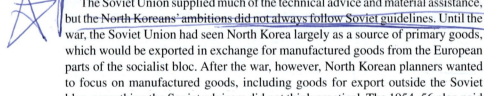

end. North Korea never joined the Soviet-directed Council on Mutual Economic Assistance (CMEA), for instance, and even scheduled its economic plans so as not to coincide with those of the other socialist countries.

In North Korea, unlike in parts of Eastern Europe, this economic mobilization did not lead to worker unrest. Economic reconstruction at this point was geared toward post-war rehabilitation, which seemed to engender genuine popular enthusiasm. Nor was the Soviet Union a domineering presence in North Korea as it was in Eastern Europe at the time. In 1953, there were major workers' protests in East Germany and Czechoslovakia, and partly as a response to this, the Soviet Union reduced its demand for reparations from the GDR, and the Czech and East German governments redirected resources toward improving living standards of ordinary citizens to some extent.[44] North Korean planners, meeting with Soviet advisors in the spring of 1954, said that they had paid careful attention to the experiences and mistakes of the "people's democracies" in economic planning, particularly the need to pay attention to the livelihoods of ordinary citizens.[45] In fact, however, DPRK economic planning was heavily skewed toward developing North Korea's independent industrial base, and in particular its military complex. But while the North Korean state may be said to have exploited its own people, North Korea was not, and certainly its citizens did not perceive it to be, the focus of Soviet economic extraction.

Reconstruction was, in a sense, war by other means. Kim Il Sung and his group of former Manchurian partisans at the center of power in the DPRK were, after all, people who had never known anything but guerrilla war, conventional war, and a brief period of Stalinist economic construction between (which could also be seen as a species of war mobilization). The production of consumer goods and the improvement of everyday life among the masses was a secondary concern to the creation of a powerful industrial state. In post-war North Korea, unlike in Eastern Europe, there were no messy workers' protests with which to contend. The population itself was a resource to be channeled into industrialization for the sake of state power, including military power.

North Korea's leaders did seem to want to move their country toward self-sufficiency – or at least the production of its own industrial necessities – as quickly as possible. In reality, post-war rehabilitation in the DPRK was overwhelmingly dependent on aid from abroad, and from the Soviet Union in particular. In 1955 Moscow agreed to transfer technology to North Korea virtually for free. Between 1956 and 1958 alone the USSR gave North Korea grants and credits in the range of 300 million rubles, and by 1959 the total amount of Soviet aid may have been as high as 2.8 billion rubles, or $690 million at then-current exchange rates.[46] According to contemporary Soviet sources, by the end of the Five-Year Plan in 1960, Soviet aid accounted for 40 percent of North Korea's electricity generation, 53 percent of coke production, 51 percent of cast iron, 22 percent of steel, 45 percent of reinforced concrete blocks and 65 percent of cotton fabric.[47] Thousands of North Koreans received technical training in the USSR and Eastern Europe, and over 10,000 North Korean students were enrolled in universities and colleges in Soviet-bloc countries during the reconstruction period.

And yet despite – or perhaps because of – this dependence, the DPRK leadership was bitterly divided over North Korea's economic relations with the Soviet Union and Eastern Europe in the late 1950s. Between 1956 and 1958, Kim Il Sung and his group opposed integration into an international division of labor led by the USSR, in which North Korea would exchange its primary products for manufactured goods from the European socialist countries. Kim's opponents argued against excessive self-reliance, and called for less emphasis on heavy industry and more on light industry and consumer goods. These arguments over economic policy became embroiled in turn with power struggles among pro-Soviet, pro-Chinese, and Manchurian guerrilla factions within the DPRK ruling group, as well as the debate over collective leadership inspired by Khrushchev's "de-Stalinization" in the USSR. In the end, Kim's line of collectivization, nationalism, self-reliance and heavy-industry-first development won the day, and those opposed to him paid, in many cases, with their lives.

Although foreign aid was drastically reduced in the early 1960s, North Korea remained dependent on long-term loans from the USSR and other socialist countries until the Soviet Union collapsed. By 1989, half of DPRK foreign trade was with the USSR, and North Korea's debts to the Soviet Union amounted to nearly a year's worth of exports.[48] It seems that DPRK planners did not seriously take into account the loss of foreign assistance when they formulated the first seven-year economic plan (1961–67). As a result, the plan could not be fulfilled and had to be extended three years, making it a de facto ten-year plan (1961–70). Thereafter, North Korea would never fulfill its economic plans on time, and after the mid-1960s would not even publish concrete statistics on economic output (as opposed to percentage increases). We can see this as the beginning of North Korea's long, protracted economic decline. The socialist economic showcase of the 1950s sputtered out in the 1960s, just as South Korea's modernization program was beginning to take off. North Korea was, in a sense, a victim of its own early economic success, entering a cul-de-sac of development from which it would not recover for decades.

This grim fate could hardly have been foreseen by anyone inside or outside of North Korea in the mid-1950s. As late as 1974, a pair of Western economists could declare the DPRK an economic success story offering "an alternative development theory which turns upside down all the accepted premises of Western economic thinking."[49] The DPRK's goal in post-war development was "socialist transformation," meaning that the state directed the economy and the people were moved into collective forms of association. State-run and cooperative industry, which had accounted for 90.7 percent of North Korea's industry before the war, was now up to 98 percent. By the end of 1956, 80.9 percent of peasant households were in agricultural cooperatives. Shiny new farmhouses on efficient cooperative farms had replaced the ramshackle huts of traditional villages, and in the words of Kim Il Sung, "Korea's countryside has now been freed forever from poverty." In the cities, North Korea's factory and office workers had received an average wage increase of 35 percent between November 1956 and June 1957 alone.[50]

The propaganda about a "heroic new age" for the North Korean people was not entirely unjustified.

If socialism meant state and collective ownership of the means of production, the DPRK had indeed accomplished the socialist revolution by the end of the 1950s, as the Party media claimed. North Korea's socialist revolution had been almost too easy. Already when the regime was founded in 1948, more than 90 percent of industrial concerns were state-owned, most of the factories simply having been expropriated from their absent Japanese owners. By the end of 1958, most of the agricultural sector was also collectivized and the land state-owned. Nationalization was more thorough in the DPRK than in any of the People's Democracies of Eastern Europe; almost nothing of the private economy remained by the beginning of the 1960s. North Korea developed what Marx might have called "barracks socialism," society as a kind of militarized factory under the leadership of a single Supreme Leader.

By the middle of the 1950s, then, North Korea had an impressive industrial economy by Third World standards, and a consumer economy able to supply its people with basic necessities on a generally stable basis. The country could have at that point focused its resources on improving the livelihood of its people, and shifted from a militaristic to a more diversified form of economic development. But, because of the instability in the communist bloc, the growing threat from the U.S. and South Korea, and perhaps the difficulty of the guerillas who now ran the DPRK in seeing economic development as anything *but* war, the regime made a conscious choice to put its resources into military build-up. The economy began to stagnate, and after a few years living conditions began gradually to decline. Perhaps if North Korea had faced a sudden shock like China's Great Leap Forward famine, the pendulum might have shifted toward economic reform and opening some years down the road. This may, in fact, be the long-run effect of the famine of the 1990s, although it is still too early to tell. In the event, from the 1960s onward, the North Korean economy suffered a protracted hollowing-out that lasted decades, the country propped up partially by Soviet bloc and Chinese assistance, its people held captive by a relentless and ubiquitous war mobilization. After a relative relaxation in the 1970s and 1980s, the acute food shortages that began in the early 1990s shifted the regime toward greater reliance on popular mobilization once again.[51]

Prospects for civil society

At the height of his dictatorship, just as industrialization in the ROK was taking off, South Korean President Park Chung Hee said, "Food comes before politics. Only with a full stomach can one enjoy the arts and talk about social developments."[52] This is one simple answer to the lack of dissent in North Korea: starving people don't revolt, and many North Koreans are starving. But this was not always the case, and even when North Koreans were better off than their Southern brethren, there was less visible dissent in the North than in the South (besides which, Park was wrong – many South Koreans enjoyed the arts, talked about social developments and engaged in protests even amidst the desperate poverty of the 1950s and 1960s). The differences between the civil societies of North and South Korea derive not just from the difference in relative economic development. They have very much to do with the way the two regimes have developed since liberation, and the models upon which these two regimes were based. The DPRK was created as a Stalinist state with Maoist influences on the foundation of Japanese colonial militarism. The ROK was an illiberal parliamentary democracy, also founded on the back of Japanese colonialism (and with far greater continuity with the colonial past, in terms of administrative personnel), but based on a liberal model which it could never entirely dismiss, however autocratic the regime became at times. In the end, the rhetoric of democracy helped to undermine autocracy.

Nor is the East European comparison apposite. As John Feffer succinctly puts it, "In Kim's North Korea, built upon the arid ground of Japanese colonial rule, there was no established civil society to contend against the imperatives of the central government."[53] No Catholic Church as in Poland, no problematic ethnic minorities as in Romania and Hungary, no workers' uprising as in East Germany, no network of critical intellectuals as in Czechoslovakia troubled the DPRK, at least after the Korean War liquidated most of the potential opposition, many of whom (such as the anti-communist Christian element) simply fled South. Far from moving toward a "thaw" that might have opened up the space for Samizdat and market reforms, such as took place in the Soviet Union, Hungary, and other East European countries in 1956, North Korea (like China) moved in the opposite direction: toward greater political restriction and an expanded cult of the Great Leader.[54] And in contrast to China, change at the top after the death of the Great Leader (Mao in 1976, Kim Il Sung in 1994) has not led to fundamental economic reform in North Korea, at least not yet. Kim wanted to ensure stability and continuity in the political system by having his son succeed him. In this regard he was probably all too successful.

This is not to say there has been no change in North Korea. On the contrary, one of the by-products of the economic crisis of the 1990s has been the gradual emergence of a market economy, now publicly acknowledged by the central state. The "Arduous March," as the DPRK government called the famine years of the mid-1990s, severely weakened the state's ability to provide for its citizens. The Public Distribution System (PDS) for delivery of food and other necessities was drastically reduced, and in some areas of the country collapsed altogether. What took its place was the market, at first clandestinely in remote areas, and then openly throughout the country. As an acknowledgement of this new reality, the Korean Workers' Party newspaper *Rodong Sinmun* announced in January 2001 a policy of "New Thinking" (*Saeroun kwanjŏm*), which called for scrapping outmoded habits and mentalities and putting all efforts into the technological reconstruction of North Korea.[55] "New Thinking" emphasized ideological and economic flexibility, industrial restructuring, and a focus on computers and information technology.[56] In order to accomplish this, the DPRK demonstrated a new willingness to learn from the outside world; after years of isolation following the withdrawal of students from Eastern Europe, North Korea again sent government officials and students abroad to study technical subjects, economics, and business, in countries as diverse as China, Malaysia, Australia and the United States.[57]

A year after the announcement of "New Thinking," the 2002 New Year's Joint Editorial in the three main official DPRK newspapers celebrated the "successes" of the previous year and renewed the call for "radical change" in the economy.[58] In March 2002, the Supreme People's Assembly, North Korea's highest legislative body, approved a budget emphasizing technical innovation and modernization.[59] In early July 2002, the DPRK began to institute some of the most far-reaching economic changes since the regime was founded in 1948. The food distribution system was modified, the price of rice was raised to near-market levels, wages were increased as much as 30-fold, the official exchange rate for the North Korean *wŏn* was drastically reduced, and taxation (abolished in 1974) was re-introduced.[60] The overall thrust of these reforms was to move North Korea away from a central planning model to a mixed social market economy. While the reforms were stalled by the crises with Japan and the United States that emerged in the fall of 2002, they were not withdrawn. In March 2006, the DPRK held a conference on national labor planning, the first in ten years, which announced the need to "strengthen economic mentality" in the country and "create in our own way the most scientific, logical and utilitarian economic management method."[61] Following closely on a visit by Kim Jong Il to China's special economic zones, the conference underscored the North Korean government's attempt to effect and control economic reform.

The social effects of the economic catastrophe of the 1990s and the subsequent economic reforms have been substantial, but political effects have yet to be felt. Against the government's heretofore strict control of movement within and beyond the country, famine forced large numbers of North Koreans to travel in search for food, including illegal travel to China. Those caught crossing the border or forcibly repatriated from China have been severely punished, many incarcerated in North Korea's notorious prison camps.[62] But the state's ability to restrict internal migration has been weakened, probably permanently. Most North Koreans now obtain the bulk of their necessities from the market (or produce it themselves) rather than from the state. The old social contract, between the paternalistic state and the dependent citizen, has collapsed.[63]

For ordinary North Koreans, the effects of the 2002 economic reforms have been mixed at best. Inflation has been high and sustained. Those with access to foreign exchange and farmers who can produce their own food have been able to cope reasonably well with these economic changes, even profit from them. Others have seen their standard of living decline, as food prices exceed the rise in wages.[64] As these new forms of division between the haves and have-nots grow, North Koreans are subject to more information from the outside world than ever before. While government control of mass media is still officially absolute, broadcasts from China and even South Korea are reaching North Korean citizens, and returned migrants from China spread news of their experiences through their networks of friends and family members. The growing presence of aid workers, tourists, and business people from Western countries, Japan, China, and South

Korea is a visible reminder of the world beyond North Korea. While far from an open society, North Korea is not the almost hermetically sealed country it was a decade ago.

The net effect of these economic changes and new access to outside information is to create a gap between what North Koreans have been taught about the world and their society, and the reality that they see around them. Will this lead to growing disenchantment with the regime and an internal opposition, as happened in Eastern Europe before 1989? Will the emerging space of autonomy from state dependence and control provide the basis for civil society to develop in North Korea? It is far too early to answer these questions with any degree of certainty, but at the moment there is little indication that an autonomous public sphere will emerge in North Korea any time soon. Dazed from the shock of one of the worst economic disasters in the late twentieth century, struggling for survival in a brave new world, ordinary North Koreans are trying to cope as best they can. Meanwhile, the North Korean state, despite its relative decline in authority, is still able to prevent the consolidation of any non-state approved association, much less opposition. Given recent changes in the country, over time the state–society relationship in North Korea could evolve into something quite different than it is today. Whether or not this new relationship would constitute a recognizable democracy, it would no longer constitute the regime of total social mobilization North Korea has been for most of its existence. But North Korea exists on a peninsula, in a region, and in a world that may not offer the DPRK the time and autonomy that would allow for such a peaceful evolution. Change may take place suddenly and violently, or peacefully and gradually. But change will come, and civil society will play an important role in Korea's political evolution whether Korea remains two separate societies, or becomes a unified whole.

Notes

1 Claude Lefort, *The Political Forms of Modern Society: Bureaucracy, Democracy, Totalitarianism*, ed. John B. Thompson (Cambridge, UK: Polity Press, 1986), p. 215.
2 See for example Nick Eberstadt, *The End of North Korea* (Washington, DC: AEI Press, 1999).
3 Niccolo Machiavelli, *The Prince*, ed. Quentin Skinner and Russell Price (New York: Cambridge University Press, 1988).
4 Slavoj Zizek, *Did Somebody Say Totalitarianism? Five Interventions in the (Mis)use of a Notion* (London: Verso, 2001), p. 90.
5 I elaborate this point in "A Socialism of Our Style: North Korean Ideology in a Post-Communist Era," in Samuel S. Kim, ed. *North Korean Foreign Policy in the Post-Cold War Era* (Oxford: Oxford University Press, 1998).
6 Ranajit Guha, *Dominance without Hegemony: History and Power in Colonial India* (Cambridge, MA: Harvard University Press, 1997).
7 Antonio Gramsci, *Selections from the Prison Notebooks*, ed. and trans. Quinton Hoare and Geoffrey Nowell Smith (New York: International Publishers, 1971), p. 12.
8 For example, in 1974 the DPRK eliminated all taxes and declared itself the first "tax-free state" in the world, yet another sign (so the regime declared) of having a materially satisfied citizenry.

9 Bradley Martin, *Under the Loving Care of the Fatherly Leader: North Korea and the Kim Dynasty* (New York: Thomas Dunne Books, 2004), pp. 514, 526, 534.

10 Stephen Epstein, "On Reading North Korean Short Stories on the Cusp of the New Millennium," *Acta Koreana* vol. 5, no. 1 (January 2002), p. 40.

11 Selig S. Harrison, *Korean Endgame: A Strategy for Reunification and US Disengagement* (Princeton: Princeton University Press, 2002), p. 25.

12 See Andrei Lankov, *Crisis in North Korea: The Failure of De-Stalinization, 1956* (Honolulu: University of Hawaii Press, 2005).

13 Robert Scalapino and and Chong-Sik Lee, *Communism in Korea, Volume 1* (Berkeley: University of California Press, 1972), p. 375.

14 North Korea's tripartite class structure is not, of course, an explicit policy of the DPRK, but North Korean defectors have consistently referred to it. See for example Minnesota Lawyers' Human Rights League, *Human Rights in the Democratic People's Republic of Korea* (Minneapolis: Asiawatch, 1988).

15 See United States Central Intelligence Agency, *Korea: The Economic Race Between the North and the South* (Washington, DC, 1978).

16 See for example Scott Lash and John Urry, *The End of Organized Capitalism* (Madison: University of Wisconsin Press, 1987).

17 Rudolf Bahro, *The Alternative in Eastern Europe*, trans. David Fernbach (London: Verso, 1981) pp. 237–8.

18 Cited in Chong-Sik Lee, "Land Reform, Collectivization and the Peasants in North Korea", *China Quarterly* no. 14 (1963), p. 71.

19 United States National Archives and Records Administration, United States Army, Far East Command. G-2 Weekly Summary no. 31 (17 April 1946), p. 6.

20 National Archives and Records Administration, Record Group (RG) 242, shipping advice (SA) 2005, item 8/59. Haeju People's Court, "Local Situation and Activities," April 10, 1946.

21 *Saegil Sinmun*, March 21, 1946.

22 RG 242, SA 2005 7/57. Supply Section, Pyongyang City People's Committee, "Distribution of Rations," January 1949.

23 For socialist systems as shortage economies, see Janos Kornai, *The Socialist System: The Political Economy of Communism* (Princeton: Princeton University Press, 1992), pp. 228–301.

24 Bruce Cumings, *The Origins of the Korean War, Volume 2: The Roaring of the Cataract* (Princeton: Princeton University Press, 1990), p. 337.

25 RG 242, SA 2007 9/61. Kim Ch'an, *Sangsa taech'a taejop'yo soron* [Outline of Industrial Balance Sheets] (Pyongyang: Munmyŏng sanŏpsa, 1947), p. 5.

26 United States Army, Far East Command. Record Group 319, *Intelligence Summary North Korea* no. 37 (15 June 1947), p. 9.

27 Kim Il Sung, "On the 1947 Plan for the Development of the National Economy," *Works* vol. 3 (Pyongyang: Foreign Languages Publishing House, 1980), pp. 79, 82.

28 United States Armed Forces in Korea, Assistant Chief of Staff, G-2. Record Group 332, box 57. "North Korea Today," p. 20.

29 *Intelligence Summary North Korea* no. 41, p. 11.

30 United States Army, Far East Command. Allied Translator and Interpreter Section (ATIS), box 4, item 25. Planning Bureau, North Korean Provisional People's Committee, "Plan of Economic Development to be Achieved by the North Korea People," 1947, p. 5.

31 Andrew Walder, *Communist Neo-Traditionalism: Work and Authority in Chinese Industry* (Berkeley: University of California Press, 1986), p. 8.

32 As Stephen Kotkin has pointed out, the Soviet Union itself emerged out of the First World War and applied the lessons of that war directly to economic development from the beginning. Kotkin, *Magnetic Mountain: Stalinism as a Civilization* (Berkeley: University of California Press, 1995).

33 *Postwar Reconstruction and Development of the National Economy of DPRK* (Pyongyang: Foreign Languages Publishing House, 1957), p. 8.
34 Soviet Embassy in DPRK Report, 30 June 1954. Foreign Policy Archives of the Russian Federation (AVPRF), Fond 0102, Opis 10, Papka 52, Delo 8.
35 Soviet Embassy in DPRK Report, 15 October 1953. AVPRF, Fond 0102, Opis 9, Papka 44, Delo 9. As it happened, the mobilization of local workers to construct East Berlin's "Stalinallee" triggered the first popular uprising in the Soviet bloc, the Berlin uprising of June 17, 1953. No such problems affected reconstruction work in Pyongyang.
36 Soviet Embassy in DPRK Report, 7 October 1953. AVPRF, Fond 0102, Opis 9, Papka 44, Delo 9.
37 Soviet Embassy in DPRK Report, 13 January 1954. AVPRF, Fond 0102, Opis 9, Papka 44, Delo 9.
38 Soviet Embassy in DPRK Report, 28 May 1954. AVPRF, Fond 0102, Opis 9, Papka 44, Delo 9.
39 Kim Il Sung to Suzdalev, July 31, 1953, enclosure, pp. 1–3.
40 Masai Okonogi, "North Korean Communism: In Search of Its Prototype," in Dae-Sook Suh, ed. *Korean Studies: New Pacific Currents* (Honolulu: University of Hawaii Press, 1994), pp. 185–6.
41 Kim, *All for the Postwar Rehabilitation and Development of the National Economy* (Pyongyang: Foreign Languages Publishing House, 1961), p. 11.
42 Kim, *Postwar Rehabilitation*, pp. 11–14; Kim to Suzdalev, Enclosure.
43 Soviet Embassy in DPRK Report, 30 March 1956. AVPRF, Fond 0102, Opis 12, Papka 68, Delo 5.
44 Martin McCauley, *The German Democratic Republic Since 1945* (London: Macmillan, 1983), p. 69.
45 Soviet Embassy in DPRK Report, 19 April 1954. AVPRF, Fond 0102, Opis 10, Papka 52, Delo 8.
46 Erik Van Ree, "The Limits of *Juche*: North Korea's Dependence on Soviet Industrial Aid, 1953–76," *Journal of Communist Studies* vol. 5, no. 1 (March 1989), p. 68.
47 Karoly Fendler, "Economic Assistance and Loans from Socialist Countries to North Korea in the Postwar Years 1953–1963," *Asien* no. 42 (January 1992), p. 42.
48 Fendler, "Economic Assistance," p. 43.
49 Ellen Brun and Jacques Hersh, *Socialist Korea: A Case Study in the Strategy of Economic Development* (New York: Monthly Review Press, 1976), p. 21.
50 Kim, "Economic Reconstruction," *Postwar Rehabilitation*, p. 13.
51 James Brooke, "North Korea, Facing Food Shortages, Mobilizes Millions From the Cities to Help Rice Farmers," *The New York Times,* June 1, 2005. http://www.nytimes.com/2005/06/01/ international/ asia/ 01korea.html.
52 Park Chung Hee, *How to Build a Nation* (1971). Cited in Yongho Ch'oe, Peter H. Lee and Wm. Theodore de Bary, eds. *Sources of Korean Tradition, vol. 2: From the Sixteenth to the Twentieth Centuries* (New York: Columbia University Press, 2000), p. 396.
53 John Feffer, "The Forgotten Lessons of Helsinki: Human Rights and US–North Korean Relations," *World Policy Journal* vol. 31, no. 3 (Fall 2004), p. 32.
54 Lankov, *Crisis in North Korea.*
55 *Rodong Sinmun*, January 9, 2002, p. 1.
56 "Let us Examine and Solve all Problems from a New Perspective and Position," *Rodong Sinmun*, January 9, 2001.
57 Nam Kwang-sik, "One Year of a 'New Way of Thinking,'" *Vantage Point* vol. 24, no. 2 (February 2002), p. 10.
58 *Rodong Sinmun*, January 1, 2002, p. 1; *People's Korea*, January 12, 2002, p. 2.
59 "SPA Approves New State Budget Featuring Technical Innovation and Modernization of Economy, *People's Korea*, March 30, 2002, p. 1.

60 "North Korea Undergoing Economic Reform," *Chosŏn Ilbo* (July 26, 2002); "Stitch by Stitch to a Different World," *The Economist*, July 27, 2002, pp. 24–6.

61 Kyungnam University Institute for Far Eastern Studies, North Korea Brief no. 06-4-03-1, April 3, 2006. http://ifes.kyungnam.ac.kr/eng/references/07_nk_brief_view.asp?nkbriefNO=46&page=1

62 David Hawk, *The Hidden Gulag: Exposing North Korea's Prison Camps* (Washington, DC: U.S. Committee for Human Rights in North Korea, 2003), pp. 56–69.

63 Stephen Haggard and Marcus Noland, *Hunger and Human Rights: The Politics of Famine in North Korea* (Washington, DC: U.S. Committee for Human Rights in North Korea, 2005), p. 19.

64 Ibid., pp. 21–2.

Index